DISCARD

Federalists in Dissent

Federalists in Dissent

IMAGERY AND IDEOLOGY
IN JEFFERSONIAN AMERICA

Linda K. Kerber

CORNELL UNIVERSITY PRESS

ITHACA AND LONDON

For Dick

Voi, che sapete
Che cosa è amor . . .

Preface

The Federalist image in American memory is a strange one. In a mere twenty years, from 1789 to 1809, the Federalists as a group are assumed to have reversed character; once representing statesmanship of the highest order and originality, they deteriorated, it seems, into a pack of quarreling, ill-tempered curmudgeons, the poorest losers in American history.

The sources of this changing image are multiple, and so familiar that it is necessary only to list them here. The most obvious source is the opposition, to whom the Federalists were a group of Anglophile monarchists unworthy of trust or even courtesy. The Federalists were themselves skilled in political invective in an era responsive to rhetorical overstatement; their colorful denunciations of the opposition increased in scurrility as those of the Republican press increased in venom. Many of the older Federalists succumbed to despair in the years of the Jeffersonian ascendancy, and historians' invasion of their personal letters has made evident a mood that they did not always display in public. Furthermore, Federalist leaders were unlucky enough to quarrel and ultimately to sever relations with President John Adams. Adams, understandably, could never forgive them; neither could his son, John Quincy Adams, nor his great-grandson, Henry Adams. The latter's volumes on the Jefferson and Madison administrations deservedly remain classics of

American historical literature, but they should not be read as nonpartisan evaluation.

Finally, the Federalists have been maligned by historians who, intent on demonstrating a Jefferson–Jackson–Franklin D. Roosevelt continuity, are unable to see Jefferson's opponents as anything but mean-spirited enemies of the republic. This view can pervade the work of otherwise careful and judicious historians; Charles Grove Haines, for example, in his magisterial volume *The Role of the Supreme Court in American Government and Politics,* can speak of a "Federalist Regime" as opposed to the "Republican administrations."

More recent historical investigations have made these assessments less tenable. Thanks to the work of historians such as Shaw Livermore and Lee Benson, we are no longer so certain of a Democratic Party continuum stretching from Jefferson to Roosevelt. Leonard Levy has forced us to approach Jefferson with a willingness to acknowledge his errors as well as his wisdom, and David H. Fischer has shown that "disintegration" is neither accurate nor sufficient to describe what happened to the Federalist Party after Jefferson took office. It begins to seem possible, at least, that intelligent men of good will might have found Jeffersonian politics distasteful.

The early national period was one of the most intellectually traumatic in modern times. Perry Miller has warned us not to let the superficial notion of nineteenth-century lawyers as men who sipped after-dinner port and dressed with old-fashioned elegance blind us to the more important undercurrents of tension beneath the ceremony. Miller's warning may be applied more broadly. The opening decade of the nineteenth century was not a placid time; social changes in the post-revolutionary era created tremendous intellectual pressures from which few were insulated. The novelty of the American political experiment and the myriad problems arising from the wars of the French Revolution are only the most obvious sources of American uncertainty and concern. A social transformation, the extent of which we are only beginning to appreciate, and which was, to many, as unexpected as it was unwelcome, seems to have been experienced by the post-revolutionary generation. Americans had from the earliest days regarded their experiment as a "City upon a Hill," as an attempt, that is, to build in the new world an exemplary civilization. The proof that such a society had been built would be found, it was thought, in certain measurable accomplishments—in the obvious ones of financial stability and commercial prosperity, and in the more subtle ones of political order, cultural sophistication, and literary and scientific achievement. How fully the revolutionary generation had succeeded in any of these accomplishments was, it turned out, debatable—not only because subjective assessments necessarily vary, but because the very terms of the debate, the definitions of the desirable political and economic order, and of the proper features of scientific inquiry and literary creativity, kept changing.

The revolutionary generation had left an ambiguous legacy. It had warned Americans against organized political parties and created an embryonic two-party system; it had endorsed popular participation in government because it expected that the citizenry would continue to accept the leadership of an educated and generally conservative elite; it had defined cultural accomplishment in the traditional terms of the study of theology, the classics, and certain experimental sciences.

Was the new nation, with its tensely mobile "middling classes," its laboring groups growing in number and in skill, its bickering party organizations, its remodeled curricula which replaced classical studies with modern languages and vocationally practical information, precisely the new society of which its founders had dreamed? Obviously not, and since it was not, what was left to justify the psychic sacrifice of the Revolution?

The answers to this last question varied, and the patterns of response are far more numerous than might be suspected from the simple distinction, so common to our historiography of a generation ago, between Jeffersonians who endorsed progressive change and Federalists who resisted it. Within each party there were many varieties of political response, from the Old Republicans on the right of the Jeffersonian spectrum to the Young Federalists on the left of the opposition, and the politics of the early republic cannot wholly be understood without a scrupulous analysis of all these factions.

This book is devoted to one of these groups, men who, for want of a better name, may be called "articulate Federalists." Representing an intellectual rather than a sociological stratum, they speak most convincingly for their party to later generations, and they have left the clearest testimony to why they could not endorse Jeffersonian democracy. They were impressed not by the accomplishments and principles of the Jeffersonians, but by the failures and contradictions. Their resentment of Jefferson was compounded not only out of jealousy for his position, but out of a genuine fear for the security and stability of the republic under his administration.

The articulate Federalists were often lawyers and politicians with literary talents. A number of them knew one another personally: John Quincy Adams and his brother Thomas Boylston Adams were distantly related to Josiah Quincy, who, in turn, corresponded with Oliver Wolcott, Jr., and Noah Webster; the Adams brothers, Quincy, Thomas Green Fessenden, and Gouverneur Morris contributed, in varying degrees, to Joseph Dennie's *Port Folio;* Rufus King was married to the niece of Richard Alsop, who came from Middletown, Connecticut, where Oliver Wolcott, Jr., made his home. John Rutledge, Jr., of South Carolina habitually spent his summers in Newport, Rhode Island, and came to know the New Englanders socially; through him, Henry William DeSaussure, who rarely left South Carolina, corresponded with Wolcott and other Federalist luminaries. But each man maintained more important connections to different political brotherhoods, and the group was, at best, an only vaguely associated intellectual community. What these men expressed was a cast of mind and a set of beliefs that constituted a significant part of a more general Federalist persuasion.

These Federalists, contemplating the American scene at the opening of the nineteenth century, concluded that an ordered world was disintegrating, and that this disintegration was encouraged by an organized group of men who joined opposition to the politics of George Washington with a skepticism of established patterns of inquiry in the arts and sciences, and a guile which enabled them to weaken the cultural fabric of the republic while purporting to strengthen it. In the heat of partisan debate, awareness of contradiction easily led to accusations of hypocrisy. Prevarication and hypocrisy seemed in fact to permeate a number of Republican concerns. Southern Republicans claimed to defend the rights of man while retaining the power of life and death over their own slaves; Republicans expressed scorn for the established educational curricula and at the same time expounded the glories of an educated citizenry; furthermore they welcomed with joy the acquisition of Louisiana, which was essentially unconstitutional.

In 1801 the Federalists became the first modern political party to accept defeat peaceably; in effect they endorsed their own defeat by their presence at the balloting in the House of Representatives which broke the electoral college tie between Jefferson and Aaron Burr. The experience was a painful one; power was not transferred without a good deal of anguish and misgiving. In their judgments of the first years of Republican rule, the most articulate Federalists revealed a conviction that the two parties were separated on practical issues because they were separated on intellectual ones. This book attempts to view the American scene at the beginning of the nineteenth century with a Federalist's eye, and, having read it in Federalist terms, to account for the opposition to Jefferson on grounds other than the obvious one of partisanship. Was there anything, we may ask, in the Jeffersonian definition of the meaning of American life which made Federalist hostility reasonable?

The articulate Federalists charged that Republican receptiveness to the crude, the novel, and the superficial in the arts and sciences imperiled the dream of founding in America a new, and higher, civilization. Federalist distrust was grounded not only in political objection but in disagreement that was ideological in the broadest possible sense. The sources of Federalist resentment are explored in the pages that follow, in the hope of broadening our understanding of American experience during the insecure days of the early republic.

In the course of writing this book, I have incurred more debts than the volume has pages. I am particularly grateful to Richard Hofstadter, who has offered good counsel from the beginning; to David H. Fischer, Eric McKitrick, Darline S. Levy, Mary-Jo Kline, Martin Roth, and James M. Banner, Jr., for their perceptive readings and helpful conversations as the work progressed; to the Danforth Foundation and the Associated Alumnae of Barnard College for funds to defray the expenses of research; to Professors Dan Vogel and Doris S. Goldstein of Stern College for Women, Yeshiva University, for providing an environment encouraging to research and for arranging leaves of absence from teaching duties. I owe a more general debt to Eleanor M. Tilton, Annette Kar Baxter, and John A. Kouwenhoven of Barnard College, who provide in their own lives invigorating models of scholarly achievement. My husband, Richard E. Kerber, criticized the manuscript at several stages with great sensitivity. My deepest obligation is to him, to our sons Ross and Justin, and to Dorothy H. Kaufman, Harry H. Kaufman, and Emilie G. Kaufman, for moral and financial support, and for patiently enduring the masses of typescripts and notes which have flooded our homes for the last few years.

LINDA K. KERBER

Menlo Park, California
March 1970

Contents

Federalists in Dissent

[1]

Journey to Laputa: The Federalist Era as an Augustan Age

> Never . . . let us exchange our civil and
> religious institutions for the wild theories
> of crazy projectors.
> —NOAH WEBSTER

"I know of only two occasions," Alfred North Whitehead once
remarked, "when the people in power did what needed to be
done about as well as you can imagine its being possible." [1] One
of these occasions Whitehead identified as the reign of Caesar
Augustus; the other, the era of the framing of the American
Constitution. The parallel was not unsuspected by the contemporaries and immediate descendants of the Founding Fathers; repeatedly they made clear a determination that their America be
as significant as Augustan Rome: as successful in the development of political power, in the building of an empire, in the construction of a civilization. Augustus had ruled Rome after a period of revolution and civil war; the American War of
Independence had been almost as much civil war as it had been
revolution. The challenge that a revolutionary generation leaves
to its sons is that the sons construct where the fathers had destroyed; that like Caesar Augustus, they keep the calm after the
storm, maintain the government steady and responsible, create

[1] Lucien Price, *Dialogues of Alfred North Whitehead* (Boston, 1954),
pp. 161, 203.

1

the excellence which the revolutionaries had demanded. The
Americans may have been luckier than most epigones, for their
fathers had left them both a completed Revolution and a constitutional blueprint for bringing its ideals into fruition, but they
still had to create reality out of words; they still had to create
an Augustan age for what they had already begun to call "our
rising empire."

The usefulness of the Roman example was blunted by the
fact that the Romans had transmuted republican precedent into
Caesarian autocracy. The Greek experience of democracy, although frequently referred to, seemed to provide as many lessons in what to avoid as in what to emulate. But another Augustan age had existed, another period of literary achievement and
political grandeur, which spoke to America's post-revolutionary
condition: England under Queen Anne and the first two
Georges. Again, the parallel was less than perfect, but there was
much in that era which directly appealed to Americans of the
post-revolutionary generation, even when it went unarticulated.
The accomplishments of the English Augustan age had in effect
justified the Glorious Revolution and the turbulence of Civil
War and Restoration which had preceded it. It was a prosperous
period, when English trade on land and sea was widely extended, and the arts and sciences flourished as they rarely had
before. Augustan Rome had sheltered Virgil, Horace, and
Ovid; seventeen hundred years later England, although she
could not claim writers quite so important, could point to Pope
and Addison, to Swift and to Dr. Johnson.[2]

With the English example in mind, Americans frequently

[2] In "The Meaning of 'Augustan,'" *Journal of the History of Ideas*
XIX (1958), 507–522, James William Johnson provides a careful analysis
of the uses of the term and the changes in its meaning. A thorough evalua-
tion of the favorite themes of Augustan satirists is found in Paul Fussell,
*The Rhetorical World of Augustan Humanism: Ethics and Imagery from
Swift to Burke* (London, 1965); Ian Jack, *Augustan Satire: Intention and
Idiom in English Poetry, 1660–1750* (Oxford, 1952); and D. Judson
Milburn, *The Age of Wit: 1650–1750* (New York, 1966).

used literary and oratorical accomplishment as an index of national greatness. It is well known that after the War of 1812 editorial demands for a "national literature" became increasingly insistent. What is not so widely appreciated, however, is that this expectation was as frequently, but far more confidently, voiced almost from the beginning of the national experience.[3] The new nation was to be justified in its novelty by its success in creating a new and better civilization, one of the marks of which was to be yet another Augustan era in arts and letters. The first post-revolutionary generation fully expected this to come to pass within their own lifetimes: they were to be bitterly disappointed. For Americans did not create a culture as distinctive and exciting as that of Augustan England until the middle third of the nineteenth century, and then it was not Augustan at all. Poe, Melville, Hawthorne, and Emerson rarely looked to the great Augustans, of Rome or of England, as models; they were largely unsympathetic to the traits that Augustans typically honored; their sensitivity was Romantic, not classic. It is no wonder that this generation did not understand its fathers; when Emerson remarked that from 1790 to 1820 there was not a thought in Massachusetts, he was not so much stating a fact as making an assessment of a cultural outlook with which he was unsympathetic. But we need not take Emerson's dismissal for our own.

If the Federalist era was Augustan, then, it cannot be because

[3] Benjamin T. Spencer, *The Quest for Nationality: An American Literary Campaign* (Syracuse, N.Y., 1957), pp. 22–72; Robert E. Spiller, ed., *The American Literary Revolution: 1783–1837* (New York, 1967), pp. 3–105. "Why," Jeremy Belknap had demanded as early as 1780, "may not *a Republic of Letters* be realized in America as well as a Republican Government? Why may there not be a Congress of Philosophers as well as of Statesmen? . . . I am so far an enthusiast in the cause of America as to wish she may shine Mistress of the Sciences, as well as the Asylum of Liberty" (Jeremy Belknap to Ebenezer Hazard, February 4, 1780, *Collections of the Massachusetts Historical Society*, 5th ser., II [Boston, 1877], 255).

its literary accomplishments rival those of Augustan England or Rome. In politics its achievements bear comparison to those of earlier Augustan eras; otherwise the nation was Augustan only in intention, in sympathy, and in ambition. The distinction between Federalist and Jeffersonian in the latter part of the early national period is as much cultural as it is political, if not more so. When Jeffersonians found that the revolution had not produced the golden age they had so confidently expected, they redefined the terms of the golden age. The Federalists tended to be men who maintained faith with the dream—and with their disappointment. Continued consciousness of disappointment makes men bitter, and the Federalists of Jefferson's time were bitter men. *Not* merely because they had lost office, patronage, and power in the election of 1800, but because America appeared to be developing a civilization which they did not understand and of which they certainly did not approve. The more they clung to their definition of what a proper Augustan age would be, the less likely it seemed that America was going to have one.

Yet at the beginning there seemed ample grounds for high expectations. For one thing, as Stuart P. Sherman has phrased it, "The public characters of Washington and his friends, like those of Burke and his friends, were in the grand style, were in a style more or less consciously moulded upon that of the great Republicans of England, Rome, and Athens." As Washington was given more honors, as he assumed in his own lifetime the mantle of the Father of his Country, his public style became a matter for emulation. When sculptors like Horatio Greenough later rendered Washington in Roman toga (for all the world, remarked Philip Hone, as though he were calling a bath attendant) they were not being frivolous: they were choosing the costume and image which would probably have pleased Washington better than any other.[4] George Washington had

---

[4] *The Genius of America* (New York, 1923), p. 200; Oliver W. Larkin, *Art and Life in America* (New York, 1949), p. 182. In *George Washington: Man and Monument* (Boston, 1958), Marcus Cunliffe sug-

played a doubly Roman role: a general as eminent for Americans as Julius Caesar, he had, like Cincinnatus, retired to his farm. It even seemed possible to imagine him as Augustus Caesar, presiding over the peaceable establishment of a new empire. He died, appropriately, at the end of his century, and the more his adherents thought about it, the more certain they became that Washington had embodied the American ideal. That no one took up his role, that his public style was not satisfactorily imitated, that partisan papers began to denounce him, was taken as a rejection of the neoclassic goals which Washington was assumed to have represented. For those who felt this way, attacks on Washington were not merely attacks on a man and his party, but on a whole set of cultural expectations.[5]

The first President's administration, it came to appear, had provided Americans with a "golden age," when, as the Constitution of Boston's Washington Benevolent Society remembered,

gests that Washington may be "better understood within a classical framework than as a man of modern times." Rome, Cunliffe points out, "was a martial civilization, always aware of unrest along the frontiers, the bringer of law and the imposer of order. . . . Rome was a slaveholding society in which (outside the capital and the provincial centers) the unit of neighborhood was a farm estate. It was a society that relied upon the family as the cohesive force. . . . This was a society that bred solid, right-thinking citizens, at once civic and acquisitive, men of a noble narrowness. . . . For 'Rome' here, may we not read 'Virginia'?" (pp. 194, 192). Among Washington's own classical models was Cato; see Fredric M. Litto, "Addison's Cato in the Colonies," *William and Mary Quarterly*, 3d ser., XXIII (1966), 441–442, 447

[5] For a perceptive assessment of Washington hagiography, see Cunliffe, pp. 3–24, 184–190. "The early American Republic, like many of the new nations, was legitimized by *charisma*," writes Seymour Martin Lipset. "We tend to forget today that, in his time, George Washington was idolized as much as many of the contemporary leaders of new states." For discussion of Washington's role as charismatic leader, see Lipset, *The First New Nation: The United States in Historical and Comparative Perspective* (New York, 1963), pp. 18–23; for a good example of this veneration, see Charles Jared Ingersoll, *Inchiquin, The Jesuit's Letters* (New York, 1810), pp. 63–65.

"the people were prosperous in their industry, the government was respected by foreign nations, and the commercial prosperity, the wealth and the power of the United States were augmented to a degree without precedent and beyond the most sanguine expectation." [6] Washington's eulogists generally found the biblical parallel the natural one: Americans, said Carter Braxton of Virginia, "wept for his loss as the Israelites did for Moses." [7] Other analogies were available. Moses had led his people only to the borders of the Promised Land; Washington, who had accompanied his people while they fulfilled their mission, was, according to one prominent Massachusetts clergyman, "truly our Joshua." And the Reverend John Snelling Popkin proceeded to find in the Book of Judges a federalist paradigm of American politics:

While, under Joshua, the Israelites adhered to their Almighty Sovereign, their success far exceeded all human efforts and credibility. . . . But when this generation were gathered unto their fathers, there arose another generation, which knew not the Lord, nor yet the works which he had done for Israel. And the children of Israel did evil in the sight of the Lord, and served other gods. . . . And the anger of the Lord was hot against Israel, and he delivered them into the hands of spoilers.[8]

[6] Quoted in William Alexander Robinson, "The Washington Benevolent Society in New England: A Phase of Politics During the War of 1812," *Proceedings of the Massachusetts Historical Society*, XLIX (March, 1916), 278. "Is there a man who contributed towards obtaining American Liberty and Independence, from WASHINGTON TO STRONG, who has not been the object of reproach and ingratitude?" asked the Boston *Centinel*. "Where are the Heroes of our revolution? How many remain, who are not exiled, *murdered*, or impeached?" (Reprinted in the New York *Evening Post*, January 26, 1805). Other complaints on the theme of "où sont les neiges d'antan?" are found in the New York *Evening Post*, January 22 and 26, 1805.

[7] Carter Braxton to John Rutledge, Jr., December 13, 1802, John Rutledge, Jr., Papers, Southern Historical Collection, University of North Carolina Library, Chapel Hill, N.C.

[8] C. C. Felton, *A Memoir of the Rev. John Snelling Popkin* (Cambridge, Mass., 1852), pp. 245, 238–239.

How would the new generation define its revolutionary heritage? Which would it choose for America's golden age? Which Washington was to be emulated and honored: Washington the Revolutionary general or Washington the cold and correct President? The problem was partly one of perspective: the men who succumbed to old age in 1800 tended to be remembered for the attitudes of their moderate middle age, rather than for those of their more radical youth. Jonathan Mason could in all seriousness report with shock that Jefferson's inaugural address "praises the *revolutionary* character of the great Washington." [9] Was Washington's "revolutionary character" to be ignored? On the other hand, did the patriots' replacements, the new generation, truly know the Lord and the works which he had done for Israel? "It is painful," commented Henry William DeSaussure, "to see the pillars of the revolution tumbling down, one after the other; and what is worse, perhaps, speaking nationally, to see the people substituting for them rotten stuff, or green materials." [10] Republicans easily assumed that their opponents were disingenuously using Washington as "a stalking horse, behind which, they may shelter themselves," but the explanation does not explain enough.[11] Was not the problem, at bottom, psychological? Might it not be suggested that one crucial distinction between Federalist and Jeffersonian in the early years of the nineteenth century was that the Federalist did not fully trust untried, "green" materials—that is, the post-Washington generation—and that the Jeffersonian did? The point must not be overstated, but it may help us to comprehend the enlargement of the Washington image to mythological and quasi-religious proportions. To William Henry Hill of North Carolina, Washington was both Moses and Joshua: "Having once led us to peace and independence, he again conducted us from weak-

[9] Jonathan Mason to J. Rutledge, March 5, 1801, John Rutledge, Jr., Papers.

[10] Henry William DeSaussure to J. Rutledge, November 2, 1801, John Rutledge, Jr., Papers.

[11] Quoted in Boston *Repertory*, March 2, 1804.

ness, wretchedness and despondence, to strength, hope, and happiness." [12] William Gaston went further: "Heaven seemed to have destined him to be our Saviour from all dangers; our Guardian and protector in all difficulties." [13] This use of imagery helped to make revolution respectable; it enabled Americans to be the proud inheritors of the American Revolution while at the same time rejecting the French Revolution as chaotic. The attitude was the more widely shared as the revolutionary era receded into the past. Alexis de Tocqueville's perceptive companion, Gustave de Beaumont, noted with some surprise that Americans did not erect statues of their heroes, and answered his own request for an explanation: "To Washington alone are there busts, inscriptions, a column; this is because Washington, in America, is not a man, but a god." [14]

The Roman model had come naturally to Washington, as it came to many of his contemporaries. To extend one's schooling beyond the three R's meant, in the early national period, to study the classics, and in the course of that study to learn not only the ancient languages, but to value, even to venerate, the stately Roman morality. For the remainder of their lives, men so educated would find the classical comparison the natural one to make. One of the more popular pseudonyms adopted by Fed-

[12] Charleston, S.C., *Courier*, March 16, 1803.

[13] "Eulogy on George Washington," n.d. William Gaston Papers, Southern Historical Collection, University of North Carolina Library, Chapel Hill, N.C.

[14] *Marie, or Slavery in the United States*, trans. Barbara Chapman (Stanford, California, 1958), p. 106. The veneration accorded to Washington may be psychologically linked to an expectation, encouraged by revolutionary rhetoric which identified all evil as British, that the new nation would be free from all taint, that is, virtually perfect. See Perry Miller, "From the Covenant to the Revival," in James Ward Smith and A. Leland Jamison, eds., *The Shaping of American Religion*, I (Princeton, 1961), 343–346. See also the extended discussion of Federalist ideology in James M. Banner, Jr., *To the Hartford Convention: The Federalists and the Origins of Party Politics in Massachusetts, 1789–1815* (New York, 1970), chs. 1, 2.

eralists was "Phocion"; the writer who used it expected his readers to know their Plutarch, and assumed that the name could
stand, in a sort of intellectual shorthand, for both the elitist variant of republican political theory popular among Federalists
and for the sense of rejection that tormented them in the years
of the Jeffersonian ascendancy. Phocion had been an Athenian
statesman of the fourth century, B.C.; a man honored for his
prudence and rectitude; a highly popular general who had been
reelected forty-five times, "although he was not even once present at the election, but was always absent when the people sum-
moned and chose him," and despite the fact that he "never said
or did anything to win their favour." Phocion was elected by a
public which could choose its own medicine; "the Athenians,"
explained Plutarch, "made use of their more elegant and
sprightly leaders by way of diversion, but when they wanted a
commander they were always sober and serious, and called upon
the severest and most sensible citizen, one who alone, or more
than the rest, arrayed himself against their desires and impul-
ses." When they eventually rejected him, Phocion complained,
like the frustrated Federalist of 1801, "I have given this people
much good and profitable counsel, but they will not listen to
me!"[15] When Alexander Hamilton searched for the worst
name he could call Aaron Burr without resorting to unprintable
language, the name of Catiline came readily to mind, and his au-

---

[15] *Plutarch's Lives*, trans. Bernadotte Perrin (Cambridge, Mass., 1919),
pp. 161–162, 177. Among Federalist users of the "Phocion" signature
were Fisher Ames (in a series of essays in the *New-England Palladium*,
April, 1801); Tapping Reeve (in the Litchfield, Conn., *Monitor*, December 9, 1803) and William Loughton Smith (in the Charleston *Courier*,
1806, published as a pamphlet called *The Numbers of Phocion . . . on
the subject of Neutral Rights* [Charleston, S.C., 1806]. Alexander Hamilton used the name in a series of articles protesting the seizure of Loyalist
property in 1783; his choice may have had certain autobiographical connotations, as John C. Miller suggests (*Alexander Hamilton: Portrait in
Paradox* [New York, 1959], p. 102n). Oliver Wolcott and Smith used
Phocion as their signature in their famous pamphlet attack on *The Preten-*

dience did not need to be reminded who Catiline had been nor why his name was odious. And to continue, after school, to read and to collect a gentleman's library meant to add to one's schoolboy editions of the ancients the works of the great English Augustans: Swift, Pope, and Dr. Johnson, who also had venerated the great heroes of the ancient world.

A classical education, a literary background in the Augustans, these were shared by most educated Americans of whatever political sympathies. But men who were disenchanted with their world found certain features of the work of the English Augustans particularly attractive. For one thing, the English Augustans were critical of contemporary changes in dress, manners, and language; American Federalists too lived in an era when the forms of social intercourse were changing, and not, they were convinced, for the better. The Augustans regularly sneered at what they called "the mob," and the more the American public rejected Federalism, the more many Federalists assuaged their feelings by sneering back at the public. The Augustans knew they lived in an age of flagrant political corruption, and sought to expose it; Federalists convinced themselves that they could not have been rejected save for political corruption, and denounced the phenomenon nearly as vigorously. Finally, the American Federalist might count himself Augustan in his expectation of literary accomplishment, in the exaggerated honor he accorded to Washington, in his gloomy cyclical reading of history.[16]

---

sions of Thomas Jefferson to the Presidency . . . (Philadelphia, 1796). Henry Steele Commager discusses this habit of "putting contemporaries into some historical niche" ("Leadership in Eighteenth-Century America and Today," in *Freedom and Order: A Commentary on the American Political Scene* [New York, 1966], p. 162).

[16] See Lewis P. Simpson, "Federalism and the Crisis of Literary Order," *American Literature*, XXXII (1960), 253–266; and Lewis P. Simpson, ed., *The Federalist Literary Mind: Selections from the Monthly Anthology and Boston Review 1803–1811* (Baton Rouge, La., 1962), pp. 31–41, for extended discussion of this analogy.

To men of such persuasion, the most useful literary form is the satire. It had been virtually the trademark of English Augustan writing from Butler to Swift, and, taking encouragement and rhetorical instruction from the great satirists of Augustan England, American Federalists scattered verse and prose satire among their jeremiads. It is not likely that Federalist pamphleteers flattered themselves they were the literary equals of Swift and Butler. They seem to have regarded satire primarily as a way of reaching the "middling classes" who failed to respond to high seriousness; given an eighteenth-century education which taught students to write by the imitation of classical models and given the obvious similarities of Augustan antipathies to their own, the Federalist turn to the Augustan model was a logical one. Federalist satire is seldom very clever, but it does help clarify those reasons for Federalist distrust of their opponents that are not linked directly to specific political issues. While their polemics attacked what the Jeffersonians did, their satire attacked what the Jeffersonians *were*, revealing in the process something of the Federalist image of the Democrat.

The satires were many and took a variety of forms. There was the witty potpourri that Washington Irving, his brother William, and James Kirke Paulding called *Salmagundi*. There were the letters of the Baron von Hartzensleigzenstoffendahl which William Tudor, Jr., wrote for the *Monthly Anthology and Boston Review*. John Sylvester John Gardiner, a Boston clergyman as pompous as his name, wrote an "Ode to Democracy" in which the lyric echoed Gray and the images imitated Pope; there were less pretentious pieces, like John Quincy Adams's drinking song "On the discoveries of Captain Lewis," or the sarcastic sketch signed "Buffon" that Oliver Wolcott, Jr., scribbled for the *Connecticut Courant*. Federalist satirists kept returning to one seemingly inexhaustible source of inspiration: Thomas Jefferson himself. Certain episodes of his career, especially his flight to Monticello during the British invasion of Virginia in 1780, and certain pieces of his writing, especially the

Notes on Virginia and the *First Inaugural Address,* became particular favorites, used to the point of redundancy and at the risk,
fatal to the satirist, of boring the reader. This singleness of focus
was due less to a failure of imagination than to the habit of
treating the Republicans not as a political party but as a faction, the personal following of a single leader, bound together
by personal loyalties rather than by ideology or by political principle. According to this reasoning, if popular faith in the person
of Thomas Jefferson could be broken, the whole opposition
could be expected to fall apart.

The Federalist satirists were not a homogeneous group. Shar-
ing primarily a technique of response to the Jeffersonian challenge, each had some acquaintance among the others, but their
interrelationship and interaction seem insufficient to justify the
rubric of "circle" or group. Some of the satirists were primarily
politicians: Josiah Quincy, for example, and his distant cousin,
John Quincy Adams. Thomas Green Fessenden was educated as
a lawyer, but spent most of his life as a writer and journalist, as
did Joseph Dennie. For others, political satire provided avoca-
tional distraction from a rather different sort of career: Timothy
Dwight, for example, was president of Yale; Oliver Wolcott,
Jr., after leaving the office of Secretary of the Treasury, was
building a mercantile trading house in New York. Surely the
satirists do not represent a cross section of Federalist society;
their family backgrounds were too upper-class, too intellectual
for that. Their fathers were too often ministers and lawyers;
their own education culminated too frequently in Harvard or
Yale to make them either sociologically or geographically typical, nor would it do to assume that they "spoke for" the Federalist party in a representative sense—if anyone, for that matter,
did or could. They were, however, authors of a particularly revealing genre of Federalist dissent, and much of what they had
to say coordinates with criticism made in more pedestrian fashion by the more typical members of their party. What is under

examination here is one variant of what might well be called "The Federalist Persuasion."

The most extended of these satires, and the ones that best repay careful analysis, were "Climenole," a dozen essays written by the Massachusetts congressman Josiah Quincy, and *Democracy Unveiled, or Tyranny Stripped of the Garb of Patriotism,* a book-length epic "of the Hudibrastic kind," by Thomas Green Fessenden, which enjoyed three printings in New York and Boston. Other satires generally concentrate on a single Democratic failing, but Quincy and Fessenden had room to expound on all they found distressing in their opponents' views of life and politics. Fessenden was a Vermont lawyer with an erratic intellectual career, which mingled poetics and polemics. During a brief stay in England he attacked the medical profession in a versified satire called *The Terrible Tractorian;* he served a brief stint in New York City as editor of the short-lived *Weekly Inspector* in 1807, and eventually returned to New England, where he edited agricultural journals and dabbled in inventing. He wrote numerous political verses, but the most vigorous are those of *Democracy Unveiled,* which is Hudibrastic both in meter and in shared antipathies.[17]

The satire of *Democracy Unveiled* was sharp, Fessenden warned, because he "cuts to cure"; a sharpness the more necessary because "our democrats, though spitted with the arrows of

[17] Written in iambic tetrameter, it was critical of the political tastes of the general public and of what Thomas Green Fessenden vaguely called "mobocracy." An antidemocratic note was characteristic of Augustan satire; perhaps the most quoted lines in *Hudibras* are these:

> "For as a Fly, that goes to Bed,
> Rests with his Tail above his Head;
> So in this Mungril State of ours,
> The Rabble are the Supreme Powers."

See Ian Jack, *Augustan Satire: Intention and Idiom in English Poetry, 1660–1750* (Oxford, 1952), pp. 34, 41.

satire, by the merciless wits of the age, and roasted before the
slow fire of public indignation, appear to possess as little feeling
as the " 'passive ox,' that graced the democratic fete in Boston,
held in honor of the French revolution." [18] He intended his
verses "as a sort of compendium of Federal principles." [19] In
cantos headed "Mobocracy," "The Jeffersoniad," and "The Gib-
bet of Satire," Fessenden took exception to, among other things,
Jefferson's *Notes on Virginia,* America's failure to take arms
against France, Tom Paine and "the Catalines of faction," ending with the pious hope that as of 1806 "the cause of Federalism
. . . has passed its most gloomy period. The *ebb tide* had arrived to its utmost point, and will shortly be succeeded by a
flood, which will overwhelm its enemies in one prodigious
ruin." [20] No accusation was too severe or vulgar for Fessenden
to endorse; he spent a whole canto chortling over the tales of
Jefferson's alleged dalliance with Mrs. Walker and a black
slave named Sally Hemings, excusing himself with the comment
that he could not be accused of libel because he did not intend to
"disturb the public peace." [21] In this respect too, he was akin to
Augustan satirists, who wrote verses as though they were stump
speeches, often concerned less with what was said than with its
impact on the audience. As Ian Jack has explained, a poem became "not so much an expression of emotion as a calculated attempt to arouse emotion in its readers. A lampooning satire, for
example, is not necessarily an expression of hatred (if it is
merely that it will hardly be a good satire): it is an attempt to
arouse hatred toward its subject in the mind of the public." [22]
Several years later an anonymous Federalist wrote in justification of his virulent invective:

[18] [Fessenden], *Democracy Unveiled, or Tyranny Stripped of the
Garb of Patriotism, by Christopher Caustic, L.L.D.,* 3d ed. (New York,
1806), I, viii, 116.

[19] *Ibid.,* I, xvi.

[20] *Ibid.,* II, 147, 214–215.

[21] *Ibid.,* I, xviii.

[22] Jack, p. 3.

Those who assert that every political transaction in this country should have its *measured share* of approbation or of censure applied to it, that just so much and no more than it intrinsically deserves, should be the quantity of either which is bestowed, know nothing of the state of politicks in the United States; and those who imagine that mere reasoning and solid argument are calculated to convince men in a republican government, of the truth or errour of opinions, know nothing of human nature. . . . Where a whole assembly is constantly brawling, he must have the lungs of a Stentor, who expects to be heard distinctly amidst the tumult.[23]

Unfortunately for Fessenden, most readers of his satires were probably already anti-Jeffersonian. At any rate, no one seems to have sued him for libel.

Josiah Quincy wrote "Climenole" in 1804, most of it in the dull months between his first election to Congress and the opening of the session. Quincy was to amass an impressively long bibliography in the course of a varied career as lawyer, congressman, judge, mayor of Boston and president of Harvard College, but virtually all of the items in it were published versions of speeches he had made or polemical pamphlets intended to endorse or attack projected legislation. "Climenole" was his sole imaginative effort, a *tour de force* written to please an old friend and college classmate, Joseph Dennie.[24] Its arrangement is peculiarly convoluted. The "I" of the narrative is not Josiah Quincy, Federalist, but Slaveslap Kiddnap, Republican author

[23] *The Ordeal*, July 1, 1809, pp. 402–403. See also Fessenden's own comments on the uses of satire in *The Weekly Inspector*, September 6, 1806.

[24] Dennie, founder and editor of the *Port Folio*, best known and most widely circulated of Federalist periodicals, was habitually in need of new contributions and constantly badgered old friends for aid. Once Quincy had obliged him with a few installments that he probably did not intend to continue, Dennie pressed him for more, and the mixture of flattery and appeal to an honorable commitment was enough to result in a total of twelve installments. The later ones were widely spaced in time, and the series eventually petered out. See also Edmund Quincy, *Life of Josiah Quincy* (Boston, 1867), p. 32.

of a fictitious book called "Memorabilia Democratica" of which Quincy purports to be merely the reviewer. The expressions of temperament and principle in the essays are thus supposed to be Republican rather than Federalist, and the absurdities in them so patent that the Republican party is condemned out of its own mouth.[25]

Quincy's rhetorical intention was to use ridicule to arouse hatred; like Fessenden, he could be nasty and at times vulgar. He found the proof-sheets of "Memorabilia Democratica," the author of "Climenole" tells the reader, among the waste papers used by Republicans, who "seldom returned from congress hall, without having their animal economy in a most deranged and turbulent state;—for being hard pressed by the federalists, and also gagged by the votes of their own party, the noxious humours, which used to vapour through the mouth, were driven to other channels." The name "Climenole" was well chosen: it was the name Jonathan Swift had given to the servants in the country of Laputa which Gulliver visited in his third voyage, who were responsible for warning their extremely absentminded masters when to speak and when to listen. "This flapper is likewise employed diligently to attend his master in his walks, and upon occasion to give him a soft flap on his eyes, because he is always so wrapped up in cogitation, that he is in manifest danger of falling down every precipice, and bouncing his head against every post, and in the streets, of justling others." [26] Quincy had

---

[25] This form was not uncommon. In 1803 the Charleston *Courier* printed a series of satirical letters signed "Habakkuk Hoecake," who pretended to be a Jeffersonian, the better to satirize them: "We drink, and smoke segars, and talk about state affairs, and argue sometimes so warmly, that we are upon the point of gouging . . . you know it would be a disgrace to democrats not to disagree, if it were for nothing else but to shew that every man has a right to do as he pleases" (February 22).

[26] "Climenole. A Review, Political and Literary.—No. 2," *Port Folio*, February 4, 1804 (all installments of "Climenole" appeared in *Port Folio* in 1804; the periodical name will be omitted in subsequent references); Jonathan Swift, *Travels into Several Remote Nations of the World. By Captain Lemuel Gulliver* (London, 1726), II, 26.

chosen a striking and perceptive illustration of the relation many
Federalists of his generation conceived they had with a largely
Republican public. If the Federalist could not awaken the public
to the dangers of democracy, then he could at least act the pro-
tective role of the flapper, the climenole, to alert the absentminded public to the dangers it ran, to keep it from "falling
down every precipice." If the master refused to heed and continued to "bounce his head against every post," the fault would not
rest with the weaker party. It was just such a definition of their
role that congressional Federalists had developed in the years
since the black day that Thomas Jefferson had been elected
President and the Federalist opposition was tempted (as a minority still, in 1804, was tempted) to sit silently by while the
nation inevitably proceeded to Hell in a Handbasket. If the
Federalists were to be flappers, they would have to pity their opponents as well as hate them; this sort of ambivalence was a
fairly standard Federalist characteristic.

Quincy was not the first Federalist to find Gulliver's Third
Voyage a highly useful source of instructive parallel. References
to Laputa appear and reappear in Federalist satirical prose.[27]
Why Federalists should have fastened on Gulliver's third voyage, the least popular, most disjointed section of the *Travels*, is
easily explained by the similarity of Swift's enmities to the Federalists' own. Federalists found that Swift had, as Quakers say,
"spoken to their condition." The hero of the Third Voyage is
Lord Munodi, a man with whom the Federalist could readily
identify. Munodi, though out of power, retains his good judgment and perceptively discerns the weaknesses of his opponents'
schemes. "While Lord Munodi tries to hold on to the living
past, which is the universally sound, the Balnibarbians sacrifice
all to the pride which they project into a utopian future."[28]
Substitute Federalist for Lord Munodi, Jeffersonian for Balni-

---

[27] E.g., Charleston *Courier*, March 14, 26, 1803; *The Ordeal*, March
25, 1809.

[28] Martin Price, *Swift's Rhetorical Art: A Study in Structure and
Meaning* (New Haven, 1953), p. 83.

barbian, and we have a statement of the Federalist definition of America's central problem. The language of Laputa, therefore, appears and reappears in Federalist satire. In Quincy's work the parallels are drawn so extensively that even the scatology so typical of Swiftian rhetoric and so foreign to Quincy's pompous, starchy prose, appears in "Climenole." [29]

Swift's satire had been directed against abstract and impractical scientific investigations, represented in fact by those that were carried on in his own day by the Royal Society of London, and in his fiction by the inhabitants of the Flying Island of Laputa, who were too engrossed in abstract speculations to cope with commonsensical problems.[30] The investigations conducted at the Grand Academy at Lagado were, as Marjorie Nicolson has demonstrated, direct lampoons of actual experiments reported in the *Transactions* of the Royal Society.[31] Swift's variants included schemes for building houses "by beginning at the roof and working downwards to the foundation," substituting spider webs for silkworm thread, and the investigations of a man who "had been eight years upon a project for extracting sunbeams out of cucumbers, which were to be put into vials hermetically sealed, and let out to warm the air in raw inclement summers." [32]

Swift's Laputan imagery proved useful to those who wished to satirize, not the Royal Society, but the Jeffersonian Republi-

[29] See Edward J. Rosenheim, Jr., *Swift and the Satirist's Art* (Chicago, 1963), pp. 230–232; Norman O. Brown, *Life Against Death* (Middletown, Conn., 1959), pp. 179–201.

[30] Laputa, the Flying Island, hovers over the domains of its monarch; Lagado, the capital city of these domains, houses a Grand Academy. Swift's description of the investigations undertaken at the Academy is a particularly pointed thrust at the Royal Society and the "new science" of Descartes, Kepler, and Newton, which had become in Swift's time fairly standard objects of Augustan attack.

[31] "The Scientific Background of Swift's Voyage to Laputa," *Science and Imagination* (Ithaca, N.Y., 1956), pp. 117–118. See also Nicolson, "Swift's 'Flying Island' in the Voyage to Laputa," *Annals of Science*, II (1937), 405–430.

[32] Swift, II, 65, 66–67, 63.

cans. One of the earliest uses, in a Fourth of July oration delivered in New Haven in 1799 by David Daggett, is engagingly entitled "Sunbeams May Be Extracted from Cucumbers, But the Process Is Tedious." Daggett prefaced a long list of recent developments he deplored in travel, in agriculture, in education, in morals as well as in politics, by the comment:

These [Laputan] theorists were very patient, industrious, and laborious in their pursuits—had a high reputation for their singular proficiency, and were regarded as prodigies in science. The common laborers and mechanics were . . . despised for their stupid and old-fashioned manner of acquiring property and character. If the inquiry had been made whether any of these projects had succeeded, it would have been readily answered that they had not; but they were reasonable, their principles just—and of course, that [they] must ultimately produce the objects in view. . . . If a further enquiry had been made what would be the great excellence of marble pin-cushions, or the superior advantage of a breed of naked sheep, the answer would have been, it is unphilosophical to ask such questions.[33]

Washington Irving's early satires abound in Swiftian imagery. Jefferson's "projects" are the targets of satire, both in *Salmagundi* and in the chapters on William the Testy in Dietrich Knickerbocker's *History of New York.* Irving reported that William "was exceedingly fond of trying philosophical and political experiments . . . much given to mechanical inventions constructing patent smoke-jacks—carts that went before the horses, and especially erecting windmills." His enemies had the effrontery to suggest "that his head was turned by his experiments, and that he really thought to manage his government as he did his mills—by mere wind!"[34] *The New-England Palla-*

[33] *Sun Beams May Be Extracted from Cucumbers, But the Process Is Tedious, An Oration Pronounced on the Fourth of July, 1799, at the Request of the Citizens of New Haven* (New Haven, 1799), pp. 6–7. Daggett made it clear that he believed similar strictures should apply to the recent social and political developments he deplored.

[34] Washington Irving, William Irving, and James Kirke Paulding, *Salmagundi; or, the Whim Whams and Opinions of Launcelot Langstaff,*

dium published a series of satires on modern trends in education
and religion headed "The Projector"; [35] a poem critical of Joel
Barlow's proposals for naval reforms stigmatized him as "Most
noble of Projectors." [36] The Hudson, New York, *Balance* ran a
poem about

> a gentleman, whose head
> Was full of philosophic notions.

Among the notions was the idea that

> To root up weeds their [*sic*] is no reason,
> Against the *rights of plants* 'tis treason.
> Each has an equal right to live.

Projector-like, he embarks on the experiment, and orders his servant to let the weeds alone.

> And why should wheat and barley thrive,
> Despotic tyrants of the field?

The result, of course, is disaster, and the story is told as an object lesson to anyone who should contemplate becoming a "Philosophical Farmer." [37]

Esq. & Others (London, 1811), I, 46; Washington Irving, *A History of
New York, from the Beginning of the World to the End of the Dutch
Dynasty . . . by Dietrich Knickerbocker* (New York, 1809), I, 194, 197–
198, 217. Irving's debt to Swift is explored in William L. Hedges, *Washington Irving: An American Study—1802–1832* (Baltimore, 1965), pp.
47–48, 58, 61, 76–78, and in Martin Roth, *Washington Irving's Contributions to "The Corrector"* (Minneapolis, 1968), pp. 33–34, 37–38,
66.

[35] *New-England Palladium*, January 2, 6, 13, 20, 23, 1801. The
similarity of the angle of vision (a satire reputedly provided by a Republican, who is made to condemn himself), the reference to Laputa,
and the easy availability of the *Palladium* to Quincy suggest that this series
may have provided the model for "Climenole," or even that Quincy had
written it himself. Another possible author of the *Palladium* series is
David Daggett.

[36] "Native Poetry," *New-England Palladium*, April 21, 1801.

[37] Hudson, New York, *Balance*, August 28, 1804.

Now, the appearance of the word "philosophical" in any Federalist tract signals invective ahead. Federalists seem to have associated the word with the French "philosophe" (which of course is not the same thing) and used the adjective to describe all that they wished to denounce, all they wished to associate with French revolutionary theory and practice, and subsequently all they deplored in Jeffersonian ideology. When a Federalist said something was philosophical, he was saying what Burke had said about the French Revolution: that it was visionary, that it was ludicrously impractical, and likely to prove dangerously unsound in practice. Another way of saying the same thing was provided by Jonathan Swift in the language of Laputa, a society formed and ruined by men who walked with their heads literally in the clouds (the island hovered in the atmosphere) and their feet dangling over precipices; a land where agriculture had been ruined by "scientific" schemes purporting to increase productivity beyond natural limits, a land where men refused to recognize the limitations of common sense, and tempted disaster by seeking to do what only God can do, as exemplified by the attempt to build houses by working downwards from the roof, imitating "the proceeding of this Sovereign Architect in the Frame of this great Building of the Universe . . . he began at the Roof, and Builded downwards, and in that process, suspended the inferior parts of the World upon the superior." [38]

"Never," warned Noah Webster in a Fourth of July Address, " . . . let us exchange our civil and religious institutions for the wild theories of crazy projectors; or the sober, industrious moral habits of our country, for experiments in atheism and lawless democracy. *Experience* is a safe pilot; but experiment is a dangerous ocean, full of rocks and shoals." [39] To the Federalist

[38] Swift, II, 65. See R. L. Colie, "Some Paradoxes in the Language of Things," *Reason and the Imagination*, ed. J. A. Mazzeo (New York, 1962), p. 128.

[39] *An Oration Pronounced Before the Citizens of New Haven on the Anniversary of the Independence of the United States* (New Haven, 1798), p. 15.

mind, Jeffersonians were Laputans, committed to an abstract impracticality which would, if not deterred, tear apart the cultural fabric of the young republic. All the famous Jeffersonian rhetoric about man's capacity to construct a better world from new blueprints was so much high-flown nonsense. It was given to man only to remodel his world, not to remake it, and then only with the greatest caution. Anything else was visionary, dangerous, "philosophical"—in short, Laputan. The Revolution and Constitution-making had been renovatory enough. The Federalist had been willing to build a new Jerusalem; he was not anxious to be absorbed into an effort to build a new Laputa.

[2]

Anti-Virginia and

Antislavery

> The republic which Jefferson believed himself
> to be founding or securing in 1801 was an
> enlarged Virginia.
>
> —HENRY ADAMS

Ridicule thrives on the disparity between profession and act. The egalitarian claims of a party which drew its leadership from slaveholders was an obvious target for satire; the Virginia Way of Life proved Virginia democracy counterfeit. The theme was employed most frequently in New England, where the contrast between northern and southern life styles was greater than in the middle states, and where the economic importance of slavery was minimal. Federalist writers used it to discredit political opponents by casting doubt on the social environment from which Jeffersonian political leadership emerged.

Democracy, Josiah Quincy suggested in serious jest, was "an indian word, signifying *'a great tobacco planter, who had herds of black slaves.'* " [1] Shocked by the more obvious excesses of the system, the New England Federalist found it difficult to credit

[1] Josiah Quincy, "Climenole. A Review, Political and Literary. No. 1," January 28. Slaveslap Kiddnap's ancestors derived their surname from "a species of patriotic labour." The given name "expresses with simplicity and neatness, a very necessary operation in raising fine crops of tobacco . . . the operator ploughs [with a cat o'nine tails] as deep into the naked back of his subject, as, in his opinion, may be necessary for the good of the tobacco" ("Climenole. No. 2," February 4, 1804).

23

southern claims for its economic utility. So far as he could tell, the greater the number of slaves, the more wretched the state of agriculture. This attitude reflected neither morality nor moralism; it was brute economics, and its clearest exponent was the Connecticut congressman Roger Griswold on his first trip South. The soil itself, Griswold asserted, was poor, and outmoded technique made it worse; farmers did not rotate their crops, they fattened their cattle by turning them loose in the cornfields. "Having never been taught to take hold of the plough themselves, or to perform any manuel [sic] labour, they cannot enter with sufficient spirit into the business to acquire any real knowledge of the best mode of managing lands." [2] Thus the primitive state of southern agriculture was both directly linked to the slave system and camouflaged by it: "The mode in which these landholders get along is, to starve their Negroes, & by that means save something for their own subsistence—They make their negroes work constantly—give them very little meat indeed, and no bread but corn meal, & the whole cost of a labourer in that way, does not cost the planter more than 30 dollars per annum including subsistence—if one of our farmers should . . . give his labourers good food and a plenty of it—the whole produce of the land wou'd not furnish subsistence much less leave any thing to pay wages or rent." [3] The contrast between the prosperous farm country of Pennsylvania and Maryland, where "poverty is legible in fair characters upon every spot inhabited by a human being," furnished the most convincing of all arguments against slavery. "If I was an enthusiast," Griswold told his wife, "I shou'd launch out into the most extravigant [sic] denunciation against slavery, and into rapturous adorations of

[2] Roger Griswold to Fanny Griswold, December 10, 1800, Griswold Papers, Yale University Library. A few years later the Boston *Repertory* made a similar comment: "[Many planters] occupy vast tracts of poor land, and have been accustomed to live among their vassals in a style of feudal hospitality, and mimick grandeur. The poorest among them, consider personal labour a *disgrace*" (October 2, 1804).

[3] R. Griswold to F. Griswold, December 6, 1800, Griswold Papers.

liberty, but being no enthusiast . . . I draw no other conclusion
. . . than . . . that it is vastly important to give the cultivators
of the soil an interest in the improvement which they make." [4]

It was a widely shared view among Federalists that the system cheated master as well as slave. Denying that the experience
of governing the miniature world of the self-sufficient plantation
prepared the Virginian to govern the real world, they asserted
that the same arrangement which brutalized the slave made the
master indolent and irresponsible.[5] The planter did not learn
sound economic practice: the wastefulness of workers deprived
of incentive for efficiency sapped profits and encouraged the
planter to bleed his estate for immediate gain. The planter's
habit of living in debt to the future, epitomized by the widespread failure to rotate crops, disqualified him for governmental
service. It seemed to northern Federalists that the luxury which
the planter enjoyed made him indolent and supercilious, and
further disqualified him for the leadership of a free people.
"There is a spirit of domination engrafted on the character of
the southern people," insisted Thomas Boylston Adams. "Of all

[4] *Ibid.*, December 28. Other Federalists were similarly distressed. "In
the Eastern states where slavery is not suffered," said Samuel White of
Delaware during the Senate debate on the Breckinridge Bill to establish
a government for the Louisiana Territory, "their lands are highly cultivated
their buildings neat, useful and elegant—and the people are strong,
powerful and wealthy. But as you travel south, the instant you arrive to
where slavery is, you find the lands uncultivated, the building decaying
and falling into ruins and the people poor, weak and feeble" (January 25,
1804, in Everett S. Brown, "The Senate Debate on the Breckinridge Bill
for the Government of Louisiana, 1804," *American Historical Review*,
XXII [January 1917], 347). See also Noah Webster, *A Collection of
Essays and Fugitiv* [*sic*] *Writings* . . . (Boston, 1790), No. 27, pp. 365–
366; and Jonathan Mason, *Extracts from a Diary . . . of a Journey from
Boston to Savannah in 1804* (Cambridge, Mass., 1885), pp. 14–29: "The
slaves of this country are its curse."

[5] Carl Bridenbaugh, "Training the Ruling Class," *Seat of Empire: The
Political Role of Eighteenth Century Williamsburg* (Williamsburg, Va.,
1950), pp. 3–17.

the inhabitants of this continent, they are the most imperious in their manners." [6] Noah Webster wrote much the same thing in his simplified spelling, ascribing it to the effect of living "remote from society, surrounded only by slaves. . . . Urbanity," he concluded, "iz acquired only in societies of wel bred peeple." [7]

On occasion, similar charges were leveled by southern Federalists. In an anonymous essay in the Charleston *Courier*, the Virginia ship of state was imaginatively—and sarcastically—described:

Near to the centre of the line [of ships representing each state] floated one much larger than the rest . . . though its anchor lay on a line with the rest, its officers had ventured to heave shorter upon the cables that it might ride foremost, and display its magnitude and its pride. Its quarter-deck was covered with a crowd of men, lolling in indolence, languishing under the enervating rays of the sun, in *ennui* and idleness, . . . some making mock races . . . between worms and other vermin . . . all laying wages and betting, a few playing for dollars—the majority *on tick*. The waist and forecastle were covered with negroes—but neither black nor white were to be seen on the masts or yards or in the rigging, the former of which seemed to be splitting with the sun, and the latter to be frittering away in white fillaments for want of varnish, grease and tar, which yet were lying in abundance on the deck.[8]

[6] [Thomas Boylston Adams] "A Looker-On," *Port Folio*, January 31, 1801. Identification of authorship in Randolph C. Randall, "Authors of the *Port Folio* Revealed by the Hall Files," *American Literature*, XI (January, 1940), p. 386. Thomas Boylston Adams was rebuked on this occasion by his elder brother, John Quincy Adams (J. Q. Adams to T. B. Adams, April 4, 1801, Adams Papers microfilms, reel 400). The Adams Papers microfilms are hereafter cited as APm, with reel numbers. All references to the Adams Papers are to the microfilm edition published by the Massachusetts Historical Society, Boston, which owns the originals. Quotations are by permission of the Society.

[7] *Essays*, p. 365. Thomas Jefferson himself considered this the most dangerous effect of slavery. See his *Notes on the State of Virginia*, ed. Thomas Perkins Abernethy (New York, 1964), p. 155.

[8] January 24, 1803.

A column in the Raleigh, North Carolina, *Minerva* discussed the difference between the attitudes of New Englanders ("If they have occasion to hire laboring men, they associate with them and eat at the same table") and of Virginia democrats ("A democrat in the southern states is a planter, or other person, who owns a large number of slaves; who is above labor himself").[9] The Washington, D.C., *Federalist* rejected the claim of the man who lived surrounded by "half-naked, ill-cared for slaves" to be "a mighty democrat—a warm stickler for the *rights* of man, for liberty—and what is more equality." The "little domestic monarch [who] writes and spouts incessantly about . . . the *danger of power*" was obviously as self-contradictory as a man could be.[10] A monologue published in the *New-England Palladium* dramatized the same point. When a Virginia planter named Fraternal is interrupted while he is apostrophizing the "divine, solacing, benevolent, convenient Spirit of Freedom," he whips the offending slave, exclaiming: " 'Oh you idle, impertinent, blundering scoundrel—to break in on me thus, when I had arrived at the most interesting, eloquent, and pathetic part of my speech, at the very instant when I was going to demonstrate the equality of all men, of what rank, station and talents soever!' " [11]

The Republican hypocrite who prattled of equality while retaining the power of life and death over his slaves was not mel-

---

[9] January 19, 1802; see also July 18, 1803.

[10] Reprinted in the New York *Evening Post*, December 30, 1801.

[11] Reprinted in the *Port Folio*, July 30, 1803. See also the Federalist pamphlet *The Political Nursery, for the Year Eighteen Hundred Two* (Norwich, Conn., 1802), p. 4:

> "These despots boast of Liberty
> Of *Freedom* and *Equality*,
> And yet O! *dire disgraceful* clan,
> They tread in dust their fellow man."

Other antislavery poems appeared in the Baltimore *Weekly Magazine*, January 28 and June 7, 1800.

lowed or educated by public service. Rather the contrary was true, according to William Tudor:

Surrounded by their slaves, the love of liberty is sublimated to a passion—and they go to the capitol with a zest for personal independence, that is whetted by the continued sight of the miseries of slavery, and which by the force of habit spurns all the frigid ceremonies and decencies, to which the rest of the world are subject—They follow an argument with a blow, and are ready to fight as well as reason.[12]

"Though the Lordlings *fatten on oppression*," complained Isaac C. Bates of Northampton, "yet we are . . . urged to colleague with them, as the guardians of Freedom, as the lovers of the poor, the friends of the unfortunate." [13]

To the Federalist mind, even the amusements of the "unrestrained aristocracy" [14] were unhealthy: Virginians were reported to amuse themselves in bear-baiting and gouging.[15] One *Port Folio* poet sang, in vague imitation of Horace:

---

[12] *Monthly Anthology and Boston Review*, VII (February, 1810), 93. Part of a series of satirical essays purporting to be a German traveler's account of life in the United States. Tudor is identified as the author by M. A. DeWolfe Howe, ed., *Journal of the Proceedings of the Society Which Conducts the Monthly Anthology and Boston Review, October 3, 1805 to July 2, 1811* (Boston, 1910), p. 327.

[13] *An Oration Pronounced at Northampton, July 4, 1805* . . . (Northampton, Mass., 1805), p. 24. See also John Arnett to Timothy Pickering, January 7, 1804, Pickering Papers, Mass. Hist. Soc.; William Vans Murray to J. Q. Adams, April 3, 1802, American Historical Association *Annual Report*, 1912, p. 405 ("as callous as is the foot's sole of one of those slaves who treads the furrows of an imperial Virginia democrat"); and Timothy Pickering to Richard Peters, December 24, 1803, *Pennsylvania Magazine of History and Biography*, XLIV, 330 ("the *aristocratic democrats* of the South").

[14] Oliver Wolcott, Jr., to Fisher Ames, January 24, 1803, Oliver Wollcott, Jr., Papers, Connecticut Historical Society.

[15] A southern Federalist pointed out that gouging was a white man's sport: "I observe . . . that the slave . . . contents himself with using his fists, and leaves, with becoming deference, the sublimer practice [of gouging] to his master" ("Babellophilos" [Love of Babel], dateline Richmond, Virginia, July 14, 1801, in *Port Folio*, August 15, 1801).

Place me at some remote Virginia inn,
Where drunken democrats the state amend
Where nought but hog and hominy is found
And toddy, tiff abhorr'd.[16]

"Where drunken democrats the state amend." There was the point. Was it wise, was it even rational, to entrust the powers of government, the power to declare war, to reorganize the judiciary system, to purchase and maintain new territory like Louisiana, to the inefficient, irresponsible, rowdy products of a slave society? When the roistering Matthew Lyon of Vermont failed to be reelected by sober, sensible New England farmers, he moved to Kentucky, where his new neighbors obligingly sent him to Congress. Southern congressmen, complained William Tudor, "rise like meteors out of the swamps and forests they inhabit; and, such is the force of their genius, trample on those who have been long accustomed to the meditations of statesmen."[17] It is perhaps an oversimplification to assume that all Federalists, including the younger generation, agreed that government might safely be entrusted only to "the wise, the rich, and the well-born," but certainly they were agreed that the government might *not* safely be entrusted to the volatile and rowdy, and they believed that southern social arrangements, far more than the northern, tended to produce such characters, even —or especially—among the rich and well-born.

Oliver Wolcott's political testament for the year 1803 summarized the accusation that Virginia society is a sick society, in which wealth is dissipated in personal luxury, slave labor drives

---

[16] December 11, 1802; imitation of Horace, *Odes*, Book I, No. 22, possibly by Thomas Cadwallader, a young Philadelphia Federalist. For descriptions of the violence endemic in southern society, see John Bach McMaster, *History of the People of the United States* (New York, 1883), II, 5; Isaac Weld, Jr., *Travels through the States of North America* (London, 1799), II, 143–144; Albert J. Beveridge, *The Life of John Marshall* (Boston, 1919), I, 22–23; Robert McColley, *Slavery and Jeffersonian Virginia* (Urbana, Ill., 1964), pp. 39–41.

[17] *Monthly Anthology and Boston Review*, VII (February, 1810), 93.

out free, and the poor white is nearly as degraded as the slave.
Virginia democrats gave lip service to the rights of man and to
republican principles, Wolcott thought, only in order to blind
slaves and poor whites to their lack of political influence and to
divert them from the assertion of their rights.[18] A year later
Wolcott was arguing that the meddling of Virginia planters also
accounted for the nation's difficulties in international relations.
His reinterpretation of American history anticipated Charles
Beard's contention that Virginia planters had supported the
American Revolution primarily to avoid paying their debts to
British creditors. The knowledge that American motives in-
cluded avarice, Wolcott thought, "deeply injured the popularity
of the *American* cause in *Great-Britain.*" [19] Wolcott believed
that both parties had broken the postwar treaty: Britain by her
refusal to abandon fur-trading posts in the northwest; the
United States by interfering with the collection of British debts.
By 1795 the two nations were so close to war that only the Jay
Treaty obnoxious as it was to Virginia Republicans, enabled
them to avoid it. But who had been responsible for the American
infringement of the Treaty of Paris, Wolcott asked. Who had
made the Jay Treaty unavoidable? Virginia—a state which, in
unenthusiastically passing laws permitting delay in the collection
of these debts, "had arrogated the right of determining, when
and to what degree a national Treaty should be executed." [20]
The Jay Treaty unavoidably exacerbated tensions with France,
and if the United States now found herself suspended between
the two great antagonists, and faced with "wretchedness & ruin,"
she had Virginia to thank. Privately, Wolcott was even sharper:
"This wicked state," he snapped to Griswold early in 1804, "has
been the principal cause of all our divisions. The dominion of a

[18] O. Wolcott to F. Ames, January 24, 1803, Wolcott Papers.
[19] *British Influence on the Affairs of the United States* (Boston, 1804),
p. 4.
[20] *Ibid.,* p. 8. For similar sentiments, see William Smith Shaw to Arthur
Maynard Walter, February 27, 1800, Shaw Papers, Boston Athenaeum.

community of beggarly Palatines and insolent slaves is intolerably odious." [21]

Imperceptibly, the Federalist image of Virginia had shifted. Once only an example, she became the epitome of a set of social arrangements and political sentiments which Federalists deplored. The Virginia Way of Life gradually ceased to be considered quaint and was regarded as an aberration; it came to seem impossible that the rest of the South could voluntarily share Virginia's *Weltanschauung*. The southern states were merely Virginia's "fiefs," Federalists tended to assume, and Virginia kept her leadership only by "fomenting faction." [22] Harrison Gray Otis compared the Jeffersonian officeholders to "tenants of a decaying estate," whose neglect would permit "the Tobacco worms [to] . . . destroy all that is flourishing and verdant, stalk and stem, and the Federal constitution in our time will I fear become literally a Virginia old field." [23] Otis made this remark in a letter to John Rutledge, Jr., of South Carolina; southern Federalists like Rutledge and William Richardson Davie confirmed their northern friends' fears. "I have long beheld in silent indignation," complained Davie, "the low degraded situation of No. Carolina, destitute of National character, self-respect, and all political importance, content with being a miserable appendage of the Ancient Dominion." The division of parties, he thought, had nothing to do with principle, but "originated in the question whether Virginia shall be every thing, and the other States

---

[21] *Ibid.*, pp. 22–23; O. Wolcott to R. Griswold, January 14, 1804, Wolcott Papers. Wolcott had been thinking along these lines for many years, at least since 1793. See C. M. Destler, *Joshua Coit, American Federalist, 1758–1798* (Middletown, Conn., 1962), pp. 42–48; George Gibbs, *Memoirs of the Administrations of Washington and John Adams, Edited from the Papers of Oliver Wolcott* (New York, 1846), I, 86.

[22] O. Wolcott to R. Griswold, January 14, 1804; Wolcott to William Bingham, February 4, 1804, Wolcott Papers.

[23] Harrison Gray Otis to John Rutledge, Jr., October 18, 1801, John Rutledge, Jr., Papers, Southern Historical Collection, University of North Carolina Library, Chapel Hill, N.C.

NOTHING." [24] What had begun as a rhetorical device was increasingly treated as a statement of fact; Virginia, not the Democratic-Republican party, was the true enemy of the Federalist cause. Thus Azel Backus of Connecticut could cheer "the Virginia defeat in Connecticut this Election," and as late as 1816 Davie was substituting the phrase "Virginia faction" for the name of the opposition party.[25]

Reliance on rhetoric could be dangerous; it could cloud the perception of reality and make oversimplification deceptively easy. When northern Federalists came to toy with secession in 1804, they reassured themselves that they were seceding from Virginian hegemony rather than from the true Union. Oliver Wolcott complained, in the months the plot was being laid, of "the abhorrent domination of the perfidious Virginians," and Roger Griswold was sure that the chief danger to the Union lay not in his own secessionist plotting, but in the "overbearing influence of Virginia." [26] This was a point of view which John Quincy Adams, first as a Federalist partisan and then as a lapsed Federalist, dedicated himself to eradicating.[27] "That New-York and Virginia, and particularly the latter, should have great influence, is so natural, that the absurdity would be in a state of things, under which they should not have it," he wrote in an article for the *Port Folio*. "They are entitled to it . . . By their proportion of territory, of population, of property, of revolutionary sufferings and exertions, and of eminent and able men, whose talents and services those important states have given to

---

[24] William R. Davie to John Steele, September 25, 1803, in Blackwell P. Robinson, *William R. Davie* (Chapel Hill, 1957), p. 374.

[25] Azel Backus to J. Rutledge, November 22, 1805, John Rutledge, Jr., Papers, Duke University Library; William R. Davie to William Gaston, April 7, 1816, William Gaston Papers, South. Hist. Coll.

[26] O. Wolcott to R. Griswold, March 3, 1804; R. Griswold to O. Wolcott, March 11, 1804, Wolcott Papers.

[27] Even he could be found, on occasion, denouncing the "Virginia faction" in the Massachusetts state legislature ("Publius Valerius" Essays, October 1804, APm reel 403).

the union." [28] When Adams came to review the writings of Fisher Ames, he noted and deplored the prominence of the anti-Virginia theme in them. George Washington had warned Americans against factional politics: men like Ames, who prided themselves on being disciples of "the Washington school of American politics," contradicted their own principles by publishing castigations of other sections of the union.[29] Adams perceived that anti-Virginia rhetoric easily led to talk of secession: "If it be true, that the people in the different quarters of this Union are not sufficiently drawn together by the ties which form the connections of a common country . . . let me ask . . . can there be any humanity, in a painful exertion of intellect, to awaken every sleeping ember of jealousy, to widen every breach . . . to stiffen coldness into frost? . . . Unjust reproach inevitably calls forth and deserves resentment, its natural offspring are hatred and revenge." [30]

To predict dissolution of the union was, in fact, a standard conversational gambit in the early years of the republic. Northern Federalists were so conscious of the differences between their

[28] *Port Folio,* July 9, 1803. He had to fight this anti-Virginia attitude at home as well; his parents and his brother all distrusted Virginians and southerners. "Your father used to say," remarked Abigail Adams, "that N. Englanders were always the dupes of the Southern States. I conjecture they are so now" (Abigail Adams to J. Q. Adams, January 9, 1806, APm reel 404).

[29] J. Q. Adams, *American Principles: A Review of the Works of Fisher Ames* (Boston, 1809), p. 38. "Is the sovereign power to be contracted to a state centre?" Ames had asked. "Is Virginia to be our Rome? And are we to be her Latin or Italian allies?" ("The Dangers of American Liberty" [1805], in Seth Ames, ed., *Works of Fisher Ames. With a Selection from His Speeches and Correspondence* [Boston, 1854], II, 353).

[30] *American Principles,* pp. 36–37. This was written in response to J. Quincy's favorable review of the *Works* of Ames, which appeared in the *Monthly Anthology and Boston Review;* in turn, John Lowell, Jr., replied to Adams in a stinging, but less logical pamphlet *Remarks on the Hon. John Q. Adams's Review of Mr. Ames's Works, With Some Stric-*

society and that of the plantation South that continued association seemed unlikely. Virginian social arrangements were incom-
prehensible in the North; the terms in which they had to be
discussed simply had no counterpart there. "Happily in these
[northern] States where the employers and the employed, are
mutually obliged and mutually dependent, where a spirit of
moderation and justice is supported by common necessities & ob-
ligations, we are unable to form a true conception of the
wretchedness and ignorance which degrade one Class [of Vir-
ginians], and the Envy & Jealousy which corrode the Bosoms
of the other," wrote Oliver Wolcott. "The Slaves and the poor
enjoy no political influence—their natural antipathies and resent-
ments are indeed stimulated and perpetuated for an obvious reason—but in the conception of a Virginian it is merely the object
of *Liberty* to secure independence to Planters; of Equality that
Palatines may know no Superior." [31] Harrison Gray Otis
warned John Rutledge, Jr., of the possibility that "want of sympathy and difference of sentiment between your people and ours,
[might] ensure the victory of the ancient dominion over
both." [32] The sections seemed so different in "manners, habits,
customs, principles and ways of thinking" that it was the persist-
ence of union which excited surprise rather than the recurring
secessionist sentiment. The colonies had originally united
through fear of a foreign enemy, and it seemed that fears rather
than hopes continued to hold them together: fear that a split between sections would be followed by further fragmentation until
the states were twenty warring nations, vulnerable to foreign attack and to their own weaknesses; and fear of a successful slave

---

tures on the Views of the Author (Boston, 1809). Adams would live to
repudiate these words, and to indulge in fierce antisouthern rhetoric himself, as a spokesman for abolition in the 1840's. See Samuel Flagg Bemis,
John Quincy Adams and the Union (New York, 1956), pp. 426, 444,
et passim.

[31] Miscellaneous notes [1802–1803], Wolcott Papers.

[32] Otis to J. Rutledge, January 29, 1802, John Rutledge, Jr., Papers,
South. Hist. Coll.

uprising should the planters attempt to govern without the support of a strong national government.[33] "The Southern Men have been actuated by an absolute hatred of New England," maintained John Adams. "Nothing but their fears ever restrained them from discarding Us from their Union. Those Fears, as their population increases so much faster than ours diminish every day; and were they not restrained by their Negroes they would reject us from their Union, within a year." [34]

"Virginia is and will be our Austria," predicted the veteran diplomat William Vans Murray as early as 1802. It is an intriguing comparison. To the Prussia of Frederick the Great, Austria was the South and, like the American South, she stood for a kind of leisured elegance, an ancient establishment reinforced by political power. Murray could not see far enough into the future to predict the military defeat of each southern province by its northern rival, in the nearly contemporaneous American Civil War and the Austro-Prussian war: all he could sense, and that was perhaps enough, was that the lines of tension were already clearly drawn. New Englanders might "talk, like Prussia, of being the Spartans of the north, but the turkey cock has too wide spread a progeny for the black or blue eagle to oppose him, now that voices decide. The wilderness is hers and those who emerge from it." [35]

[33] A similar sense of disparity between the sections is revealed in an article, headed "FAREWELL, A LONG FAREWELL TO ALL OUR GREATNESS" (*Port Folio*, March 13, 1802), which concluded: "Far, far distant be the day, when these injured slaves shall PRACTICE on those empty declarations of EQUAL RIGHTS, which yet exist but in theory among masters. May the time never come, when these slaves rise against their masters. But the possibility that such a time may come, ought to teach the southern states, that to them union is far more necessary than to the people of New-England; for should there ever be a spirit of general insurrection among the blacks, that spirit will rage uncontroued [*sic*] in the blood of the whites, till quelled by the people of the northern states."

[34] John Adams to J. Q. Adams, January 8, 1805, APm reel 404.

[35] William Vans Murray to J. Q. Adams, April 3, 1802, American Historical Association, *Annual Report*, 1912, p. 705.

Thus Virginia and her satellites appeared doubly blessed. Not only did those who emerged from the wilderness of the newly organized western states and territories invariably vote as Virginia voted, but her own representation in Congress benefited from the three-fifths rule. The three-fifths clause began to come under especially heavy attack in the early years of the nineteenth century, as Federalists located in it the legal mechanism responsible for their declining power. "There are above 500,000 negro slaves in the United States," complained the *Gazette of the United States*, "who have not more voice in the Election of President and Vice-President . . . than 500,000 New-England horses, hogs, and oxen. Yet . . . their masters for them choose 15 Electors!"[36] The Boston *Repertory* asked the question more directly. "Are the rotten boroughs of England more infamous than our Negro boroughs? Why should *their* slaves be represented if denied the rights of suffrage, in preference to *our* horses and oxen?"[37] It is true enough that had the three-fifths clause not existed, John Adams would have won another term in office; but one must be permitted to wonder whether the most vigorous opponents of the three-fifths clause would have been pleased with *that* eventuality. The inclusion of the clause had been part of a fairly complicated tacit understanding in the Constitutional Convention, the other part of which had been that the federal government could make no Navigation Acts; but no Federalist who proposed giving up the three-fifths clause ever proposed giving something in exchange. The attitude was irreproachable in legal terms, but perhaps not in political ones.

These repeated criticisms of the three-fifths clause resulted, before very long, in a formal proposal to eliminate it from the Constitution. The amendment was drafted by Congressman William Ely and submitted by the Massachusetts General Court to other state legislatures in the spring of 1804. It was widely assumed that the amendment was a trial balloon for the seces-

[36] N.d., quoted in the Washington *Federalist*, January 14, 1801.
[37] Boston *Repertory*, April 24, 1804.

sionist plots of Roger Griswold and his friends, and the amendment was greeted with skepticism in Massachusetts and hostility elsewhere. During the brief period of its serious consideration, it received its most coherent defense from Josiah Quincy, then a Massachusetts state senator. "The operation of this [three-fifths] principle," Quincy argued, "has deprived, and so long as retained, must forever deprive the States, in which slaves do not exist, of their due weight in the political scale, and transfers, in effect, all power into the hands of the slave holding States." [38] Eastern Virginia alone, with 354,000 whites and 322,000 slaves had nearly as many representatives in Congress—and therefore in the electoral college—as New York, with 535,000 whites and 20,000 slaves. Five slave states, Quincy argued (Maryland, Virginia, North Carolina, South Carolina, and Georgia), with a total white population of 1,400,000 had three more electoral votes than seven nonslave states (Pennsylvania, New Hampshire, Massachusetts, Rhode Island, Connecticut, Vermont, and Ohio) with 1,800,000.[39] This discrepancy had given slaveholding regions sufficient additional electoral votes in 1800 to throw the election to Jefferson.[40]

Josiah Quincy's accounting was sloppy. Instead of counting the number of congressional districts in each state, he estimated the number of representatives to which certain selected states were entitled at the standard ratio of one congressman per 30,000 population. On this basis he assumed that eastern Virginia had eighteen votes when in fact the Eastern District of Virginia (a census division which excluded the District of Columbia and most of what is now West Virginia) included only fifteen of the

[38] *Ibid.*, September 21.

[39] *Ibid.*, September 25. Quincy believed the trend would continue, as the slave population increased both by birth and by a renewal of importation, which he expected to be resumed after 1808; the availability of plantation land in the Louisiana territory would, he believed, encourage the use of slaves.

[40] *Ibid.*, September 21. For similar assertions, see "A Plain Fact," *New-England Palladium*, January 20, 1801.

House districts in the state. Eastern Virginia did *not* outvote New York, which had seventeen House seats, but certainly it wielded an influence disproportionate to its population. Similarly, Quincy estimated that five slave states had a "political weight" of 63½ votes in the Senate and House combined, while seven nonslave states had only 60. Again, the accurate figures shift the balance: the five slave states had 55 representatives and 10 senators; the seven free states, 54 representatives and 14 senators. Five southern states did not outvote seven northern states, but they did exercise a clearly disproportionate influence, and they did outvote six northern states. However, if all the states are included in the tally, the nonslave states had the advantage: 77 representatives and 18 senators in the North; 65 representatives and 16 senators in the South.

However representation were to be arranged, Quincy insisted, it ought to be consistent. "The question is not whether property is a right measure of representation, but whether if it be a right measure for a part, it be not for the whole?" [41]

The proposed amendment failed to receive the necessary endorsement of three-quarters of the state legislatures. Undaunted, its supporters arranged for Timothy Pickering, now a senator from Massachusetts, to introduce it in Congress. He did so, on December 7, 1804; it was promptly laid upon a table from which it was never removed. Pickering had expected that it would at least come to debate, and in his notes for the speech he would have given he makes the point that since slaves are only "a species of property," and "Freemen alone can exercise the powers of government," the Constitution should be amended so that the powers of all freemen are equal. [42]

[41] Boston *Repertory*, September 21, 1804. Note that he does not say if it be *wrong* for a part it is wrong for the whole. See also the series of articles in support of the Ely amendment signed "Hortensius" (*Port Folio*, September 1801).

[42] Octavius Pickering and Charles W. Upham, *The Life of Timothy Pickering* (Boston, 1873), IV, 64–65; U. S. Congress, *The Debates and*

The extra power which the three-fifths clause gave a southern candidate for federal office was a consideration which was linked, in Federalist minds, to the belief that the slaveholder's "spirit of domination" disqualified him for leadership in a free society. The extra representation enjoyed by the white men of the South benefited unfairly the regional type which was of all regional characters the most autocratic and therefore the least deserving. The Boston *Repertory* found exceedingly distasteful a report that a jubilant crowd had carried "a triumphant Democrat" on their shoulders after his election victory: "*To ride or not to ride* [the people]—*to carry or not to carry—that is the question.*" And when they thought of Jefferson, invariably the first image that came to mind was the lord of plantation society who had been carried into office by the extra votes of the three-fifths arrangement; "his triumphal car drawn by a million of enslaved Negroes, drives over the necks of those who have not bent the knee to Baal. And are we to submit to the guidance and the tyranny of the South?" [43]

Federalists objected to the presence of the slave, then, partly because existing political arrangements permitted the slaveholder to derive political as well as economic value from his

---

Proceedings of the Congress of the United States (Washington, D.C., 1851), 8th Cong. 2d sess., Senate, pp. 20–22 (hereafter referred to as *Annals of Congress*). Objection to the three-fifths clause was also articulated in the South. In 1803, the Federalists of western Virginia, where there were relatively few slaves, supported a reapportionment of the state senate in order that each district include an equal number of free, white inhabitants. They made clear their resentment of the three-fifths clause and of the bill's defeat by a tidewater-based Jeffersonian majority. Federalists continued to display an interest in reapportionment in the state House of Delegates, and the few old Federalists who attended the Virginia Constitutional Convention of 1829–1830 aligned themselves with the supporters of manhood suffrage and the omission of the three-fifths clause in state affairs. The sole exception was John Marshall (Norman K. Risjord, "The Virginia Federalists," *Journal of Southern History*, XXXIII [1967], 507–508, 514–516).

[43] Boston *Repertory*, June 8, April 24, 1804.

property. They also came to suspect that the slave system represented a potential military liability. Many Federalists lived in
momentary expectation of war with France after Napoleon had
subjugated Europe, a war which the slaveholding South would
be ill prepared to fight. "Take away those whites who must remain to watch over the Slaves," asked the Boston *Repertory,*
"and how many will there be, to act against the enemy?—Officers enough. Yes, the South is the seat of our privileged orders.
But Soldiers? As before, in the yeomanry of the Northern
States. Who fought the battles of Independence? Who freed
Virginia and the Carolinas from the British troops when aided
by their slaves? It was the men of the North." [44] Slavery weakened the state: "In case of foreign war," Timothy Pickering
warned, "Virginia must keep at home half her force to prevent
an insurrection of her negroes: and if attacked in her own do-
minions her danger and imbecility would be still more manifest." [45] Federalists argued that wherever the slave system was
established, there the nation was most vulnerable to infiltration
by foreign radicals. When, for example, it was learned that
the French had re-established slavery in Santo Domingo, the
Boston *Centinel* logically assumed that many Negroes would refuse to return to bondage. "Will they not seek a shelter among
the slaves on the plantations of the Southern States, and after
having inculcated their crude notions of freedom, and the theory
of murder, fire, and pillage, will they not then proceed to the
practice?" [46]

[44] *Ibid.,* April 24. When France took possession of Louisiana, John Cotton Smith commented, "Much evil is apprehended . . . from the spirit
of insurrection which will inevitably be infused into the slaves by their
Gallic brethren" (to Tapping Reeve, March 8, 1802, E. A. Park Papers,
Yale University Library).

[45] T. Pickering to Stephen Higginson, January 6, 1804, Pickering
Papers.

[46] Boston *Columbian Centinel,* October 9, 1802. See also T. B. Adams
to Joseph Pitcairn, September 30, 1800, *Historical and Philosophical
Society of Ohio Quarterly Publication,* XII (1917), pp. 41–42; and

Although escaped Negroes from Santo Domingo had not arrived in large numbers, slaveholders had, and they brought
their slaves with them. The acquisition of Louisiana, with its
large population of slaveholding Frenchmen, seemed to multiply the dangers of slave insurrection. It brought other problems
with it as well. The French in New Orleans openly resented the
prospect of rule from Washington. In the summer of 1804,
New Orleans was the scene of a popular uprising; there were tur-
gid public meetings. Finally a three-man lobby was dispatched
to Washington to dissuade Congress from assuming the powers
of government in Louisiana, but despite support from Federalists, it was unsuccessful.[47] The French argued that they had
never been asked for and had never granted their consent to be
governed. They found an ardent supporter in John Quincy
Adams, who thought a constitutional amendment was in order.
"I never knew nor heard of an instance before of any Sovereign
however despotic undertaking to exercise the highest powers of
Government over a people, without something like the consent
of that people, by treaty, by popular acclamation, or at least by
requiring an Oath of Allegiance[;]. . . although there were popular acclamations, it is carefully remarked, that they were uttered
by Americans, and not by the antient Inhabitants. . . . This at
least is setting out upon the profess'd avowal of *force,* as the

"Levity," *Port Folio,* March 5, 1803: "A patriotic song, intended to be
published, should we be obliged to declare war against the French, for
attempting, (as some think they will, soon after their arrival in Louisiana),
to deprive our southern democratic citizens of their property, by exciting
their negroes to run away from them." In *White Over Black: American
Attitudes Toward the Negro, 1550–1812* (Chapel Hill, 1968), pp. 375–
402, Winthrop D. Jordan suggests that a primary reason for the failure
of the early abolition movement was the fear of Negro rebellion elicited by
the revolution in Santo Domingo.

[47] Jean Nöel Destrehan, Pierre Derbigny, and Pierre Sauvé. See
E. S. Brown, "The Orleans Territory Memorialists to Congress, 1804,"
Louisiana Historical Quarterly, I (1917), pp. 99–102; R. Griswold to
O. Wolcott, November 11, 1804, Wolcott Papers; and J. Q. Adams to A.
Adams, December 19, 1804, APm reel 403.

only basis of our dominion," he wrote to his brother Thomas Boylston Adams. Years later, he recalled that the purchase had been made "at an immense price, not of money, but of principle," and linked the crisis to the New England secessionist movement of the following year: "The Constitution cannot thus be treated, not even for objects of highest interest to the nation, with impunity." [48] One breach of the Constitution suggested—perhaps justified—another.

The objections offered most frequently by the inhabitants themselves were not, however, so theoretical. They disliked Jefferson's gubernatorial appointee, W. C. C. Claiborne, who could not speak French, and, more significantly, they objected to the possibility, the prospect, and finally the fact that Congress had and chose to exercise its power to prohibit the international slave trade in their territory. [49] The decision to prohibit the slave trade, distasteful as it may have been to residents of Louisiana, represented something of a congressional compromise. When the resolution to prohibit the trade was introduced it was paired with one to prohibit slavery entirely in Louisiana—which did not pass. When Congress, having ratified the treaty of acquisition, proceeded to establish regulations for the government of the new lands, the obvious legislative models were the old ordinances for the Northwest and the Mississippi Territories. The major difference between them was that slavery and the impor-

---

[48] J. Q. Adams to T. B. Adams, January 27, 1804, APm reel 403; J. Q. Adams, *Parties in the United States* (New York, 1941), pp. 37, 38. Adams's speech on this subject is recounted by William Plumer, in E. S. Brown, ed., "Documents: The Senate Debate on the Breckinridge Bill for the Government of Louisiana 1804," *American Historical Review*, XXII (1917), 361–363. See also Worthington Chauncey Ford, ed., *Writings of John Quincy Adams* (New York, 1914), III, 2–21; J. Q. Adams to John Adams, November, 1804; to [T. B. Adams?] January 31, 1804; to A. Adams, January 27, 1804, APm reel 403.

[49] See Walter Prichard, "Selecting a Governor for the Territory of Orleans," *Louisiana Historical Quarterly*, XXXI (April 1948) pp. 269–393; and *Memoirs of John Quincy Adams* (Philadelphia, 1874), I, 321.

tation of slaves was forbidden in one and not in the other; a choice of precedents had to be made. The final decision to permit slavery but prohibit the slave trade merely brought Louisiana law into conformity with the laws of other states and territories and was perhaps only to be expected. It is not the outcome of the vote, but the debate that is most revealing of developing Federalist sentiment on the subject of slavery.

"I consider slavery as a serious evil," announced James Hillhouse, "and wish to check it wherever I have authority." [50] The debate which this comment introduced, although it foreshadowed the debate on the Missouri Territory fifteen years later, did not turn out to be as divisive because of the care with which most participants (including Hillhouse, after his opening statement) clung to practicality. Even so, it was painful enough; "The prohibition of the admission of slaves into Louisiana, is like the drawing of a jaw tooth," remarked John Quincy Adams.[51] Hillhouse appealed to Southern self-interest: "Will not your slaves, even in the southern states, in case of a war, endanger the peace and security of those states? Increase the number of slaves in Louisiana, they will in due time rebel—their numbers in the district of Orleans, are now equal to the whites —Why add fuel to this tinder . . . [?]" [52] He was seconded by John Smith of Ohio, who reminded his hearers that runaway and rebellious slaves might easily hide in the swamps that were so characteristic of the Louisiana country. "Will you increase there [sic] number, and lay the necessary foundation for the horrors of another St. Domingo? If slaves are admitted there, I fear . . . that country . . . will prove a curse." [53]

[50] E. S. Brown, ed., "Documents: The Senate Debate on the Breckinridge Bill [January 25, 1804]," *American Historical Review*, XXII (1917), 346.

[51] J. Q. Adams to [T. B. Adams?], January 31, 1804, APm reel 403.

[52] E. S. Brown, p. 346.

[53] *Ibid.*, p. 347. Samuel White of Delaware also sought "to prevent, as far as possible, the horrid evil of slavery—and thereby avoid the fate of St. Domingo."

The Santo Domingo analogy was one which even southern Democrats could accept: "I fear," agreed Breckinridge, "our slaves in the South will produce another St. Domingo." [54] But their opponents also suspected that the northern Federalist position was primarily motivated by political considerations. "It has been said on this floor that I am an *Eastern-man*," protested Hillhouse. He admitted the charge, but went on to make a thinly veiled secessionist threat: "*While* I am the representative of a State which is *yet* a member of the *Union*, I hope I shall have as much influence as if I was a *southern man*. I did not expect *so soon* to hear on this floor the distinction of *eastern* and *northern*, and *southern* men. Has it indeed come to this—are we to be designated by a geographical line?" [55] It was, of course, coming to that; the debaters were largely distinguishable by geographical lines. A Georgia Democrat, James Jackson, pointed out that as a southeastern landowner his self-interest was aligned to that of his northeastern colleagues in dictating that he support the prohibition of slavery in Louisiana in an attempt to inhibit its settlement and keep eastern land prices high. "But my duty is opposed to my interest." [56]

The Federalist case was somewhat akin to the one they would formulate later that year in support of the Ely amendment. In seeking to keep slaves out of Louisiana, they were not only trying to keep eastern land prices high and avoid a situation conducive to domestic rebellion; they had come to believe that an increase in the number of slaves threatened to overbalance an already lopsided constitutional arrangement in which the presence of the slave acted to increase the weight of his master's vote. The difficulty of preparing a code of regulations for the government of Louisiana added to the catalogue of objections to the purchase which Federalists had already compiled. Payment for Louisiana meant pouring money into Napoleon's treasury for

[54] E. S. Brown, p. 345.
[55] *Ibid.*, p. 348.
[56] *Ibid.*, p. 349.

use in prosecuting a war against England of which Federalists vigorously disapproved; the eventual creation of new states in the west would further undermine the already declining power of the original states in Congress; the cotton and tobacco grown in Louisiana would lower prices for southeastern produce; and New Orleans might attract commerce away from eastern ports.[57] As men who had read their Montesquieu, they were skeptical of an extension of territory in what seemed to them an already over-large Republic; as men who had speculated heavily in what, after 1803, had to be regarded as *mid*-western lands, they had reason to fear that their investments would fall in value.[58] In short, as one sneering Federalist toast phrased it, Louisiana seemed to be "a country of golden dreams and leaden realities." [59]

As the Senate debate on the Hillhouse amendment suggests, to talk of Louisiana meant, almost inevitably, to talk of Santo Domingo; and talk of Santo Domingo led invariably to talk of slavery. One feature of the Federalist prosecution of the quasi-war with France in 1799 had been support for Toussaint L'Ouverture in his struggle to oust the French from the island. As Secretary of State, Timothy Pickering had worked intensively to encourage American trade with Santo Domingo; de-

[57] Thomas Evans to O. Wolcott, August 8, 1803, Wolcott Papers; Washington *Federalist*, reprinted in Boston *Repertory*, February 17, 1804.

[58] E.g., Arthur Maynard Walter to William Smith Shaw, July 26, 1803, Shaw Papers; J. Quincy to O. Wolcott, September 5, 1803, Wolcott Papers; T. Pickering to Winthrop Sargent, January 6, 1804, Pickering Papers. "Our country was sufficiently extensive before the acquisition of that boundless wilderness," said Archibald Henderson in the North Carolina House of Commons. "The best informed statesmen were fearful that our empire would ere long be dismembered; but when this new world is added, that which we supposed doubtful before is reduced almost to a certainty" (December 11, 1807, Archibald Henderson: Papers relating to the Henderson Family, South. Hist. Coll.).

[59] Boston *Repertory*, December 25, 1804. Federalists had insisted that first priority be given to the acquisition of New Orleans, even at the risk or cost of war. It was the larger Purchase that distressed them.

spite some reservations, President John Adams endorsed the policy, and kept an American consul general on the scene to deal with Toussaint and smooth the way for American merchants who traded there.[60] Neither Adams nor Pickering could have been unaware that their support, although given primarily for commercial reasons, made possible a government in which Negroes ruled a society of whites, mulattoes, and former slaves; refugee whites with horrible atrocity stories to tell were crowding into American port cities like Philadelphia and Baltimore, and the South vociferously shuddered in fear that Toussaint's army, once victorious over the French, would turn its energy toward freeing its enslaved brethren in America.[61] But Toussaint and Adams shared an enemy; French efforts to reestablish rule in Santo Domingo were obviously tied to their hopes of reestablish-

[60] John C. Miller, *Alexander Hamilton: Portrait in Paradox* (New York, 1959), p. 559.

[61] "Our Southern States," wrote T. Pickering, "altho' not equally with Jamaica, are yet in much danger from attempts to excite the blacks to insurrection." He thus advised that the President "guard against the danger to be apprehended from St. Domingo" (T. Pickering to John Adams, June 7, 1799, Wolcott Papers). Timothy Dwight versified the same point in "Triumph of Democracy" (*New-England Palladium*, January 6, 1801):

> "remember ere too late,
> The tale of St. Domingo's fate.
> Tho' *Gabriel* dies, a host remain
> Oppress'd with slavery's galling chain.
> And soon or late the hour will come
> Mark'd with Virginia's dreadful doom."

The atrocity stories were not fabrications; see R. R. Palmer, *The Age of the Democratic Revolution* (Princeton, 1964), II, 514. For Santo Domingo refugees in America, see Frances Sergeant Childs, *French Refugee Life in the United States, 1790–1800: An American Chapter of the French Revolution* (Baltimore, 1940), pp. 23, 65, 142–143. See also Ralph Korngold, *Citizen Toussaint* (Boston, 1944), p. ix; and Charles Callen Tansill, *The United States and Santo Domingo, 1798–1873: A Chapter in Caribbean Diplomacy* (Baltimore, 1938), pp. 13–18, 34–69, 73–109.

ing French influence and rule elsewhere in the Western Hemisphere.

When he assumed the presidency, Thomas Jefferson substituted for the Federalist policy one which was hostile to Toussaint. This behavior seemed to support Federalist accusations that Jefferson's foreign policy unduly favored France. A major point in the Federalist indictment was the charge that Jefferson had failed to pressure Napoleon to abandon Santo Domingo in 1802, even though once Napoleon did so, it was logical for him to decide to sell Louisiana. Jefferson thus received unearned credit for a diplomatic coup. Jefferson's behavior seemed even more pro-French in 1805, when administration spokesmen pushed through Congress first a law requiring ships clearing for Santo Domingo to post bond that any arms they carried would be used only for defense, and subsequently a full embargo on all trade with Santo Domingo. Most of that trade was in provisions, but some of it was in arms and ammunition, for which the rebels were willing to pay black market prices.[62] Napoleon insisted that the trade, largely emanating from Philadelphia, was a contraband one and, uncomforted by the American minister's assurance that Quakers were forbidden to deal in tools of war, set up a paper blockade of the waters around Haiti.[63] Meanwhile, Talleyrand continued to press for an interdiction of the trade; when George Logan introduced an embargo bill, letters from Talleyrand were among the supporting papers he submitted to Congress. The debate on the Santo Domingo embargo is revealing; ostensibly it was about neutral trading rights, but it kept sliding into the subject of slavery and of whether free Negroes could behave responsibly. That the embargo would hurt American commerce was undeniable; the damage might be lasting since, denied the convenience supplied

[62] J. Q. Adams to John Adams, November 3, 1804, APm reel 403.
[63] Tansill, pp. 97–98. The names Haiti and Santo Domingo are here used interchangeably, as they frequently were in the nineteenth century.

by American carriers, the Haitians might well develop their own shipping. If not, Britain would monopolize the extremely lucrative trade of the sugar island, which before its revolution had accounted for over half the French import and export trade.[64] Why do for France what she could not do for herself?

The answer is to be found in the Republican defense of the bill; where northern Federalists talked of commerce, profits, and embargoes, southern Republicans seemed unable to stay on the obvious subject. It was not for them a question of neutral rights and of contraband; it was a question of American support for a Negro republic. Joseph Nicholson of Maryland defined the terms: "If we are inclined to favor the revolt of the blacks in St. Domingo, let us make the bill such that it cannot stop the intercourse. If we are enemies to the revolters, let us make the provisions of the bill such that they cannot be eluded." [65] J. C. Clay was willing to give up the trade entirely: "We cannot trade with them without acknowledging their independence. If gentlemen are ready to do this, I shall consider it as a sacrifice on the altar of black despotism and usurpation." [66] John W. Eppes started to defend his party against the charge of taking orders from Napoleon: "Every nation, when injured, has a right to demand redress. Has not France, then, this right?" But he too drifted off the subject: "Some gentlemen would declare St. Domingo free; if any gentlemen harbors such sentiments let

[64] See New York *Evening Post*, April 29, 1806; and *Annals of Congress*, 9th Cong., 1st sess., House, February 25, 1806, p. 513. Sugar production had made Santo Domingo, before it exploded in revolution, "the most profitable European colony in the world" (John Edwin Fagg, *Cuba, Haiti, and the Dominican Republic* [Englewood Cliffs, N.J., 1965], p. 4). The turbulent history of the island is summarized in Fagg, pp. 114–120. See also Alexander DeConde, *The Quasi-War: The Politics and Diplomacy of the Undeclared War with France: 1797–1801* (New York, 1966), pp. 130–141, 206–211, 322–325.

[65] *Annals of Congress*, 9th Cong., 1st sess., House, p. 498, February 24, 1806.

[66] *Ibid.*, p. 512, February 25, 1806.

him come forward boldly and declare it. In such case, he would
cover himself with detestation. A system that would bring immediate and horrible destruction on the fairest portion of America." In short, the embargo provided an opportunity not only
for sidestepping the paper blockade and the risk of war with
France; it had the added advantage of helping to suffocate Hai-
tian independence. It had all the advantages of counterrevo-
lution, and none of its burdens. William Ely rose to reply:
"Have these Haytians no rights? If they were once subjects of a
Government that can no longer hold them, has that nation any
right to call on us to starve them out . . . ? I deny the necessity
or policy of yielding to the orders of the French Minister." [67]
An embargo might avoid the risk of drifting into another undeclared war with France, but there was much commerce to be
lost, and no equivalent concession was proffered by Napoleon. It
seemed to Federalists that Republicans endorsed the measure
primarily because of their preoccupation with slavery, ignoring
the effect upon the nation's commerce. Preoccupation with slavery was the Republicans' special weakness, and even those Federalists who were not particularly abolitionist in sentiment could
not resist playing up to it.

> sad Domingo's isle!
> Ill-fated Isle! what crime unknown
> Has drawn from Heav'n its vengeance down,
> To whelm your fields with Ruin's flood,
> And float your streets with murder'd blood?
> Is it that Afric's ceaseless groan

[67] *Ibid.*, p. 515. George Logan introduced the bill in the Senate; his
opening words contained the same fears that the House displayed: "Whilst
we are anxious to have our own national rights respected, is it honorable to
violate the rights of a friendly Power with whom we are at peace? or is it
sound policy to cherish the black population of St. Domingo whilst we
have a similar population in our Southern States, in which should an insurrection take place, the Government of the United States is bound to render
effectual aid to our fellow-citizens in that part of the Union?" (*ibid.*,
Senate, p. 28). See also continuation of Senate debate, pp. 28–38 *et passim*.

At length had reached mild Mercy's throne,
Who calling Justice (not in vain)
Justice has slept on earth again?
Columbia! let Domingo's fate
Give warning ere it prove too late;
Rouse! and pronounce the bold decree,
'Death to the Monster, Slavery!' [68]

Their condemnation of slavery enabled Federalists to regard politicians and customs of Southern origin superciliously, but it seldom drove them to abolitionism and still less frequently made them integrationists. When they called, for example, for an end to the fictitious slave representation of the three-fifths compromise, they did not seek to replace it with true representation for the Negro, but rather, as Josiah Quincy phrased it, with representation "of civil beings, of beings possessing political capacities, having rights to be protected and interests to be advanced." [69]

When Virginia's slaves were implicated in Gabriel's abortive conspiracy in 1800, northern Federalists were not surprised, but neither were they sympathetic to the rebels. The reaction of President Adams's youngest son, Thomas Boylston Adams, is probably representative: the slaveholders, he thought, were reaping the harvest "of those seducing theories" of equal rights which slaves had been allowed to hear "discussed, with great zeal . . . at the tables of their owners," but he had only scorn for the "distracted blacks." [70] When James Callender "re-

[68] "New Year's Address of the Carrier of the [New York] *Mercantile Advertiser* to his Customers," reprinted in *Port Folio*, February 2, 1805. See also Tansill, pp. 108–109; Miller, p. 559; Henry Adams, *John Randolph* (Boston, 1899), p. 185; Henry Adams, *History of the United States . . .* (New York, 1889), III, 142.

[69] Boston *Repertory*, September 21, 1804. Only in sarcasm did the *Repertory* suggest that the three-fifths members should be "real Negroes" (April 24, 1801).

[70] T. B. Adams to J. Pitcairn, September 30, 1800, *Pub. of the Hist. and Phil. Soc. of Ohio*, XII, 41–42. The method Adams proposed to prevent

vealed" that Jefferson had a black mistress, Federalist pamphleteers were only too happy to help spread the slander; that the President indulged in impropriety seemed not nearly so unfortunate as the color of his partner's skin. From Joseph Dennie, who parodied Henry Carey's well-known poem "Sally in our Alley," to the thirteen-year-old William Cullen Bryant, who, in his versified compilation of Federalist slanders entitled "The Embargo" ordered the "philosophist" to "sink supinely in her sable arms," Federalist satirists made "dusky Sally" a standard weapon in their arsenal. Scarcely a month passed for a year after Callender's outburst that the *Port Folio* poets did not have something to say on the subject. Even John Quincy Adams joined in the game with an extremely loose imitation of Horace's "Ode to Xanthia Phoceus"; as Achilles had loved Briseis, Jefferson should "deem it no disgrace / With slaves to mend thy breed." [71]

a recurrence was not amelioration of the slave system, but greater discretion in the use of "inflammatory language." For accounts of the Rebellion, see Herbert Aptheker, *American Negro Slave Revolts* (New York, 1943), pp. 219–226; Robert McColley, *Slavery and Jeffersonian Virginia* (Urbana, Ill., 1964), p. 111.

[71] The subject of Jefferson and Sally Hemings is subtly and perceptively discussed in Jordan, pp. 461–469. Dennie's parody was published in the *Port Folio* on October 2, 1802; ascription to Dennie by John Cook Wyllie, *New York Times Book Review*, May 16, 1965. Similar poetic effusions appeared in the *Port Folio* on July 10, October 30, November 6, 13, December 4, 1802; February 19, March 19, August 20, 1803. Perhaps the most famous of all was written by the Irish poet Thomas Moore:

"The patriot fresh from Freedom's councils come,
Now pleased retires to lash his slaves at home:
Or woo, perhaps, some black Aspasia's charms,
And dream of freedom in his bondmaid's arms."

For J. Q. Adams's authorship of the "Ode to Xanthia Phoceus," in the *Port Folio* on October 30, 1802, see J. Q. Adams, *Memoirs* (Philadelphia, 1876), VIII, 339; Linda K. Kerber and Walter John Morris, "Politics and Literature: The Adams Family and the *Port Folio*," *William and Mary Quarterly*, 3d ser., XXIII (1966), 457, 470. The future defender

Their excessive reaction to Callender's rumor hints at the concern with which many Federalists viewed the mulatto, and points, by inference, to their distaste for the social arrangements implied by the mulatto's presence. Thus another item was added to the Federalist case against southern society as immoral and unfit for leadership in a republic. "Climenole" mocked Jefferson's first inaugural: "Intimacy . . . with all women—matrimonial alliance with none." [72] In the course of his unveiling of democracy, Thomas Green Fessenden found the tale proof that Jefferson was "nine times as able / as Mazarine or Machiavel"; the more illegitimate children sired by planters the greater the usefulness of the three-fifths clause.

> A southern negro is you see, man,
> Already three-fifths of a freeman,
> And when Virginia gets the staff,
> He'll be a freeman and a half.

> Great men can never lack supporters,
> Who manufacture their own voters;
> Besides 'tis plain as yonder steeple,
> They will be *fathers* to the people.

Remarking that hybridization improved the breed, Fessenden sardonically hailed "Columbia's transmutation / to one great grand mulatto nation!" [73]

---

of the Amistad rebels was to outgrow the prejudices of his younger years, but that he had them at the turn of the century is shown by other productions of his pen. See Fugitive Pieces, APm reel 223; and Robert A. East, *John Quincy Adams: The Critical Years* (New York, 1962), pp. 113–114, 223–224, note 31.

[72] "Climenole, No. 3," February 11, 1804. See also "Climenole, No. 6," March 3.

[73] *Democracy Unveiled* (New York, 1806), II, 18–19, 21, 25. A minute section of American opinion was wiling to take Fessenden at his word, if only for the purpose of argument. As early as 1790, Webster suggested that extensive intermarriage would be the easiest way to abolish slavery and absorb blacks into white society. With sudden emancipation

Thomas Jefferson's deism and latitudinarianism were another source of shock to Federalists, especially to a number of ministers who rallied to the defense of the account of creation as given in Genesis. In the course of this defense, they were impelled by the force of their own rhetoric to endorse the essential humanity of the Negro and found themselves, therefore, in a quasi-abolitionist position. This line of reasoning is most fully developed by Clement Clark Moore, a New York minister who was a federalist pamphleteer before he achieved more lasting renown as the author of "A Visit from Saint Nicholas." His critique of the impious implications in *Notes on Virginia* proved Moore to be one of the more fundamentalist of Jefferson's critics in matters of religion. Incensed at Jefferson's implication that the events in the Garden of Eden were merely "a pretty . . . tale" and irritated by a vague and undefined group of men he called "modern philosophers . . . whose industry is equalled by nothing but their vanity, whose pursuits are impeded . . . by no law, human or divine; who think nothing too great for them to grasp, and nothing too minute to be observed," he demanded the purpose of their inquiries, and answered his own questions: "Is it to render more stable the uncertain condition of man? Is it to alleviate one of the miseries which afflict his nature? No; it is to banish civilization from the earth, that we may be reduced to the state of savages; to pluck from the wretched their sweetest consolation; to extinguish the only light by which the Christian hopes to cheer the gloomy hour of death; to quench the thirst for immortality which the Creator has attached to our nature; to degrade us from the rank of angels, to which we are taught to aspire, that we may complete the catalogue of brutes." [74] But

---

appearing too dangerous and wide-scale colonization too expensive, racial amalgamation was an appealing solution because it included the possibility of the literal disappearance of the Negro (Webster, *Essays*, p. 366).

[74] *Observations upon Certain Passages in Mr. Jefferson's Notes on Virginia, Which Appear to Have a Tendency to Subvert Religion, and Establish a False Philosophy* (New York, 1804), p. 18, 30–31.

the same conservatism of approach to revealed religion that required Moore to be distressed by Jefferson's use of the word "perhaps" in a sentence like: "For two dialects to recede from one another till they have lost all vestiges of their common origin, must require an immense course of time; perhaps not less than many people give to the age of the earth," [75] also alerted him to its appearance in another context: " . . . the rank in the scale of being which their Creator may perhaps have given [the Negroes]." Jefferson is very cautiously advancing an argument for black inferiority; Moore will not permit him the protection of caution, and fastens on the phrasing as proof of Jefferson's infidelity. "Very pretty truly! the scale of beings which their Creator may *perhaps* have given them!" [76]

Moore distrusted the very concept of a "scale of beings" as an artificial one, developed by "modern philosophers" and imposed by them on the natural world to make it appear more orderly, more comprehensible, and to free them from the necessity of crediting man with a separate and miraculous creation in the Garden of Eden. "It is a favourite object with modern philosophers to persuade themselves and others, that man is of the same nature with the rest of the animal creation," wrote Moore. "They have observed how wonderfully minute the gradations are from the inanimate spar, up to man, the lord of the creation. . . . They have perceived that an uniformity of design prevails in the structure of every part of the animal creation, from the skeleton of a man down to that of a mouse. . . . This view of nature . . . offers a very delusive spectacle; . . . the intellectual faculties of man were found to set him at such an immense distance from all the other animals, that it was absolutely necessary to devise some scheme for filling up the chasm. The resemblance of the bodily structure of the orang-outang to that of the human species, and consequent similarity in many of its actions to those of men, were not to be overlooked. . . . But as there

[75] *Ibid.*, p. 17.
[76] *Ibid.*, p. 27.

was still a long jump from an ape to a man, some happy geniuses bethought them of setting the Africans as a step which would make the transition perfectly easy. So that in the same proportion as the ape was raised above its proper sphere, the inoffensive negro was pulled down from his just rank in the creation. And thus was the golden chain of nature strained and new-linked, to serve the purposes of these gentlemen." [77]

Similarly, William Linn, pastor of the Dutch Reformed Church in New York, found in the Bible grounds for his opposition to Jefferson. In a political sermon of "Serious Considerations on the Election of a President," Linn voiced his skepticism of a man who could employ the phrase, "perhaps not less than *many people give to the age of the earth,*" warned against making mountains "older than Moses," and moved from that point straight to the crucial question: "Would a man who believes in a divine revelation even hint a suspicion" that blacks are a separate race? [78] He thundered the answer:

Sir, we excuse you not! You have degraded the blacks from the rank which God hath given them in the scale of being! You have advanced the strongest argument for their state of slavery! You have insulted human nature! You have contemned the word of truth and the mean |ing| ot salvation! [79]

Moore, a slaveholder himself, was no abolitionist, but for the purpose of argument he was willing to imply that he was. Jefferson had to be attacked where he was most vulnerable; if Jefferson endorsed emancipation when accompanied by colonization, Moore had to question Jefferson's unwillingness to live

---

[77] *Ibid.*, pp. 19–20.

[78] *Serious Considerations on the Election of a President* (New York, 1800), pp. 9, 12. Shortly before his death in 1808, Linn, a liberal theologian, was elected president of Union College. His son was the Presbyterian minister and poet John Blair Linn.

[79] *Ibid.*, p. 13. Linn admitted that Jefferson had endorsed emancipation, but suggested that the endorsement was only verbal and that Jefferson's deprecations of racial equality counteracted it.

with freed Negroes.[80] Therefore Moore professed his horror at a "scientific" outlook which "debases the Negro to an order of creatures, lower than those who have fairer skin and thinner lips"; he denied Jefferson's contention that difference in color necessarily implies difference in race; and when he found Jefferson arguing that Negroes themselves testify to white superiority by their "preference of them, as uniformly as is the preference of the Oranootan for the black woman over those of his own species," [81] he threw up his hands in dismay. "Where Mr. Jefferson learnt that the orang-outang has less affection for his own females than for black women, he does not inform us. . . . If it be true that the negroes entertain so great an affection for us, the swarms of West-Indian mulattoes testify that the regard is mutual." [82] Moore refused to countenance Jefferson's suggestion that when Negroes were brave it was from their inability to recognize danger, and he was properly scornful of comparisons between American slaves and their Roman counterparts. "The negroes who are brought to this country," Moore wrote, "are poor uncivilized creatures, as ignorant as they are unfortunate, and the greater part of them brought up in servitude before they came: but the ancient slaves, all know, were captives in war, ofttimes equally civilized with their conquerors, and frequently far superior to them in all the fine arts and useful sciences. . . . A precious sample this of philosophical reasoning: because the uncivilized Africans are not as good sculptors and poets as were the enslaved Greeks, they are not worthy to be called men." [83] And no Garrisonian abolitionist of the next generation could have drafted a more heartfelt reply to Jefferson's naive demand that a superior people would have made "affecting . . . poetry" out of the experience of their enslavement.

[80] Jefferson, *Notes on the State of Virginia*, ed. T. P. Abernethy (New York, 1964), Query XIV, pp. 132–133.
[81] *Ibid.*, p. 133.
[82] Moore, pp. 22–23.
[83] *Ibid.*, p. 27.

That the contemplation of misery in others often gives birth to affecting poetry, is true enough: and many a wretched mortal, who has been left to reflection, has endeavored to solace his grief by pouring forth his complaints in numbers. But one would have thought that modern philosophy herself could not have the face to declare that the wretch who is driven out to labour at the dawn of day and who toils till evening with the whip flourishing over his head, ought to be a poet.[84]

The antislavery arguments which Federalists found so congenial were not theirs alone. Federalists shared their suspicions of the slave system with many non-Federalists, including Jefferson himself, who had voiced, in a section of *Notes on Virginia* which his opponents never quoted, similar castigations of the system they took him to represent.[85] George Mason, for example, had his doubts about slavery; George Wythe judged runaway slave cases on the supposition that a Negro is considered free until proved to be a slave. St. George Tucker maintained that gradual emancipation was essential "not only to our moral character and domestic peace but even to our political salvation," and published a plan for gradual emancipation. The scheme, however, required over a century to achieve full emancipation and did not admit blacks to social equality.[86] James Madison was probably representative of Virginia slaveholders; he regarded slavery as a contradiction of American ideals, but did not trust the morality of the free black man and endorsed emancipation only if coupled with colonization in Africa or the removal of blacks to separate communities in the American west.[87]

[84] *Ibid.*, p. 24.

[85] Jefferson, p. 155.

[86] St. George Tucker, *A Dissertation on Slavery: With a Proposal for the Gradual Abolition of It in the State of Virginia* (Philadelphia, 1796), pp. 66–106.

[87] James Madison to Joseph Jones, November 28, 1780, *The Papers of James Madison*, ed. William T. Hutchinson and William M. E. Rachal (Chicago, 1962), II, 209; James Madison to Robert J. Evans, June 15, 1819, *The Complete Madison*, ed. Saul K. Padover (New York, 1953),

More significantly, Federalists might have claimed, with some accuracy, that antislavery was part of their heritage from the Revolutionary generation. It had been a common habit among revolutionary pamphleteers to justify resistance to England on the ground that the regulatory legislation of the 1760's and 1770's was intended virtually to enslave the colonists. As Bernard Bailyn has explained, slavery was equated with

the inability to maintain one's just property in material things and abstract rights, rights and things which a proper constitution guaranteed a free people. Both symptom and consequence of disease in the body politic, it was the condition that followed the loss of freedom. . . . "Slavery" in this sense, far from being mere exclamation and hyperbole, was a term referring to a specific political condition, a condition characteristic of the lives of contemporary Frenchmen, Danes, and Swedes as well as of Turks, Russians, and Poles. And it applied equally to the black plantation laborers on the southern American colonies. For their condition was only a more dramatic, more bizarre variation of the condition of all who had lost the power of self-determination.[88]

Among those who explicitly denounced the slavery to which they believed the American colonists were reduced were Joseph Warren, John Dickinson, John Adams, and Josiah Quincy, Jr. Loyalists seeking to discredit the Patriots' integrity found it use-

---

p. 325. See also Richard Beale Davis, *Intellectual Life in Jefferson's Virginia* (Chapel Hill, 1964), pp. 411–419; and Robert McColley, *Slavery and Jeffersonian Virginia* (Urbana, Ill., 1964), pp. 124–162. McColley feels that when Virginians attacked slavery they generally did so in letters to foreigners or Northerners; they seldom criticized slavery to other Southerners and seldom sought practical schemes for abolition. The few Virginians who acted on their verbal castigations of the system tended to be the elderly who manumitted slaves in their wills, *after* they had enjoyed their services, or Quakers who ran Negro schools and investigated the legality of the titles by which slaves were held, with an eye toward bringing lawsuits in cases of doubtful title. These efforts were generally frustrated by the rest of the public and by the state legislature.

[88] Bernard Bailyn, ed., *Pamphlets of the American Revolution: 1750–1776* (Cambridge, Mass., 1965), I, 141.

ful to emphasize the paradoxical spectacle of slaveholders protesting the principle of slavery; inevitably Patriot rhetoric, in response, was threaded with increasingly general and explicit antislavery argument. Some of the clearest expositions came from clergymen, frequently from those most conservative in their outlook and fundamentalist in their theology, who insisted that God would not approve of Americans' fight for liberty so long as they denied freedom to their own slaves.[89]

The Quincy family provides a suggestive generational paradigm: from Josiah Quincy, Jr., a Revolutionary patriot highly suspicious of slavery; to his Federalist son Josiah, equally skeptical of the slave system, less perhaps on social grounds than on political ones; to Josiah's son Edmund, who would become one of William Lloyd Garrison's closest associates in a radical and humanitarian campaign to which his father, Federalist though he claimed to remain to the end of his life, appears not to have objected. Virtually all the themes of the Federalist indictment of Southern society were present in a journal kept by Josiah Quincy, Jr., during a tour through the South in 1773. The author of "Climenole" had not known his patriot father, who died while Quincy was still a young child, but he knew his father's journal and some years later edited and published it as part of his father's biography. The elder Quincy's reaction to Southern society was disconcertingly similar to the reactions of his son's contemporaries. "Having now finished my tour through those Southern provinces which boast most of their politeness, taste, and the art of true living," the journal began, "I am naturally led to consider the justness of their good opinion of themselves." [90] Like Roger Griswold, Quincy had been shocked at the Southern landscape and was certain that the fewer the slaves, the more thriving the state of agriculture. Thus he preferred

[89] *Ibid.*, pp. 141–149.

[90] M. A. DeWolfe Howe, ed., "Journal of Josiah Quincy, Jr., 1773," *Proceedings of the Massachusetts Historical Society*, XLIX (June, 1916), 467.

North to South Carolina; in the former the lower profits of tobacco plantations meant there were fewer slaves. Since they were less able to afford slaves,

you see husbandmen, yeomen and white laborers . . . instead of herds of negroes and tawny slaves. Healthfull countenances and numerous families become more common as you advance North. . . . The slaves in North Carolina are fewer in number, better clothed and better fed, than in South, and are of consequence better servants.[91]

Like Thomas Boylston Adams and Thomas Jefferson himself, Quincy observed that the institution of slavery had an unfortunate effect on the slaveholders:

The brutality used toward the slaves has a very bad tendency with reference to the manners of the people, but a much worse with regard to the youth. They will plead in their excuse "this severity is necessary." But whence did or does this necessity arise? From *the necessity* of having vast multitudes sunk in barbarism, ignorance and the basest and most servile employ! By reason of this slavery, the children are early impressed with infamous and destructive ideas, and become extremely vitiated in their manners, they contract a negroish kind of accent, pronunciation and dialect, as well as ridiculous kind of behaviour: even many of the grown people, and especially the women, are vastly infected with the same disorder. Parents . . . [talk] to their very young children . . . as though they were speak[ing] to a new imported African.[92]

He was distressed at the laws governing slaves, especially when Charles Cotesworth Pinckney told him that "any two justices and three free-holders might and very often did *instanter* upon view or complaint [i.e., without warrant] try a negro for any crime, and might and did often award execution of death, . . . that neither negroes nor mulattoes could have a Jury; . . . that

[91] *Ibid.*, pp. 462–463.
[92] *Ibid.*, pp. 456–457.

(further) to *steal* a negro was death, but to *kill him* was only fineable." [93]

Their Legislators [have] enacted laws touching negroes, mulattoes and masters which savor more of the policy of Pandemonium than the English constitution: —laws which will stand eternal records of the depravity and contradiction of the human character: laws which would disgrace the tribunal of Scythian, Arab, Hottentot and Barbarian are appealed to in decisions upon life limb and liberty by those who assume the name of Englishmen, freemen and Christians: . . . the Judges . . . would do well to remember that no laws of the (little) creature supersede the laws of the (great) creator. Can the institutions of man make void the decree of GOD? [94]

Like Moore, Quincy's dislike of slavery was linked to his dismay at the laxity of religious observance. In their behavior toward their slaves, Southerners ignored the will of God; in their use of the sabbath as "a day of visiting and mirth" they gave further evidence that the "state of religion here is repugnant not only to the ordinances and institutions of Jesus Christ, but to every law of sound polity." [95] The presence of mulattoes led Quincy, like Moore, to draw highly unfavorable conclusions about the character of the slaveholder: "It is far from being uncommon to see a gentleman at dinner, and his reputed offspring a slave to the master of the table. I myself saw two instances of this. . . . The fathers neither of them blushed or seem[ed] disconcerted. They were called men of worth, politeness and humanity. Strange perversion of terms and language!" [96] Finally, like Oliver Wolcott a generation later, the elder Quincy entertained serious suspicions about the depth of Southern commitment to the revolutionary cause. Wolcott had suggested that Southern planters were motivated primarily by a selfish desire to avoid payment of debts owed to British merchants.

[93] *Ibid.*, p. 446.
[94] *Ibid.*, p. 457.
[95] *Ibid.*, p. 455. *See also* pp. 462–463.
[96] *Ibid.*, p. 463.

Quincy thought he sensed that Southerners gave only lip service to the patriot resistance. "Their fiercer passions seem to be employed upon their slaves and here to expend themselves"; he expected that they could be easily bought off, not by the annullment of debts, but by the offer of privileges.

Let us suppose a change in British policy.

Compose the Council of the first planters, fill all the Public offices with them, give them the honours of the State, and though they don't want them, give them it and emoluments also: introduce Baronies and Lordships—their enormous estates will bear it—what will become of Carolinian freedom? The luxury, dissipation, life, sentiments and manners of the leading people naturally tend to make them neglect, despise, and be careless of the true interests of mankind.[97]

Other families display a similar continuum, suggesting that the political abolitionism of an earlier generation was transformed into a humanitarian abolitionism by sons who took their fathers at their word. Judge John Lowell had been a delegate to the Continental Congress, and, as a member of the Massachusetts State Constitutional Convention, had introduced a famous clause abolishing slavery. His son John was a Federalist very much of Josiah Quincy's uncompromising cast of mind, but his grandson (son of John's brother Charles) was James Russell Lowell, an ardent abolitionist who contributed his "Biglow Papers" to the *National Anti-Slavery Standard* during the years that Edmund Quincy was serving as an assistant editor.

The career of Wendell Phillips' father, John Phillips, provides certain rough parallels to Josiah Quincy's. The two men were members of the same lower house of the Massachusetts General Court in 1803; when Quincy returned from Congress in 1815 to take a seat in the State Senate, he found Phillips still a colleague. When neither Harrison Gray Otis nor Quincy won a clear majority in the Boston election of 1822, John Phillips was the compromise candidate for mayor; when he died the fol-

[97] *Ibid.*, pp. 454, 455.

lowing year Quincy succeeded him. Phillips' son Wendell, like Edmund Quincy, would be one of Garrison's most ardent supporters: more Garrisonian than Garrison, perhaps, he kept the abolitionist movement in being as an agency to assist the freed Negro long after Garrison himself, satisfied by the formulae of war and emancipation proclamation, moved to disband the movement.

Theodore Sedgwick, Jr., one of the most articulate of the abolitionist spokesmen, was the son of Theodore Sedgwick, who illustrated in his career as congressman, lawyer, and judge a typically Federalist ambivalence on the subject of slavery. Believing in the necessity of sustaining constitutional guarantees, Theodore Sedgwick had been a leading member of the congressional committee which reported the first fugitive slave law, and he insisted that any proposal for the "abolition of slavery in this country would be the height of madness." [98] But as a practicing lawyer in Stockbridge, Massachusetts, Sedgwick undertook the defense of Elizabeth Freeman, a slave who sued for her liberty on the ground that slavery had been effectively abolished in the state by the Bill of Rights of 1780,[99] and as a judge on the Massachusetts Supreme Court Sedgwick refused to sustain an African slave trade contract on the ground that "the law of nature should be the law of the land; that one man could not have a legitimate property in the person of another man; and that therefore a contract made in *Rio Pangos,* on the coast of Africa, was . . . *malum in se,* and void as against the law of God." [100] Theodore Sedgwick, Jr., credited his family with providing a home atmosphere conducive to the development of abolitionist

[98] Richard E. Welch, *Theodore Sedgwick, Federalist: A Political Portrait* (Middletown, Conn., 1965), pp. 102, 135. Welch calls him "virtual author" of the fugitive slave law.

[99] The case is extensively discussed in Arthur Zilversmit, "Quok Walker, Mumbet, and the Abolition of Slavery in Massachusetts," *William and Mary Quarterly,* 3d ser., XXV (1968), 614–624.

[100] [Theodore Sedgwick, Jr.], *The Practicability of the Abolition of Slavery* (New York, 1830), p. 35.

beliefs. Elizabeth Freeman came to work in Sedgwick's home and be nurse to his children: "Having known this woman as familiarly as I knew either of my parents," Theodore Sedgwick, Jr., recalled, "I cannot believe in the moral or physical inferiority of the race to which she belonged." [101]

Garrison himself seems to have been molded by a similar set of relationships. His own family was too poor to be political, and his father deserted the family when his son was a small child. But Garrison found his politics in the Federalism of the *Newburyport Herald* for which he went to work as a printer's apprentice in 1818, and a model, perhaps a father image, in Timothy Pickering. Pickering's Federalism was "high" enough to set a standard definition of what party loyalty meant, and his endorsement of abolition dates from at least as early as 1785, when, with Rufus King, he attempted to convince the Continental Congress to prohibit slavery in the entire transappalachian territory. Pickering's politics included more than a touch of anti-southern feeling, and his secessionist plot of 1804 perhaps suggested Garrison's own later demand for the secession of the free states from a constitution which was a "compromise with the devil and a compact with hell." [102]

In their endorsement of the Ely amendment, Timothy Pick-

---

[101] *Ibid.*, p. 18.

[102] See John L. Thomas, *The Liberator: William Lloyd Garrison* (Boston, 1963), pp. 31–40; Robert Ernst, *Rufus King: American Federalist* (Chapel Hill, 1968), pp. 54–55; John Marshall to Pickering, March 20, 1829, in A. J. Beveridge, *The Life of John Marshall* (New York, 1919), IV, 473. Pickering is generally regarded as a bitter old curmudgeon, a characterization based largely on John Adams's descriptions. "Mr. Pickering," complained Adams, "would have made a good collector of the customs; but he was not so well qualified for a Secretary of State." Adams's friend Benjamin Waterhouse described Pickering as a man "who like spoilt wine, grows every day more sour, & is in a fair way of becoming first rate vinegar." But Pickering had other faces. Abijah Bigelow found him "a very sociable man, of rather blunt manners," who spent occasional evenings in Washington, D.C., teaching his landlady how to make Indian pudding for homesick New Englanders. When his son John hesitated to take part in oratorical exhibitions at Harvard, Pickering wrote a very human

ering and Josiah Quincy had carefully avoided any hint of abolitionist sentiment. But Quincy's son was to argue that modern abolitionism began with his father's speech in defense of the Ely amendment, and Pickering's grandson insisted that the effect of the amendment would have been abolitionist. Like those modern historians who doubt the economic viability of the slave system, Pickering and Quincy believed that it was kept alive by the excessive political power vouchsafed to it by the three-fifths compromise; that without that false vitality the system would die of its own weight.[103] "It is for thoughtful minds," wrote Pickering's grandson, ". . . to judge whether, if a persistent agitation had been confined [to the Ely amendment] . . . it would not [have put an end to slavery], without involving the subject in personal criminations or moral reproaches, thus maddening the passions and blinding the eyes of the people, [and] have accomplished the great end without drenching the country with fraternal blood." [104]

In a famous phrase, Thomas Jefferson called the Missouri

letter of advice and confession: "At this early period [of your life] the more frequently you enter into the company and conversation of respectable strangers of both sexes, the sooner you will secure an easy freedom, which will contribute to your happiness, and certainly guard you from the awkward pains of a recluse. For want of such advice and of corresponding opportunities, I have suffered all my life long anxieties from which I wish you may be exempt" (John Adams to William Cunningham, Oct. 15, 1808, *Correspondence Between the Hon. John Adams, Late President of the United States, and the Late William Cunningham, Beginning in 1803, and Ending in 1812,* ed. E. M. Cunningham [Boston, 1823], p. 40; B. Waterhouse to John Adams, February 19, 1811, APm reel 411; Abijah Bigelow to Hannah Bigelow, December 29, 1810, *Proceedings of the American Antiquarian Society,* new ser., XL [1930], 312; T. Pickering to J. Pickering, May 7, 1794, in Mary Orne Pickering, *The Life of John Pickering* [Boston, 1887], p. 61).

[103] See Harold D. Woodman, "The Profitability of Slavery: A Historical Perennial," *Journal of Southern History,* XXIX (1963), 303–325; and Eugene D. Genovese, *The Political Economy of Slavery: Studies in the Economy and Society of the Slave South* (New York, 1965), pp. 85–179, 275–287.

[104] O. Pickering and C. Upham, IV, 65.

Compromise debates "a firebell in the night"—dangerous because party divisions coordinated with geographic divisions. But the first firebells were not rung in 1820; long before, in the debates on Louisiana and Santo Domingo, northern Democrats and southern Federalists had been conspicuous by their silence, while northern Federalists and southern Republicans were permitted to speak for their respective parties. John Quincy Adams had recognized that although the Ely amendment would be given only brief attention in the Senate it was not for that reason unimportant; "It is a speck," he told his mother, "deeper in the flesh, than from its present treatment may be thought." [105] Federalists who found slavery repugnant also found that the issue of slavery could be used to good effect against their political opponents, and they began to develop a political antislavery case to set beside and to reinforce religious, humanitarian abolitionism. By their ideas—and their sons—they helped to found the larger antislavery crusade of the Jacksonian generation. That this crusade was being demanded as early as 1811 is suggested by the verses of a sixteen-year-old Yale freshman, whose youthful writing directly and unselfconsciously reflects what he heard from adults around him:

> Swains of New England you I call to stop
> That horrid trade which grows in human blood
> And from the oppressor's iron grasp to wrench
> The crimson scourge dripping with negro's gore.
>
> . . . . .
>
> Then will the slave from toil and hardship free
> Beneath the spreading Bohab loudly sing
> Thanks to New England's sons.[106]

[105] J. Q. Adams to A. Adams, December 3, 1804, APm reel 403.
[106] James Gates Percival, "The Seasons of New England," in Julius H. Ward, *The Life and Letters of James Gates Percival* (Boston, 1866), p. 18.

[3]

The Objects of
Scientific Inquiry

Whenever modern philosophers talk
about mountains, something impious
is likely to be at hand.
—CLEMENT CLARKE MOORE

Jefferson the hypocritical politician was, after all, only one
among many politicians whom Federalists found odious. But
there appears to have been something particularly objectionable
to the Federalist mind about Jefferson the inventor, Jefferson
the anthropologist, Jefferson the president of the American
Philosophical Society. Satirists frequently scant Jefferson's political errors (there is, for example, no extended satire on Jefferson's replacement of the midnight judges) in order to concentrate on what they evidently considered his more vulnerable
roles.

Whereas sympathizers saw in the President's limitless curiosity and inventiveness evidence of an imaginative and far-ranging
mind, Federalists, using the same evidence, found a mind that
was flighty and irresponsible. Hamilton, for example, once
claimed that Jefferson's opinions were as "versatile" as the
swivel chair he had invented: "As in schools, applications to the
breach are said to have a wonderful effect on the head, by driv-
ing up learning, so there appears to be such a wonderful connexion between the seat and the head of this great politician, and
the motions of the one have such a powerful effect on the opera-

tions of the other." [1] In 1804, when Jefferson was exhibiting a model of a dry dock to White House guests, the Boston *Repertory*, ever critical of Jefferson's naval policies, scoffed at the inventor as a man who exercised his speculative mind upon "this knotty question solving, / how *salt* can be of *use* without *dissolving*," and who had found his answer in the mountain of salt long rumored to exist in the distant west:

> ah! this will do,
> docks shall be scooped, . . .
> And in this mountain shall our ships be *salted*.[2]

"The truth is," Josiah Quincy complained, "that ever since putting together watchwork, and measuring bones, and making mould-boards, have been sufficient qualifications to entitle men not only to set up for great philosophers themselves, but to be rated as such by others. . . . A man . . . need ask no other boon of providence than to be enabled to discover *a mammoth pit*." [3]

That Quincy should include measuring bones and the invention of the mold board plow in the same recital of distasteful activities is not unusual. Federalists seem to have assumed that Jefferson the natural historian and anthropologist was as open to ridicule as Jefferson the visionary inventor, although on the face of it Jefferson's work in this field does not appear particularly vulnerable. His major effort, of course, was the *Notes on Virginia*. Drafted during the darkest year of the American Revolution, when the British under General Tarleton had forced Jefferson, then Governor of Virginia, to abandon Richmond for the comparative safety of Monticello, and then to abandon Monticello for a still more secluded retreat, the book is vibrant testimony to Jefferson's faith in the American cause and the

[1] Quoted in John C. Miller, *Alexander Hamilton: Portrait in Paradox* (New York, 1959), pp. 347–348.

[2] Boston *Repertory*, February 10, 1804. The salt mountain was reported by Lewis and Clark, who located it one thousand miles up the Missouri and gave its dimensions as 180 miles long and 45 miles wide.

[3] "Climenole, No. 8," March 24, 1804.

strength of his conviction that American society and the American land could sustain a viable state and, in fact, a new civilization. The *Notes* are readable despite their format, which is a series of straightforward answers to a set of rather dull questions posed by the secretary of the French legation,[4] beginning with Query I: "An exact description of the limits and boundaries of the State of Virginia?" going on through Query VI: "A notice of the mines and other subterraneous riches; its trees, plants fruits, etc." and ending with Query XXIII: "The histories of the State . . . and the pamphlets relating to its interior or exterior affairs present or ancient?" But in the election year of 1800, two new editions of the *Notes* were published, and the first year of Jefferson's administration saw the appearance of no fewer than five new editions.[5] Once the volume was thus forcibly brought to their attention, Federalists were not slow in finding much to criticize, in obvious chapters like those on the state constitution, the administration of justice, and the religious beliefs of the citizens,[6] and in chapters on natural history whose titles give no hint that they would lend themselves to political contention.

Jefferson was one of the earliest American students of what is now called vertebrate paleontology; he collected the bones of extinct animals, and sought to reconstruct them as they must have been. Much of his work is still considered respectable, but one of its limitations was the notion, which he shared with many contemporaries, that forms of life, once created by a God who

[4] François Barbé-Marbois, who was perhaps wondering whether the colony was worth defending.

[5] Hamilton Bullock Tompkins, *Bibliotheca Jeffersoniana: A List of Books Written by or Relating to Thomas Jefferson* (New York, 1887), pp. 71–75; Thomas Jefferson, *Notes on the State of Virginia*, ed. Thomas Perkins Abernethy (New York, 1964), pp. xv–xvi.

[6] In which Jefferson (p. 152) made the remark for which thousands of fundamentalists would never forgive him: "It does me no injury for my neighbor to say there are twenty gods, or no God. It neither picks my pocket nor breaks my leg."

does not waste energy in useless effort, last perpetually and are not subject to extinction. In the answer to Query VI, he therefore accepted the Indian "tradition" that the "tusks, grinders, and skeletons of unparalleled magnitude" which had been uncovered in large quantities on the banks of the Ohio, "some lying on the surface of the earth, and some a little below it," belonged to the mammoth, a sort of giant buffalo which "still exists in the northern parts of America." [7] It was a thought which raised John Quincy Adams's ever-skeptical eyebrows, and when he came to list in doggerel verse the things Jefferson's protégé Meriwether Lewis did *not* find on his famous expedition, Adams began:

> He never with a Mammoth met,
> However you may wonder;
> Nor even with a Mammoth's bone,
> Above the ground or under.

Adams reproached Lewis and Clark for failing to find other wonders: "the hog with navel on his back," or "mountain, soil'd in pickle," the latter, like the salt mountain of the *Repertory* poet, probably a reference to Jefferson's discussion of limestone caves in the Allegheny hills from which large quantities of salts and nitrates might be extracted.[8]

In his reply to Query VI, Jefferson cited the size of the mammoth bones as evidence in his refutation of Buffon's claim that

---

[7] *Ibid.*, pp. 37–38.

[8] *Monthly Anthology and Boston Review*, IV (1807), 142–144. Nor had Lewis and Clark found "an Indian tribe / From Welchmen [*sic*] straight descended," although in 1804 it had been rumored that there lived "high up the Missouri" a tribe of white-skinned, Welsh-speaking Indians, descended from the legendary prince Madoc, who had once sailed west and never returned (*Kentucky Palladium*, December 12, 1804, reprinted in Richard Alsop *et al.*, *The Echo* [New York, 1807], pp. 324 ff; Jefferson, p. 30). See also Edwin T. Martin, *Thomas Jefferson: Scientist* (New York, 1952), pp. 227–228.

American animals were naturally smaller than European animals; in a subsequent chapter he defended the American Indians against Buffon's remark that they, like other forms of life indigenous to the New World, were smaller, weaker, and sexually less adequate than those of Europe.[9] That Jefferson chose to oppose him was nearly enough to make Buffon an honorary Federalist. Oliver Wolcott, for example, chose "Buffon" for his *nom de plume* when he came to write a series of strictures on Jefferson's hesitant suggestion that Indian criminals facing capital punishment be shot rather than hanged, because in their culture hanging was "particularly repugnant." His tongue firmly in his cheek, "Buffon" doubted that it would be possible to settle the matter by treaty, "even consistently with the extravagant ideas heretofore advanced by the federalists respecting the nature of the constitutional power vested in the President and Senate." Perhaps, after all, Wolcott went on, reluctance to be hanged was a reliable identifying mark of species; during Tarleton's invasion the best specimens of Homo Sapiens Virginianus had "preferred the chance of being *hanged as a rebel,* to the rigor of being *shot as an Enemy.*"[10]

His critics gradually transformed Jefferson's interest in natural history into a senile fixation. Irving's William the Testy "confused his brain with abstract speculation"; in *Salmagundi* the president is dismissed as "a very plain old gentleman something they say of a humorist, as he amuses himself with impaling butterflies and pickling tadpoles."[11] The implication of dotage cannot be missed, nor is it absent from Bryant's harsher dismissal:

[9] For a discussion of this debate with Buffon, see Martin, ch. 7.

[10] Oliver Wolcott Papers, Connecticut Historical Society; *Connecticut Courant,* March 15, 1802. Jefferson (p. 59) had referred to "Homo Sapiens Europaeus."

[11] Washington Irving, *A History of New York, from the Beginning of the World to the End of the Dutch Dynasty . . . by Dieterich Knickerbocker* (New York, 1809), I, 197–198; Washington Irving, *et al., Salmagundi,* February 13, 1807 (London, 1811), I, 46.

Go search, with curious eye, for hornéd frogs,
'Mongst the wild wastes of Louisianian bogs;
Or, where Ohio rolls his turbid stream,
Dig for huge bones, thy glory and thy theme.[12]

Jefferson's best-known work as a paleontologist was a paper he read before the American Philosophical Society on March 10, 1787. Since it was not published until the next issue of the Society's *Transactions* appeared in 1799, Federalists did not pounce on it until after its author had become President. The title is harmless enough: "A Memoir on the Discovery of certain Bones of a Quadruped of the clawed kind in the Western Parts of Virginia." In it, Jefferson described the discovery of animal bones in a limestone and nitre cave west of the Blue Ridge. Among the remnants was a fragment of a great claw, several times the size of the lion's, which Jefferson suggested belonged to an animal rumored to have appeared to the first explorers of the region. "He went round and round their camp," Jefferson wrote. "At times they saw his eyes like two balls of fire, . . . their horses were so agonized with fear that they couched down on the earth, and their dogs crept in among them, not daring to bark." Visualizing the animal as a sort of giant lion, Jefferson suggested that it be named the Megalonyx, or Great Claw, after its most distinctive trait, and the name has stuck, although before long Baron Cuvier and Caspar Wistar, working independently, more accurately identified the animal as an extinct giant sloth.[13] Like the Mammoth, the Megalonyx began to make its

[12] William Cullen Bryant, *The Embargo; or Sketches of the Times. A Satire* (Boston, 1809), p. 12.

[13] American Philosophical Society, *Transactions*, IV (Philadelphia, 1799), 246–260. Jefferson's essay still makes delightful reading, but even in his time it was something less than a model of scientific method. "As scientific research," writes George Gaylord Simpson in an article appearing in the *Proceedings* 144 years after Jefferson's, "it departs from inaccurate observations and proceeds by faulty methods to an erroneous conclusion" ("The Beginnings of Vertebrate Paleontology in North America," *Proceedings of the American Philosophical Society*, volume 86, no. 1 [1943], p. 157). See also Martin, pp. 107–130.

appearance in Federalist satires. In one of these, Jefferson suggests a design for the nation's coat of arms: on a sable field, "the skeleton of a mammoth passant, *argent*. Crest; on a fascis, *or*, a sinister hand plumed, *argent*. Supporters; two great claws." [14] In the *New England Monthly Magazine*, a thinly disguised Jefferson turns up as a Dr. Gall, who studies his large collection of human skulls for hints as to the "powers and dispositions of the soul." [15] And in the final installment of "Climenole," Jefferson's pregnant mother is visited by a vision of crossed bones, but cannot decide whether the omen means her son is destined to become a warrior, a surgeon, or a sexton. As a child the prodigy retrieves chicken bones from the family cook, and assembles skeletons of a mouse, two kittens and a bullfrog.[16] The obvious implication of all this is that an active interest in bones is at least dim-witted, and possibly evidence of mental disturbance.

Once Quincy's philosopher had found his mammoth pit, renown would follow as a matter of course:

If he happen to have his scale and dividers in his pocket, and should submit to the drudgery of making a drawing and description, for the benefit of the curious, he will have ill luck indeed, if, in consequence of these rare exertions, he be not elevated, for life, to the presidency of the American philosophical society.[17]

It is startling to find the American Philosophical Society, that dignified and deservedly honored organization which, as Jefferson remarked, embodied "whatever the American world has of distinction in philosophy and science in general," [18] a target of political satire, but the Society was one of Josiah Quincy's favorite targets. Although in private correspondence with the Society he maintained the tone of a modest admirer of its work, in public he identified it with its execrable president and suggested that Jefferson's remark was accurate only insofar as it implied

[14] *Port Folio*, March 13, 1802.
[15] Quoted in the Boston *Repertory*, February 28, 1804.
[16] "Climenole, No. 12," November 17.
[17] "Climenole, No. 8," March 24.
[18] American Philosophical Society, *Transactions*, IV (1799), pp. xii–xiii.

that "the members of that society were not famous for A PARTIC-
ULAR AND ACCURATE KNOWLEDGE OF ANY THING, but were distinguished only by a *general acquaintance* with philosophy." [19]
Even the *Transactions* of the Society, a series of scientific reports
which constitute the young republic's proudest contribution to
the literature of science, were, in Quincy's view, just so much
printed paper, published by men who believe that *"in literature,
bulk is as necessary to respectability, as it is, in nature, to the
sublime,"* [20] and whose only practical aim was "the encouragement of paper, and other infant manufactures of our
country." [21] The *Transactions* were expressly made bulkier,
Quincy suggested, in order to render them fraudulently impres-
sive; properly edited, he added, they would make excellent
"three penny gifts for children," since there is so much in them
that children admire. In support of this last contention, Quincy
listed John Heckewelder's observations on grasshoppers, Dr.
Benjamin Smith Barton's account of a hunt for "frozen rattle-
snakes," and Jefferson's memoir of the Megalonyx, "an unknown and *unseen* animal . . . *whose roaring resembled thun-
der,"* and which, Quincy reported, reminded his three-year-old
son of the wolf in "Little Red Riding Hood." [22]

Yet Quincy was no ordinary anti-intellectual. Twenty-five

[19] Josiah Quincy to John Vaughan, December 31, 1801, May 12, 1803,
American Philosophical Society Archives; "Climenole, No. 9," September
15.

[20] "Climenole, No. 11," October 13. The reference is to Edmund
Burke's essay "On the Sublime and the Beautiful."

[21] "Climenole, No. 9," September 15. Volume IV, for example, was
over six hundred pages long, but could have been two hundred pages
shorter had the printer eschewed three-quarter-page margins, and not
reproduced all five lines of the complimentary close on reprinted letters:
"I am, with great respect / Dear Sir / Your most obedient and / humble
servant / signature / as though they were a description of the title of a
real estate, which it was dangerous either to destroy or mutilate" (Climenole, No. 11," October 13).

[22] American Philosophical Society, *Transactions*, IV, 124 ff, 326 ff;
"Climenole, No. 12," November 17.

years later he would become a distinguished president of Harvard; in 1804 he was treasurer of the Massachusetts Historical Society, a founder of the Society for the Study of Natural Philosophy, and a member of Boston's American Academy of Arts and Sciences. The Academy, which had a heavily Federalist membership, had been chartered forty years after the Philadelphia Society, and if its *Memoirs* were less bulky than the *Transactions,* they were equally learned. (They were printed, it must be observed, on widely margined—and cheaper—paper.) And Quincy's suspicions of Jeffersonian science were shared by others who were serious and enthusiastic students themselves, among them John Adams, Thomas Boylston Adams, Winthrop Sargent, and even a few democrats like Hugh Henry Brackenridge.[23]

Federalist skepticism about "Jeffersonian science" is not easily explained. Part of the answer, however, may lie in diverging definitions of the proper object of scientific investigation. Natural history and astronomy were, as the visiting Marquis de Chastellux had suggested in 1782, the "peculiar appendages" of a new nation whose vast extent enabled her citizens to survey "a large portion of heaven and earth."[24] Almost from the beginning, an informal division of labor had prevailed; the sea-faring New Englanders had come naturally to astronomy by their need to plot the positions of heavenly bodies and to determine longitudes, and Benjamin Franklin's omission of astronomy from his original prospectus for the American Philosophical Society

[23] Dirk J. Struik, *Yankee Science in the Making* (Boston, 1948), p. 153; Thomas Boylston Adams, "Levity," *Port Folio,* March 13, 1802; Winthrop Sargent, "Letters to Leinwha," *Monthly Anthology and Boston Review,* II (1805), 74; Hugh Henry Brackenridge, *Modern Chivalry* (Philadelphia, 1846), I, 41–42. See also Van Wyck Brooks, *The World of Washington Irving* (New York, 1944), p. 92n. The development of this satirical theme culminated in Dickens, with Mr. Pickwick's theory of tittlebats.

[24] Daniel J. Boorstin, *The Americans: The Colonial Experience* (New York, 1958), p. 164.

serves as an indication that astronomical interest was less pervasive further south. Since, as Dirk Struik puts it, the path to navigation and astronomy went through Newton's *Principia*, Newton was greatly honored at Harvard, where mathematics and astronomy had been well and competently taught since the eighteenth century.[25]

By the turn of the nineteenth century, comparison of the published papers of the two leading scientific societies suggests that the Boston-based American Academy of Arts and Sciences tended to stress mathematical and astronomical studies at the expense of natural history; Philadelphia's American Philosophical Society encouraged descriptive work in botany, geology, and paleontology, placing comparatively less emphasis on the mathematical sciences.

Increasingly, the old division of labor came to take on a political dimension: while Jefferson occupied the White House it was widely assumed that the Philosophical Society was Democratic and the Academy Federalist.[26] Although the Society's membership rolls included Federalist names, its best-known members were Democrats. Just as Jefferson's association with the salt-mountain rendered it suspect, Jefferson's long identification with the American Philosophical Society meant that the Society's claim to intellectual pre-eminence would have to be disputed if Jefferson's own claim to honor as a scientist were to be undermined. Automatically, then, the Society became an object of Federalist suspicion, and the information published under its auspices a target of Federalist ridicule. When, for example, Francis Adrian Van der Kemp submitted an essay on Jefferson's debate with Buffon to the American Academy of Arts and Sci-

[25] Struik, pp. 20, 30, 66, 150; Brooke Hindle, *The Pursuit of Science in Revolutionary America: 1735–1789* (Chapel Hill, 1956), pp. 69, 87. There were exceptions to this pattern, for example, the work of Benjamin Silliman at Yale, or of David Rittenhouse, the astronomer who was a member of the Jeffersonian circle in the American Philosophical Society.

[26] Lewis S. Feuer, *The Scientific Intellectual* (New York, 1963), p. 363; Struik, pp. 44–45; Martin, p. 219.

ences, John Adams, president of the Academy and Van der Kemp's old friend, had to warn against disappointment. "I think it a learned and ingenious Performance and the compliments to Jefferson and Buffon, have no weight with me, but I am apprehensive will form an objection to the Publication in the Minds of the Committee and the Academy: Neither of these illustrious Personages is held in much Veneration among our New England Philosophers." A year later, Van der Kemp's manuscript was returned, unpublished. "All who have looked into it, express themselves handsomely of it, as ingenious and learned, but all agree that it cannot be inserted in the Transactions." [27] New York and Pennsylvania scientists like Samuel Latham Mitchill and Thomas Cooper began to credit their inspiration to contemporary French scientists instead of Newton, and the pervasive feeling that there was a radical flavor to geology, zoology, and botany led Dr. Benjamin Waterhouse to decry the intrusion of "a streak of party politics" into the discussion of natural phenomena.[28] The crude syllogism seemed to run: Democrats are suspect. The American Philosophical Society is largely Democratic, and concentrates on natural history. Therefore there is something suspicious about natural history.

Waterhouse's own experience provided one example of how party politics might intrude on scientific discussion, and might,

[27] John Adams to F. A. Van der Kemp, August 1, 1803; November 5, 1804, John Adams Letters, Historical Society of Pennsylvania.

[28] Benjamin Waterhouse to Benjamin Russell, February 8, 1804, in Boston *Centinel*, February 22, 1804. Feuer (pp. 344–347) states that the Quaker identification of most members of the American Philosophical Society was largely a matter of form; like most practicing scientists in all societies, they tended to be anti- or a-religious in temper and to espouse what he calls a "hedonist-libertarian ethic." But the Congregational-Unitarian identification of most members of the Academy was *not* at all a matter of form; such men would be likely to find their suspicions of the American Philosophical Society on political and intellectual grounds reinforced by their distrust of the Society and its work on religious grounds; thus they would build a case against the Society as a menace to the community at large.

in fact, shape scientific decisions. At the turn of the century, as one of a few well-informed physicians who sought to substitute Jenner's technique of vaccination with mild cowpox virus for the more dangerous older method of inoculation with smallpox itself, Waterhouse faced "a host of enemies" apparently inspired more by their political hostility to his outspoken Republicanism than by contradictory evidence. Since it was difficult to predict accurately the precise effect of small amounts of the smallpox virus, the older method had often proved to be merely the voluntary contracting of a virulent and sometimes fatal disease; among Waterhouse's defenders were ex-president Adams, who could remember his own experience of the "cure" in 1764, and Thomas Jefferson, who, as Waterhouse later remembered, "strengthened my hands and encouraged my heart." [29] But at the same time that Waterhouse was endorsing the new technique, he was engaged in other campaigns which had the effect of arousing hostility against him and, by extension, against all his works. He was opposed, for example, to the removal of Harvard's medical school from the Cambridge campus, where its course of instruction was of necessity largely theoretical, to the city of Boston, where, in association with an active hospital, it could offer clinical training. Furthermore, the same newspaper columns that were filled with Waterhouse's public letters in defense of inoculation also carried his letters defending the existence of that salt mountain which Federalist publicists had already committed themselves to deriding. The doctor's arguments were calm and reasonable; he could not provide legal proof of the mountain's existence, but other traveler's tales of strange phenomena, "a bird with the make of a turtle, and the qualities of a sloth; . . . animal flowers, resembling the water-lilies, that seek their food, eat and digest like other animals; . . . [and] an enormous quadruped [that] walks for hours on the bottom of the deep, like an Elephant on dry ground," sug-

[29] B. Waterhouse to James Tilton, March 24, 1815, in Massachusetts Historical Society, *Proceedings*, LIV (1920–1921), 161.

gested that the salt mountain was not beyond the realm of the probable. "If we determine to disbelieve every phenomenon that we cannot explain, our knowledge will soon be reduced to a very narrow circle." These notions (some valid, some mythological) smacked too much of the medieval for Federalist editors to let pass; to accept "the narrative of a notorious visionary"—i.e., Jefferson—was to display "the credulity of a bigot rather than the circumspection of a philosopher." As for the quadruped who walks on the bottom of the deep, he, commented a *Repertory* writer, obviously lived in a *"Waterhouse."* [30]

Thus if Federalists discounted natural history it was not only for political reasons. Those whose road to the sciences had begun with the *Principia* were naturally slow to acknowledge the claims of natural history to the category of professional science, distinct from a gentlemanly and amateurish curiosity about the plants that grew on one's farm. Any man who stumbled on a fossil in his backyard, anyone who, as Quincy said, fell upon a mammoth pit, might demand recognition as a scholar. This accusation has some merit; the same issue of *Transactions* which printed Benjamin Smith Barton's classic debunking of the belief that snakes had the power to hypnotize their victims contained John Heckewelder's ludicrous account of hibernating grasshoppers. As proof of the existence of the Megalonyx, Jefferson introduced old rumors of unknown animals which roared in the dark along with the evidence of the bones. The physical sciences, or Natural Philosophy, as they were then called, left less room for the inclusion of myths and legends, and with Natural Philosophy, Federalists may have felt more secure.

The study of science automatically raised questions about the relationship of God to the physical world. Puritans had encouraged the study of God's works on the ground that there could be no possible contradiction between the artifact and its Maker, for Reason led inevitably to recognition of the Divine. An early

[30] B. Waterhouse to B. Russell, February 8, 1804, in Boston *Centinel*, February 2, 1804; Boston *Repertory*, February 24, 1804.

denial of necessary contradiction is found in a comment by Robert Hooke, one of the founders of the Royal Society of London: "And as at first, mankind fell by tasting of the forbidden tree of knowledge, so we, their Posterity, may be in part restor'd by the same way, not only by beholding and contemplating but by tasting of those fruits of Natural Knowledge, that were never yet forbidden." [31] It is well known that Newton pored over the Apocrypha during the day while he searched the heavens at night, and even Priestley, a radical in politics, fully expected his permanent reputation to rest on his theological musings. The attitude percolated down to nonspecialists and is perhaps best illustrated by the effusions of the Harvard senior who scribbled, at the conclusion of his astronomy course in 1790:

What a Delightful & extensive subject of speculation is astronomy. The Luminaries of heaven form a glorious spectacle to the eye & How majestic do they shine forth! . . . How regular their courses! How large is the circumference of their orbits! . . . During the solemn silence of the nights, with what pleasing astonishment do we gaze upon these glorious works of God! [32]

Even when he had apparently made his peace with science, even with the reassuring precedent of ancestral Puritan scientists, even when he limited himself to the seemingly rational and

[31] Feuer, p. 51.

[32] Tom Chandler to J[oseph] Dennie, April 9, 1790, Dennie Papers, Houghton Library, Harvard University. Examples of this sort could be multiplied, and the authors were not only the young. Francis Adrian Van der Kemp wrote to John Adams in 1804: "A correspondence with a German Mineralogist induced me this winter to take a course of chemistry, and how deeper I dive in this and other branches of Nat. Philosophy, how more glorious appears to me—the goodness—the wisdom—and our thought surpassing greatness of our glorious maker" (February 15, 1804, quoted in Harry Jackson, *Scholar in the Wilderness: Francis Adrian Van der Kemp* [Syracuse, N.Y., 1963], p. 167). Whitfield J. Bell, Jr., suggests that Quakers found it easier to balance the contradictory demands of science and faith; see "The Scientific Environment of Philadelphia, 1775–1790," American Philosophical Society, *Proceedings*, vol. 92 (March, 1948), 9.

mathematical study of natural philosophy (rather than natural history, which carried with it disturbing questions about the age of the earth and the development of animal life), the believing scientist could hardly help but feel some ambivalence toward the knowledge he sought. Federalists found "French Science"—and, by extension, "democratic science"—suspect perhaps partly because contemporary French investigators had ignored the divine creation of the objects of their study even when they did not explicitly deny it.

One of those who sought to maintain the old delicate balance between theology and science was Jean André DeLuc, a widely respected Genevan chemist, geologist, and physicist, whose work was introduced to the American audience by John Quincy Adams.[33] Between 1799 and 1802, Francis Bacon's works had been translated into French by Antoine de Lasalle, a merchant-turned-writer who had enjoyed something of a critical success in the years before the French Revolution. The translation, fitted out with interpretive footnotes whose purpose was to transform Bacon into a radical *philosophe* was, even before the final volume had appeared, subjected to a lashing attack by DeLuc, in a pamphlet titled *Bacon As He Is*. It was published in French in 1800 at Berlin, where John Quincy Adams was serving as American minister to Prussia. Adams agreed with DeLuc and thought his work important; he gave the pamphlet an extended review in a series of "Letters from an American, Resident Abroad, on Various Topics of Foreign Literature" published in the *Port Folio*.[34]

[33] Charles Coulston Gillispie, *Genesis and Geology* (New York, 1959), p. 32. DeLuc was important enough to have had a chair of geology created for him at the University of Göttingen. In 1773 he settled in London, and in English scientific circles he was hailed as a man whose works would be honored "so long as sound reasoning and physical logic [*sic*] have any claims to the attention of mankind" (George Adams, *Lectures on Natural Philosophy* [London, 1799], I, xi). In 1788, the American Philosophical Society had acquired two hygrometers made by DeLuc (Hindle, p. 348).

[34] June 6, 1801. In this series Adams attempted to publicize worthy arrivals on the European literary scene. Other installments included an

Some of DeLuc's objections to Lasalle's translation were made on technical grounds, but his more serious protest was, as Adams put it, to the attempt "under colour of a *translation,* to palm upon the public . . . principles of philosophy, of theology, of morals and of politics, absolutely contrary to those of the author translated." Thus Lasalle ignored Bacon's own profession of faith and his long service to the crown, and added a preface, purportedly by Bacon, declaring that "the *throne* [and] . . . the *altar* . . . lean upon each other, and resting both, upon the three-fold basis of *long ignorance, long terror, and long habit.*" Where Bacon had explicitly insisted on the separation of science from religion, Lasalle insisted that the two are inextricably tangled, on the naive ground that God is the mainspring of the world, "the theory of *springs* being a part of *mechanics,* and mechanics a part of *physics.*" Adams applauded DeLuc's added castigation of "theologicans" whose new criticism revised the Bible out of recognition just as Lasalle's edition had resulted in a non-recognizable Bacon. "The writings of Bacon," Adams concluded, may be considered as the sources of our natural, as the Bible is the great source of our divine learning. . . . It is a melancholy prospect, to observe the indefatigable industry, the fanatic enthusiasm . . . with which both the great fountains of human science have been poisoned." [35]

"The writings of Bacon . . . are the source of our natural . . . learning." What did they teach? Among other things, that

---

introduction to the work of the poet Gellert and a lengthy critique of a discussion of French foreign policy by Hauterive.

[35] *Port Folio,* June 6, 1801. DeLuc's pamphlet was followed two years later by a two-volume *Précis de la philosophie de Bacon . . .* (Paris, 1802), in which he reiterated his argument that "Bacon had always professed the greatest regard for revelation," and included a detailed refutation of the notes to Lasalle's edition, in which Bacon's thoughts "sont complètement dénaturés." DeLuc later wrote treatises on electricity and geology, and engaged in ardent debate on the origins of the earth, taking the Neptunist view that geological changes were the result of major biblical catastrophes like the Flood. He died in 1817, aged 96.

revelation might be supplemented (not necessarily corrected or changed) by Natural Theology, which Bacon defined as "that spark of knowledge of God which may be had by the light of nature and the consideration of created things; and thus can fairly be held to be divine in respect of the object, and *natural* in respect of the source of information."[36] The Baconian attitude was prevalent in New England in the eighteenth century, and when, in 1802, William Paley provided convenient documentation for Bacon's remarks, demonstrating "the existence and perfections of God from the evidences of design in the adaption of creatures and objects to nature," Harvard hurried to adopt it as a text.[37] Timothy Pickering owned a copy of Paley's *Evidences of the Truth of Christianity*, which included similar arguments, and advised a dejected son to read it as an antidote to religious skepticism.[38] New England scientists did not think they were afraid of the wonders of the universe; they were used to viewing them as extensive evidence of the Lord's might.

A New Englander could be startled, therefore, by other interpretations of physical phenomena. When the Yale-educated Benjamin Silliman went to study chemistry under James Woodhouse at the University of Pennsylvania, he reported, with some surprise:

His lectures were quite free from any moral bearing, nor, as I remember, did he ever make use of any of the facts revealed by Chemistry to illustrate the character of the Creator as seen in his works. At the commencement of the course he treated with levity and ridicule the idea that the visitations of the yellow fever might be visitations of God for the sins of the people. He imputed them to the ma-

[36] Quoted in Gillispie, p. 31.

[37] Struik, p. 299. William Paley, *Natural Theology* (Philadelphia, 1802); Justin Winsor, ed., *The Memorial History of Boston* (Boston, 1884), IV, 302.

[38] Timothy Pickering to Henry Pickering, February 1, 1805, in Octavius Pickering and Charles W. Upham, *The Life of Timothy Pickering* (Boston, 1873), IV, 78.

terial agencies and physical causes,—forgetting that physical causes may be the moral agents of the almighty.[39]

It is at least suggestive that when a group of prominent Boston Federalists organized a "studying Society" [40] to acquaint themselves with recent scientific progress, they largely eschewed natural history and chose for their first text a book by George Adams with the following magniloquent title: *Lectures on Natural and Experimental Philosophy, Considered in its Present State of Improvement. Describing in a Familiar and Easy Manner, the Principal Phenomena of Nature: and Shewing that they all Co-operate in Displaying the Goodness, Wisdom, and Power of God.*[41] The introduction informed its readers, who included John Quincy Adams, Josiah Quincy, Judge John Davis, and William Emerson, that it had been written with the intention of discrediting "modern philosophers" who, frequently "pensioned by republicans," sought to propagate principles "that are subversive of all order and religion," and of proving "that physics, properly understood, would ever go hand in hand with religion . . . to enlighten the mind, to comfort the heart, to establish the welfare of society, and promote the love of order." [42] A close reading of George Adams's book suggests the coloration of the turn-of-the-century scientific frontier: wherever the author excessively reassures his reader that no impiety is possible, one can be sure that impiety seemed too close for comfort. The five volumes include nearly as much reassurance as they do science.

The Society for the Study of Natural Philosophy chose to

[39] John F. Fulton and Elizabeth H. Thomson, *Benjamin Silliman, 1779–1864: Pathfinder in American Science* (New York, 1947), p. 29.

[40] James Jackson to John Pickering, January 8, 1803, in J. J. Putnam, *A Memoir of Dr. James Jackson* (Boston, 1906), p. 249. The records of the Society for the Study of Natural Philosophy are in the collection of the Boston Athenaeum.

[41] Five vols.; 2d ed., London, 1799.

[42] *Ibid.*, I, vii–x.

concentrate on the chapters dealing with electricity, a subject which Benjamin Franklin's kite experiments had long since endeared to the lay mind. Their text tended to treat the subject as one of harmless amusement, which sometimes verged on the grotesque:

[Electricity] . . . furnishes matter of entertainment for all persons promiscuously, while it is also a subject of important speculation for the most philosophic minds. . . . For it exhibits to you bodies rising and falling, moving this way and that, and suspended by others contrary to the principles of gravitation, and this by powers which have been put in action only by a very slight friction. Here you may see a piece of cold metal, or even water or ice, emitting strong sparks of fire. . . . When a single person receives a shock, the company is diverted at his sole expence; but all contribute their share to the entertainment. . . . When the whole company form a circle by joining their hands, the person at one extremity of the circle touching the outside coating, while he, who is at the other extremity touches the ball of the [Leyden] jar [a primitive battery]. All the persons who form this circle being struck at the same time, and with the same degree of force, it is pleasant to see them all start at the same moment, to hear them compare their sensations, and observe the very different accounts they give.[43]

But even natural philosophy had its dangers. It had to be admitted that in many electrical demonstrations "you see the course of nature overturned to all appearance."[44] The fear of impiety became more pronounced, the reassurances less confident, when electrical experiments were extended to the animal kingdom. These were reported, Adams explained apologetically, only so that performing these distasteful experiments again would be rendered unnecessary by a promulgation of the results. For example, that an electrical shock administered to the exposed nerve of a dead animal might cause a limb to contract or a

[43] *Ibid.*, IV, 341–342, 344.
[44] *Ibid.*, p. 341–342. Therefore instructions on how to perform experiments were often accompanied by the reiteration that these supernatural changes were only apparent.

heart to resume beating: "Animals which were almost dead, have been found to be considerably revived by exciting this influence."[45] The power to accomplish these mysterious phenomena seemed almost supernatural; it still savored of the alchemist's forbidden magic, and required the reassurance that "he who gave curiosity to his creature, man, gave it for good and great purposes." "Chemists . . . hunt, perhaps, after chimeras and impossibilities, and find something valuable by the bye." "The word of God is as perfect as his work. Both proceed from the one fountain of truth, who cannot contradict himself. His word and His work mutually illustrate each other."[46] The excessive repetition of these statements suggests that neither author nor audience was fully convinced of them.

Thus studying science, especially for nondeists who held traditional religious beliefs, was permeated with tension. Republicans and Federalists, conservatives and liberals would have agreed with Silliman that God manifests himself in Nature; but the manner in which that manifestation took place was increasingly open to question, and the debate took on a political coloration. If man could imitate God by causing, via electric shock, a heart to beat, what became of God? If man could explain the physical development of the globe without recourse to divine intervention, what became of God? In Europe the latter debate was carried on by Vulcanists, who argued that geological change results from the "cumulative effects of minute forces and infinitesimal changes [which] can produce results equal to those of any sudden cataclysm . . . [implicitly] superseding the necessity for any divine intervention," and Catastrophists, who postulated that the vast geological changes indicated by fossil remains required for their explanation more violent upheavals than the ordinary op-

[45] *Ibid.*, pp. 425, 426, 414, 428. For a summary of progress in the study of electricity, see Samuel Miller, *A Brief Retrospect of the Eighteenth Century*, I, 21–32, 441–453.

[46] *Monthly Anthology and Boston Review*, VI (1809), 280; George Adams, IV, 300, 301, 430.

eration of the universe.[47] These violent upheavals might be due to natural causes, like volcanoes, or they might be taken to imply the needful existence of a God. Most Americans of 1800, insofar as they thought of it at all, counted themselves as Catastrophists.[48] But they differed greatly in their definition of the nature of the geological rearrangement required to place marine fossils on mountains; some thought of natural causes only; others identified the crucial catastrophe with the Biblical Flood. In this they agreed with DeLuc, which may explain why John Quincy Adams chose his work for translation.[49]

But catastrophism did not necessarily imply acceptance of DeLuc's brand of biblical interpretation; the catastrophes that had molded the surface of the earth might as readily be assumed to result from natural causes alone. William Wirt, for example, could wax just as romantic as Chandler over Nature's wonders:

Over this hill on which I am now sitting and writing at my ease, and from which I look, with delight on the landscape that smiles around me—over this hill and this landscape, the billows of the

[47] Gillispie, p. 49.

[48] See Boston *Repertory*, April 24, 1804.

[49] DeLuc was a highly competent geologist, and Baconian induction enabled him to square most geology with the Flood; when it did not, he was willing to twist it until he had, in Gillispie's words, displayed "the structure and development of the material world as the history of an intending Providence with a moral purpose," that is, until the fossils illustrated the Natural Theology of the Bible. (A similar attitude had enabled young Tom Chandler to find a purpose in the sun: not only does it heat the ground, but the warmth of its rays "raise up the bowed down . . . comfort the broken-hearted.") DeLuc's insistence on biblical verities led him to discourage a group of German Jews from conversion for political reasons; he assured them that "the history of the earth, and its present appearance, are the strongest of all possible testimonies, to the truth of the Mosaic history, and that, if they will only take the pains to become better *natural* philosophers, they will not be so ready to renounce their faith as Jews" (Gillispie, p. 147; T. Chandler to J. Dennie, April 9, 1790, Dennie Papers, Houghton Library, Harvard University; John Quincy Adams, "Letters from an American . . . No. III," *Port Folio*, June 20, 1801).

ocean have rolled in wild and fearful fury, while the leviathan, the whale, and all the monsters of the deep, have disported themselves amid the fearful tempest.

When it came to explaining them, however, the Bible seemed insufficient. It was obvious enough that the land had once been covered by water, "But that this emersion is, even comparatively speaking, of recent date, cannot be admitted; unless the comparison be made with the creation of the earth; and even then, in order to justify this remark, the aera of the creation must, I fear, be fixed much further back, than the period which has been inferred from the Mosaic account." [50]

Read literally, the "Mosaic account" kept getting in the way of scientific interpretation, an unfortunate development for those who clung to a Baconian Nature which could not, by definition, contradict theology. It was time for a choice, Benjamin Waterhouse announced: "If we judge the powers of Nature by our own narrow prejudices, we shall always be oppressed by wonder, and wonder is the suspension of reason." [51] Some, like Wirt, were not seriously disturbed at the prospect of giving up wonder in favor of reason; it was a confident Rembrandt Peale who reprinted Baron Cuvier's summary of the history of the earth:

It is now universally known that the globe which we inhabit, on every side presents irresistible proofs of the greatest revolutions: the varied productions of living nature, which embellish the surface, is but a garment covering the ruins of an antecedent state of nature. Whether we turn up the plains, whether we penetrate the cavernous mountains, or climb their broken sides, the remnants of organized bodies are everywhere found, buried in the various strata which form the external crust of this globe. Immense collections of shells lie buried far from any sea, and at heights inaccessible to its waves: fishes are found in veins of slate, and vegetable impressions at heights and

[50] William Wirt, *Letters of a British Spy* (Newburyport, 1804), pp. 15, 12.

[51] B. Waterhouse to B. Russell, February 8, 1804, in Boston *Columbian Centinel*, February 22, 1804.

depths equally astonishing. But what is most surprising is the disorder which reigns in their relative positions; here a stratum of shells covers another of vegetables; there, fishes are found over terrestrial animals, which in their turn are placed over plants or shells. . . . In short, although nature has thus embellished the actual residence of living beings, although so much care is shewn in their preservation and happiness, she seems equally pleased with exhibiting the monuments of her power in this disorder and apparent confusion—all evident proofs of the total overthrow which must have preceded the present order of the universe.[52]

A Nature who disported herself in "disorder and apparent confusion" was not the Nature regulated by God's power who appears in Genesis, nor was she a Nature whose every operation was designed to demonstrate God's foresight, as explained by William Paley; she was not even Jefferson's Nature, through which the logical operations of Nature's God are visible. To accept a capricious Nature, whose laws, if any, were her own, was to experience an intellectual *bouleversement* quite as radical—if not more so—as the one presided over by Darwin two generations later.[53]

Jefferson did not go so far as Cuvier in postulating a capri-

---

[52] Rembrandt Peale, *An Historical Disquisition on the Mammoth, or, Great American Incognitum, An Extinct, Immense, Carnivorous Animal, Whose Fossil Remains Have Been Found in North America* (London, 1803), pp. 2–4.

[53] Simpson, pp. 143–144. The discovery of the bones raised a host of questions. It was not known what the animals had looked like, where and how they had lived, whether or not they were extinct. Cotton Mather had suggested the bones were the remains of human giants. Simpson remarks, "The questions are simple now only because they have been answered. Every answer was contrary to the accumulated lore of all the millenniums before 1700. They required not only the rejection of some of the fondest beliefs of mankind but also the development of fundamentally new ways of thinking and of an apparatus for scientific interpretation. It was the great achievement of the eighteenth century that it made *this revolutionary advance, even more basic than that wrought by the doctrine of evolution in the nineteenth century*" (italics added).

cious Nature. He believed in a Creator and criticized Vulcanists on the grounds that once a Creator is postulated, one might as well suppose He had made the earth properly in the first place. Jefferson's vision of how major geologic change had been accomplished made use of large quantities of water, but not those provided by forty days of rain; he gave the Biblical Flood credence only as "a partial deluge in the country lying round the Mediterranean sea." [54] His depiction of what might be called "vestiges of creation" is poetic:

The passage of the Potomac through the Blue Ridge is, perhaps, one of the most stupendous scenes in nature. You stand on a very high point of land. On your right comes up the Shenandoah, having ranged along the foot of the mountain an hundred miles to seek a vent. On your left approaches the Potomac, in quest of a passage also. In the moment of their junction, they rush together against the mountain, rend it asunder, and pass off to the sea. The first glance of this scene hurries our senses into the opinion, that this earth has been created in time . . . that the rivers began to flow afterwards, that in this place, particularly, they have been damned up by the Blue Ridge of mountains, and have formed an ocean which filled the whole valley; that continuing to rise they have at length broken over at this spot, and have torn the mountain down from its summit to its base. The piles of rock on each hand, but particularly on the Shenandoah, the evident marks of their departure and avulsion from their beds by the most powerful agents of nature, corroborate the impression.[55]

It began to seem that Jefferson, Wirt, and Peale were engaged in reducing the Flood—and therefore the Bible—to mythology.[56] Like Macbeth's witch whose thumbs pricked at

---

[54] Martin, pp. 127–128; Jefferson, p. 27. In *Salmagundi*, Washington Irving stigmatized Jefferson as "antediluvian" (April 4, 1807 [London, 1811], I, 134).

[55] Jefferson, pp. 16–17.

[56] A myth suggested, according to Cuvier, by scattered marine fossils, just as the folk "memory" of giants was suggested by the chance discovery of mammoth bones (Peale, p. 4).

the approach of the wicked, Federalist critics learned to raise an eyebrow when the talk turned to geology. "Whenever modern philosophers talk about mountains," thundered Clement Clarke Moore, "something impious is likely to be at hand."

Rousseau says, that on the summits of high mountains all our cares are forgotten. . . . This is certain, that whenever these pigmy philosophers get perched upon their beloved heights, they seem not only to be insensible of their own insignificance, but to lose even their boasted reason.[57]

The irrationality of Jefferson's argument was located in its implicit contradiction of Genesis: mountains gradually eroded were not the mountains God had created by His Will. There were other grounds for Moore's dismay. He could understand that Voltaire had probably erred in suggesting that fossil shells on mountain tops had grown there in a sort of spontaneous generation. But Moore could not understand why the accepted explanation should be that the shells furnish evidence that the sea once covered the mountains, rather than his own explanation that they are remnants of primordial Chaos.[58] Quite as disturbing, in Moore's opinion, was Jefferson's willingness to define the Old Testament as the written tradition of a tribal people, with the implication that other ancient peoples had equally valid traditions. Moore was distressed by passages like the following:

[the lands] of Egypt and Armenia, which, according to a tradition of the Egyptians and the Hebrews, were overflowed about two thousand three hundred years before the Christian era; those of Attica, said to have overflowed in the time of Ogyges, about five hundred years later; and those of Thessaly, in the time of Deucalion, still three hundred years posterior.

[57] Clement Clark Moore, *Observations upon Certain Passages in Mr. Jefferson's Notes on Virginia, which Appear to have a Tendency to Subvert Religion, and Establish a False Philosophy* (New York, 1804), pp. 6–7.

[58] Jefferson, p. 28.

But what distressed him was less the information than the diction, the unwelcome implication that "Jewish history and Grecian stories, Lucian, Ovid, and Moses, are all considered as of equal authority." [59]

Moore's scorn was shared by William Linn, who called on the Scriptures to testify against Jefferson's refusal to believe that the biblical Flood had accounted for major geological changes in America: "And the rain was upon the earth forty days and forty nights . . . *and all the high hills that were under the whole heaven were covered.* . . . But Mr. Jefferson . . . cannot . . . get water enough to cover the mountain." If forced to choose between Jefferson and revelation, Linn would choose revelation, wherever it might lead: "It is safest [for one] . . . to believe in the Mosaic account of the deluge, though he should never find out a satisfactory solution; yea, though he should adopt the wrong one." [60]

Benjamin Waterhouse had a direct answer to Federalists like Linn, but it was of a sort calculated to heighten rather than ease their distress. "If we determine to disbelieve every phenomenon that we cannot explain, our knowledge will soon be reduced to a very narrow circle. . . . [We cannot] restrict the power of Nature to our own narrow conceptions. No study expands the mind like Natural History." [61] In the physical sciences, experiments and observations may be repeated. But most of the phenomena "that we cannot explain" were reported, with little if any corroborative evidence, by travelers in the western wilderness, [62] and

[59] Moore, p. 11. Wirt had similarly reported Flood traditions among American Indians, both in the West and in Virginia, and among the Greeks, suggesting that the Indian tradition postulated a larger and therefore more reasonable event than "the petty territory that was innundated by Deucalion's flood" (*Letters of a British Spy*, pp. 19–20).

[60] *Serious Considerations*, pp. 7–8.

[61] B. Waterhouse to B. Russell, February 8, 1804, in *Columbian Centinel*, February 22, 1804.

[62] Natural history, especially in the eighteenth century, was preeminently a cataloguing enterprise; emphasis was placed more on collecting and identifying than on use or interpretation.

there were those who were not ready to have their minds expanded by lists of artifacts which may or may not have existed. "There is so much Rhodomontade of Travellers in our Wilderness which have proved in the end to be mere delusions," protested John Adams, "that I give little attention to them. The Country is explored and thinly planted much too fast. . . . Speculations about Mammoths . . . are all pitifull Bagateels, when the Morals and Liberties of the Nation are at hazard, as in my Conscience I believe them to be, at this moment." [63]

The wilderness, of course, was the newly purchased Louisiana, of whose value Federalists were extremely skeptical. The obvious reasons for this skepticism were political; primary among them was the fear that to add to American possessions in the South would deprive New Englanders of their power in the political balance. Some of the opposition was legal, arising from the *way* in which Louisiana had been purchased and absorbed into the American political structure rather than from the fact; and some of the opposition, as we have seen, was motivated by a refusal to add to the slaveholding territory in the nation. But it also seems likely that Federalist skepticism was grounded in an image of the West as "the land of Marvels . . . the Ultima Thule," as Van Wyck Brooks has phrased it, a weird country, which lent itself to the uncontrolled investigations of natural historians, and which remained mysterious even after Lewis and Clark's expedition. [64] Only recently convinced by Madison's tenth *Federalist* essay that an eighteenth-century republic might be risked on the vast eastern seacoast, how else than skeptically *could* Federalists be expected to react when for these already dangerously extensive limits were substituted boundaries so far in the distant west and so vaguely defined that no one could be sure where America ended? They would not join in Jefferson's hunt for the great mammoth or the salt mountain, a hunt that

[63] John Adams to F. A. Van der Kemp, November 5, 1804, John Adams Letters.

[64] Van Wyck Brooks, *The World of Washington Irving* (New York, 1944), p. 90.

seemed to them no more sensible than a hunt for the unicorn—and what if the unicorn should be found? Jefferson did not find a unicorn, but he had found the megalonyx, whose claws were five times the length of a lion's, and, extrapolating its dimensions from its remains, concluded that logic "would give us a being out of nature." Jefferson comfortably remarked that "Our entire ignorance of the immense country to the West and North-West, and of its contents, does not authorize us to say what it does not contain." [65] Man, as Waterhouse had suggested, may not set nature's limits. The typical natural historian was not anxious to discover Nature's limits, preferring to seek for and delight in the revelations of her limitless inventiveness. But his quest made Federalists uneasy.

[65] American Philosophical Society, *Transactions*, IV, pp. 249, 252. See also Daniel Boorstin, *The Americans: The National Experience* (New York, 1966), pp. 221–222.

[4]

Salvaging the Classical Tradition

Some wicked people in the nation
Find fault with our administration;
But if the whole truth were unfurl'd,
They're not the worst men in the world:
They lack but two things, I suspect,
Viz. *honesty* and *intellect.*
—*The Weekly Inspector,*
September 6, 1806

From the earliest Indian missions to twentieth-century "Americanization" programs for immigrants, Americans have habitually treated formal education as a civilizing and socially useful process—the means by which one generation transfers its knowledge to the next. Federalists and Jeffersonians alike assumed that social stability in a republic requires an educated and politically sophisticated citizenry; in this context, argument over educational policy often took on political overtones. The post-Revolutionary generation faced an unusually severe problem in the transfer of culture. Few desired or expected their sons to inaugurate another generation of violence, and nearly all dreaded a possible repetition of the French cycle of revolutions. Could the next generation be educated so that political leadership would be given to men of high moral and intellectual caliber? Could a community be developed in which political and intellectual abilities would be coordinated? These were among the questions that an extensive, and often heated, public discussion of educational policy sought to answer.

In that discussion, political lines were not always clearly drawn, and it seems clear that what united the members of the post-Revolutionary generation on matters of educational theory was quite as significant as what divided them. At the same time, substantial disagreements often existed among supporters of the same party. Federalists, as a group, displayed mixed feelings about a problem that was central to the debate—the role of the classics in the curriculum. For example, while many of his fellow partisans were vigorously arguing the classics' continued vitality, Samuel Stanhope Smith, the president of Princeton, was moving to replace classical studies with modern languages and philosophy. The Federalist arguments against curriculum reform are useful to trace not only because of what they reveal about Federalist notions of the proper function of education in the republic, but also because they show a prevalent Federalist image of the opposition party.[1]

Much of the debate on educational policy centered around the work and recommendations of Noah Webster. When Thomas Jefferson took office Webster was one of his best-known Federalist opponents. Webster's "blue-backed speller," produced in numerous editions by many different publishers, was well on its way to making its author's name a household word. Shortly after the Revolution, Webster had discovered that his first book, *A Grammatical Institute of the English Language,* required thirteen separate copyrights, one for each state in the Confederation. No state had yet established a copyright law, and Webster undertook to prod state legislatures himself, reflecting as he did so that a national copyright law under a national constitution would have saved him much exhausting travel.[2] The *Grammatical Institute* was therefore followed by *Sketches of American*

---

[1] See Rush Welter, *Popular Education and Democratic Thought in America* (New York, 1962), pp. 36–41, who argues that standards and expectations were shared by leaders of both parties in the early republic.

[2] Horace E. Scudder, *Noah Webster* (Boston, 1899), pp. 53–56.

Policy, an ardent and widely read defense of federal union: Webster could claim himself to be one of the earliest Federalists. Webster subsequently published several political pamphlets of a generally Federalist persuasion, edited one magazine and two newspapers, began work on his dictionary, and wrote seven other books, including the famous reader, grammar, and speller. Reforming the speller suggested reforming the spelling, and Webster acquired a reputation as an authority who wrote "music" instead of "musick," "favor" instead of "favour," and was at least tempted to substitute "laf" for "laugh" and "greef" for "grief." [3]

Although Webster began to attack Jefferson in print only six months after his inauguration, other Federalists—quite to Webster's surprise—refused to regard him as an exemplary member of their party. [4] In the course of his career he had come to espouse precisely those features of the changing American cultural scene which many Federalists most deplored. That Webster, in the internecine feud preceding the presidential election of 1800, had enthusiastically favored the election of John Adams was disappointing, but no more disappointing than the behavior of other "Adamites," and, since Webster's sister-in-law was married to Adams's nephew, perhaps only to be expected. Political error was easily met by economic reprisal: Hamilton and his friends regularly bypassed Webster's two newspapers as a means of disseminating party gossip and political opinion, and turned instead to William Coleman's new *Evening Post,* which their patronage had helped to establish. [5] But when many Federalists, casting

---

[3] Harry R. Warfel, *Letters of Noah Webster* (New York, 1953), p. xliii; Ervin C. Shoemaker, *Noah Webster: Pioneer of Learning* (New York, 1936), pp. 259, 284. See also pp. 243–302, and Noah Webster, "An Essay on the Necessity, Advantages and Practicability of Reforming the Mode of Spelling . . . ," in *Dissertations on the English Language: With Notes, Historical and Critical* (Boston, 1789), pp. 391–398.

[4] Webster to Thomas Jefferson, October, 1801, in Warfel, pp. 241–242.

[5] Webster to Oliver Wolcott, October 1, 13, 1801, in Warfel, pp. 237–240. Webster was eventually forced to give up journalism.

about for emblems of America's loss of honor and dignity as a
result of Jefferson's election, found what they were looking for
in Webster's work as grammarian and lexicographer, no similar
reprisal was available. Webster's books were paid for by subscrib-
ers and booksellers all over the country; their circulation did
not depend on party patronage. The only possible answer was
ridicule, and Federalist satire during Jefferson's years in office is
sprinkled with allusions to Webster's work.

Among those for whom Webster's words epitomized a de-
plorable cultural trend was the Connecticut lawyer David Daggett, who solemnly predicted that men who endorsed such absurd reforms as Webster's might next abolish language entirely,
in the interest of brevity and general well-being. "For it is plain
that every word we speak is an injury to our lungs, by corrosion,
and consequently contributes to the shortening of our lives."
The eventual solution would be Swift's: if "words were only
names for things," Americans, like the inhabitants of Laputa,
would soon be found carrying the things with them wherever
they went, and holding conversations by *showing* them.[6]

A more fully developed criticism appeared in a series of sa-
tiric articles headed "The Restorator," written by the Boston
clergyman John Sylvester John Gardiner.[7] Gardiner denigrated
Webster's attempt to provide dictionaries and grammars keyed
to American speech on the ground that they would formalize a
dialect of the English language, and an awkward and ugly dia-

---

[6] David Daggett, *Sun Beams May Be Extracted from Cucumbers, but
the Process Is Tedious. An Oration Pronounced on the Fourth of July,
1799, at the Request of the Citizens of New Haven* (New Haven, 1799),
p. 5.

[7] The essays were originally published in the *New-England Palladium:*
according to Josiah Quincy, against the editor's better judgment (J. Quincy
to Webster, December 8, 1805, in Emily Ellsworth Fowler Ford, *Notes
on the Life of Noah Webster* [New York, 1912], I, 552–553). They
were later reprinted in the *Port Folio*. Gardiner is identified as the author
in Harold Milton Ellis, *Joseph Dennie and His Circle: A Study in
American Literature from 1792 to 1812* (Austin, Texas, 1915), p. 185.

lect at that. Mixing politics with his philology, he suggested entries for Webster's dictionary:

La, sus! is a very beautiful exclamation, and a great improvement on the English original, *Lord, sirs. Sus* is Latin for sow. This consideration greatly increases the propriety of its use among the "swinish" multitude.

and even a title: "Let, then, the projected volume of *foul* and *unclean* things, bear his own christian name, and be called NOAH'S ARK." The authentic American language, Gardiner pointed out, was spoken by the Indians: consistency therefore required that Webster adopt one of the Indian languages directly, leaving English intact, if only to be studied "as a *dead* language" by antiquarians. To remodel English by the adoption of awkward spellings and "Colloquial barbarisms" was an effort which could only please those who believed that

if we can once become unintelligible to foreigners, one great source of corruption will be dried up. Whilst we retain the language of *Britain,* we cannot forget that we were once a colony. . . . To coin new words, or to use them in a new sense, is, incontrovertibly, one of the unalienable rights of freemen; and whoever disputes this right, is the friend of civil tyranny, and an enemy to liberty and equality.[8]

It was not a far-fetched accusation. Webster did regard his work as a contribution to a cultural separation from Great Britain, an aim that Gardiner, for his part, deplored. "For more than twenty years," Webster wrote to Joel Barlow in 1807, "since I have looked into philology, and considered the connection between language and knowledge, and the influence of a national language on national opinions, I have had it in view to detach this country as much as possible from its dependence on the

---

[8] *Port Folio,* October 10, November 21, 1801. Dennie gave his own suggestions for the forthcoming "Dictionary of the *American vulgar* tongue," including "Lengthy," "Strengthy," "If I was he," and "Caucus" (*Port Folio,* August 28, 1802).

parent country. . . . Our people look to English books as the
standard of truth on all subjects and this confidence in English
opinions puts *an end to inquiry.*" Webster said he would have
felt the same had the cultural ties been to France or Spain
rather than to England: "All nations have their interests and
prejudices." But those who did not accept Webster's claims of
neutrality continued to question his purposes. "As he hates England," Joseph Dennie plaintively inquired, "why not murder
English?"[9]

Josiah Quincy, who in 1805 counseled Webster to ignore Gardiner's castigations, was himself unable to resist imitating the
Restorator's technique. Quincy's private endorsement of Webster suggests that his own attacks were not personal. He denounced not Noah Webster the "Adamite" or even Webster the
lexicographer, but rather the tendency of Americans to welcome
innovations in words (as they welcomed, to Quincy's dismay, innovations in the world itself), a weakness to which Noah Webster catered. Where Gardiner had scoffed at the claim that the
coining of new words is an inalienable right of free minds, in
"Climenole" Quincy introduced a series of tangential remarks
by ironically suggesting digression as another. In a republic writers were excused from the exigencies of the classic unities. "For
melancholy, indeed, would be our lot, if we, in these free states,
in executing our immortal works, were under the necessity of
conforming ourselves to what are called rules of taste and laws
of good writing." Since these rules had never been assented to in
person or by representative, Quincy sarcastically maintained,
they were, like any political law, obviously arbitrary and
despotic.[10]

"In such a country as this," remarked Josiah Quincy, "indeed

[9] N. Webster to Joel Barlow, November 12, 1807, in Ford, II, 31.
Dennie is quoted in A. H. Smyth, *The Philadelphia Magazines and Their
Contributors* (Philadelphia, 1892), p. 97.
[10] J. Quincy to Webster, December 8, 1805, in Ford, I, 552;
"Climenole, No. 8," March 24, 1804. On occasion, Quincy's satire
endorsed Webster's work. In the early editions of his *Grammar*, Webster

in all, writers will bring passions acquired among political contests to the judgment of works merely literary." [11] Webster's linguistic reforms seemed tinged with his political heresies. Federalist critics quickly convinced themselves that what they were observing was the application to linguistics of an opposition *Weltanschauung* which had already wrought a political revolution. The next step, they predicted, would be a cultural revolution for which they had no sympathy.

Among those Federalists who opposed the general thrust of Webster's work was Timothy Pickering's son John, a prominent philologist. John Pickering agreed with Dennie that the introduction of "colloquial barbarisms" into the language should be resisted, on the ground that the intellectual community was already sufficiently capricious. He feared that the development of an American dialect would encourage the drift away from the mainstream of European culture. There was, in fact, a logical relationship between philological theory and political attitudes. Those who were not distressed by the speed of social change readily welcomed, with Webster, the accompanying modifications in language. But to those who shared Pickering's skepticism of the rate and tendency of contemporary change, it seemed all the more necessary to keep at least the signals of communication stable. If all were slipping away, even the symbols by which men explained themselves to each other, how could society possibly be saved from disintegration? [12]

Reforming the spelling suggested reforming the way in which

---

worried about the American habit of using singular verbs with plural nouns, as in "What is the news?" One of the "Climenole" essays purports to excuse Jefferson's use of a singular pronoun to refer to a plural noun: "His tender, philanthropic soul has been wrung with anguish, at that cruel despotism . . . whereby the pronoun is kept in slavery, and is obliged to follow the fates of the noun" (Climenole, No. 10," September 22, 1804; Shoemaker, p. 128).

[11] J. Quincy to Webster, December 8, 1805, in Ford, I, 552.

[12] Daniel H. Calhoun, "From Noah Webster to Chauncey Wright: The Intellectual as Prognostic," *Harvard Educational Review*, XXXVI (1966), 432.

spelling was taught. "The more I look into our language and methods of instruction," Webster observed, ". . . the more I am convinced of the necessity of improving one and correcting the other." When he "kept a classical school" Webster's classroom procedure no doubt followed the standard practices of his day. Commonly students began by learning the alphabet, then they learned to spell common words, and then to read them in sentences. Classes tended to be large and ungraded: the primary skill demanded was memory, and the instructors, in order to keep their classes quiet while hearing individuals recite, might resort to corporal punishment; if we are to trust the reminiscences of their pupils, most of them did. When the children had learned to read, write, and do simple arithmetic, most of them left school, and those who stayed were set to work doing the same procedures again, this time in Latin. Entrance requirements set by the colleges measured the applicants' proficiency in classical studies; the assumption was that other subjects could be learned in college.[13]

As early as 1783, Webster was arguing that classroom procedures should be drastically reorganized, and he pressed these views in print for at least a decade. His ideas, as they were developed in an essay "On the Education of Youth in America," were largely commonsensical: he wanted schoolmasters to be more carefully chosen and better trained, schools to be provided with modern books about the child's own country, and to be more numerous and easily available. But if educational reform failed to recommend itself to public sympathy by its obvious practicality, then it could be endorsed on the grounds that the subjects of the schoolmaster's realm were future citizens of a real political world. Webster drew on Montesquieu:

[13] Webster to John Canfield, January 6, 1783, in Warfel, pp. 3–4; Scudder, p. 32. See also R. Freeman Butts and Lawrence A. Cremin, *A History of Education in American Culture* (New York, 1953), ch. 8; Clifton Johnson, *Old-Time Schools and School-Books* (New York, 1917), pp. 100–125.

In despotic governments, the people should have little or no education, except what tends to inspire them with a servile fear. Information is fatal to despotism.

In monarchies, education should be partial, and adopted to the rank of each class of citizens. But "in a republican government . . . the whole power of education is required." Here every class of people should know and love the laws.[14]

Webster did not rule out corporal punishment altogether, for he believed that children must be taught respect for authority, but he insisted that it was preferable to teach obedience and respect in milder ways, and at home. "A proper subordination in families would generally supersede the necessity of severity in schools; and a strict discipline in both is the best foundation of good order in political society." [15] If the home did its job properly the school would not need corporal punishment. Webster thought that impersonal practices and corporal punishment inspired only servile fear in the child; suitable, perhaps, for the subject of a tyrant, but highly unsuitable for those who would have to learn to live as free men in a democratic republic.

Webster was not alone in his insistence that political reform in America made pedagogical reform necessary. In 1793, for example, the American Philosophical Society, which took all knowledge for its province, had offered a prize of one hundred dollars for an essay on "the best system of liberal education and literary instruction, adapted to the genius of government, and best calculated to promote the general welfare, of the United States; comprehending also a plan for instituting and conducting public schools, in this country, on the principles of the most extensive utility." [16] The prize was divided between Samuel Knox, a

---

[14] Webster, "On the Education of Youth in America," *A Collection of Essays and Fugitiv [sic] Writings* . . . (Boston, 1790), pp. 15–19, 23, 26.

[15] *Ibid.*, p. 16.

[16] American Philosophical Society, *Transactions*, IV (Philadelphia, 1799), iv.

Maryland minister and educator, and Samuel Harrison Smith, editor of a Philadelphia magazine called *The New World,* who in 1800 would establish the Jeffersonian *National Intelligencer.* Both men emphasized the need to avoid rote learning and to make elementary instruction meaningful in the child's own terms. Knox thought children might be taught reading before spelling, so that instead of beginning their education by memorizing long lists of words, they would understand that reading is primarily a way of gaining ideas.[17] Smith thought that children learned best by doing, and that even young children could and should be taught the sciences by experiments.[18] Within a decade, Jefferson's friend P. S. DuPont de Nemours would endorse learning by doing as an education in democracy; even more to the purpose, he thought, would be a system in which older children taught younger children, and both thereby learned to carry out their own work with a minimum of external control.[19]

To many of Webster's contemporaries, these plans appeared as startling as John Dewey's espousal of progressive education would seem a century later. It was perhaps not accidental that most of those who insisted on reformed classroom procedures were liberal Democrats or, like Webster and Dr. Benjamin Rush, factional Federalists. The educational reformers, said David Daggett, acted as though the commandment "Train up a child in the way he should go, and when he is old he will not depart from it" should be modernized to read "Let a child walk in his own way, and when he is old he will be perfect."

As Daggett defined the reform effort, its goal was "to shew that all reproof, restraint and correction, tend directly to extin-

[17] Samuel Knox, *An Essay on the Best System of Liberal Education, Adapted to the Genius of the Government of the United States* (Baltimore, 1799), p. 99.

[18] Samuel H. Smith, *Remarks on Education* (Philadelphia, 1798), pp. 51–52.

[19] Allen Oscar Hansen, *Liberalism and American Education in the Eighteenth Century* (New York, 1926), pp. 186–187.

guish the fire of genius, to cripple the faculties and enslave the understanding." [20] Daggett feared that the most serious threat posed by the Democratic opposition was to a social order underwritten by a stable family structure, and he accused the reformers of assuming "that the prejudices of education, and an inclination to imitate the examples of parents and other ancestors, is the great bane of the peace, dignity and glory of young men, and that reason will conduct them, if not fettered with habits, to the perfection of human nature. Obedience to parents is expressly reprobated, and all the tyranny and despotism in the world ascribed to parental authority." [21] In "Climenole," Josiah Quincy attempted to account for Democratic espousal of permissiveness in the classroom: since they had been poor students themselves, he alleged, the Democrats' school-boy memories presumably were colored by rather more than the usual share of whippings. Democrats did not respect traditional education, Quincy suggested, because they had not enjoyed their own exposure to it, whereas the brighter boys (who presumably grew up to be Federalists) had behaved well and therefore remembered their learning experience with pleasure.[22] Three essays of the series called "The Projector" in the *New-England Palladium* were devoted to assorted sarcasms on the education of children. Traditional studies were being abandoned in the colleges, the "Projector" explained, because "a close application to the languages, logic, mathematics, &c. is extremely apt to give the body an *unseemly* and *awkward* leaning forward, which com-

[20] Daggett, p. 37. Nearly the same words appear in "The Projector, No. 4," *New-England Palladium*, January 13, 1801.

[21] Daggett, p. 37. Certainly Smith, at least, had laid himself open to this charge. Evidently influenced by a reading of Rousseau's *Emile*, Smith declared that parents and nurses exercise "despotic authority" and that in their formative years infant minds must be protected from these misconceptions; therefore public education should begin early, ideally at birth (Hansen, pp. 156–157).

[22] "Climenole, No. 8," March 24.

monly ends in actual *crookedness*. And how monstrous it is, that a man made *upright* should become *crooked*." There was no point to the study of medicine, since man was destined to reach perfection; theology was outdated in a deistical world; the only thing left to do after college was to dissipate one's energies on a Grand Tour of Europe.[23] In a parody of reformers' complaints Quincy suggested that reformers turn their attention to the American classroom of 1800, where children spent their formative years in a system analogous to an unlimited monarchy, where unlimited power lay in the hands of a schoolmaster "who restrains their natural liberty, or punishes the exercise of their unalienable rights, by those ancient instruments of despotism, the rod and the ferula."[24] If the reformers really sought to undermine old authorities, if they were really serious in their demand for freedom from the illogical restrictions of the traditional past, then it was only to be expected that they would focus their attack on the schoolroom and what was taught there.[25]

Proposals for reforming classroom procedure were frequently associated with plans for establishing a coherent national educational program for the preparation of patriots, capped by a national university. The most formal of these proposals was the bill for the establishment of a National Academy presented to

[23] *New-England Palladium*, January 13, 20, and 23, 1801. Federalist opposition to the reformed curricula was, it seems, characteristically ambivalent: at the same time that reform was attacked in the Federalist press, several college faculties of a generally Federalist persuasion, like those of Princeton and Yale, were modifying their own courses of studies.

[24] "Climenole, No. 5," February 25.

[25] The *Monthly Anthology and Boston Review* reprinted a similar parody of the reformer's case, found in an essay written in England in 1769 by Dr. James Beattie: "How debasing to an ingenuous mind is the drudgery and discipline of our publick schools! That the best days of youth should be embittered by confinement, amidst the gloom of solitude, or under the scourge of tyranny; and all for no purpose, but that the memory may be loaded with the words of two languages that have been dead upwards of a thousand years?" (VII [1810], 228–229).

the Senate by George Logan early in 1806.[26] The bill provided for an institution which would combine advanced research with undergraduate instruction, with as many branches across the country as funds would permit; it would have printing presses to publish and distribute cheap and uniform schoolbooks in order to "give a uniformity to the moral sentiment, a republican energy to the character, a liberal cast to the mind and manners, of the rising and following generations."[27] The fact that the bill had been drafted, as was widely known or suspected, by Jefferson's friend Joel Barlow shortly after his return from France made it *documentum non gratum* to Federalists from the outset, by they had other, more serious grounds for objection, among them the suspicion that Barlow had in mind the model of the University of Paris and the national network of secular schools then being established in France by Napoleon's regime.[28] Barlow believed that a national system of education would go far toward counteracting separatist tendencies (which, since the abortive effort of 1804, could hardly help but be associated with the Federalist Party): "The liberal sciences are in their nature republican; they delight in reciprocal communication; they cherish fraternal feelings, and lead to a freedom of intercourse."[29] One may well suspect that Federalists would resent even the hint that the humanities were the preserve of a single political party. Nor could they be expected to endorse the trend toward a uniform curriculum with books provided by a central agency whose funds came from a Republican-controlled Congress. In a previous plan for a National University, Benjamin Rush had shown how far the demand for uniformity might go by arguing that once a national university was established, attendance at it

[26] *Annals of Congress*, 9th Cong., 1st sess., Senate, p. 161, March 4, 1806.

[27] Joel Barlow, *Prospectus of a National Institution, to Be Established in the United States* (Washington City [*sic*], 1806), pp. 3–4, 30, 32, 35.

[28] See Timothy Pickering to Timothy Dwight, March 7, 1806, Pickering Papers, Massachusetts Historical Society.

[29] Barlow, p. 5.

(and a degree from it) should be required of every federal officer, including congressmen and other elected officials.[30]

Opponents of reform often responded to these suggestions in inappropriately apocalyptic terms. The real subject of the debate, however, was not mere technique, but what Benjamin Rush had called "the Mode of Education Proper in a Republic." [31] Federalists and Republicans alike were familiar with Montesquieu's warning that republics are viable only if geographically small. Madison's tenth *Federalist* essay may have convinced them that they might ignore this warning, but they still believed that only a virtuous population could create and maintain a republic. "Virtue" was regularly used to imply not merely morality, but all the qualities that are associated with the Italian *virtù*—manliness, vigor, capacity; and these qualities, it seemed to a pre-Romantic generation, could be instilled by the proper kind of education. Their disagreements were not over the desirability of an educated populace, and they agreed that the purpose of education is a virtuous citizenry. But many of the reformers couched their arguments in a rhetoric that foreshadowed Mazzini's fierce romantic nationalism, and men who found the terminology of the French Revolution distressing could not be expected to endorse the reforms thus proposed. When Rush's essay on education, first published in 1786, was reprinted in the *New England Quarterly Magazine* in June, 1802, its arguments were still disturbingly novel. Its readers may well have found their worst fears of the reformers' intentions realized in the following passages:

Our schools of learning, by producing one general, and uniform system of education, will render the mass of people more homogeneous,

[30] Benjamin Rush, "Plan of a National University," quoted in Harry G. Good, *Benjamin Rush and His Services to American Education* (Berne, Indiana, 1918), p. 211.

[31] B. Rush, "Of the Mode of Education Proper in a Republic," *Essays, Literary, Moral and Philosophical* (Philadelphia, 1798), pp. 6–20 (originally written in 1786).

and thereby fit them more easily for uniform and peaceable government. Our country includes family, friends, and property, and should
be preferred to them all. Let our pupil be taught that he does not
belong to himself, but that he is public property. Let him be taught
to love his family, but let him be taught, at the same time, that he
must forsake, and even forget them, when the welfare of his country
requires it. He must watch for the state, as if its liberties depended
upon his vigilance alone. . . . I consider it is possible to convert men
into republican machines. This must be done, if we expect them to
perform their parts properly, in the great machine of the government of the State.[32]

One can easily guess that Federalists were not anxious to turn
citizens into "Republican machines." The term may have
sounded harmless enough when Rush wrote it, but sixteen years
later it had taken on the connotations which it still carries.

Federalists were the more dubious about modifications in educational procedure because their goals seemed to be a leveling
down, rather than up. Webster had remarked that the colleges
had become "nurseries of Inequalities, the enemies of
liberty."[33] More to the point was the comment in Samuel
Knox's prize-winning essay: "A general system of education
ought rather to be adapted to those whose parts may be more
properly assigned to mediocrity, than to excellence."[34] By the
turn of the century, Democrats like William Manning had come
to argue that the only proper purpose of the college was to turn

[32] *Ibid.*, pp. 7–8, 10–11, 14–15. Reprinted in *The New England
Quarterly Magazine*, June, 1802, pp. 133, 135, 136–137. In his *Remarks
on Education*, Samuel H. Smith had drawn upon Cambacères: "It is
proper to remind parents, that their children belong to the state, and that
in their education, they ought to conform to the rules which it prescribes"
(quoted in Hansen, pp. 149–150).

[33] Quoted in Hansen, p. 232.

[34] P. 20. In New York City the Republican mayor DeWitt Clinton
organized a society to promote the Lancastrian system of cheap mass education in which older pupils assisted a single head teacher to instruct hundreds
of children in a single hall. See Harvey Wish, *Society and Thought in
Early America* (New York, 1950), pp. 286–287.

out instructors for the elementary classrooms so that the common man could have "larning": that other uses of higher education and delicate scholarship were a waste of private time and public money.[35] The Boston *Repertory* willingly agreed that, according to sound republican doctrine, "knowledge ought to be as extensively diffused as possible" but insisted that cheaper education should not mean cheapened education. Expanding the common schools was an admirable goal, but it should not be pursued at the expense of the universities, which should "be devoted and confined to the important object of . . . qualifying gentlemen . . . for the highest duties of professional life." [36] It was perhaps not accidental that the same issue included an announcement that Harvard was about to raise its admission requirements. The shifting emphasis struck Rufus King sharply on his return from England:

In nothing has this Country suffered a greater and more injurious change of Opinion, than on the Subject of Education; which is known to have excited the earliest and most anxious Solicitude of our Forefathers: they in the midst of their difficulties founded Colleges,

[35] William Manning, *The Key of Libberty*, [*sic*] ed. Samuel Eliot Morison, *William and Mary Quarterly*, 3d ser., XIII (1956), pp. 202–254. See also Richard Hofstadter, *Anti-Intellectualism in American Life* (New York, 1963), pp. 151–154.

[36] Boston *Repertory*, February 7, 1804. Interest in schools on both lower and higher levels was not uncommon among Federalists, and the concentration on the growth and expansion of universities did not necessarily eclipse all interest in the expansion of the common schools. James Hillhouse, commissioner of the school fund of Connecticut in 1810, untangled its finances and substantially increased its size; Archibald D. Murphy in North Carolina and Charles Mercer in Virginia also worked to increase funds for the support of grammar schools. Mercer led the Federalists of Virginia to the support of a statewide system of grammar schools at a time when the Jeffersonians were stressing the use of state funds for the support of the University of Virginia only. See Welter, pp. 24–32; Merle Curti, *The Social Ideas of American Educators* (Totowa, N.J., 1935, 1966), 46n; Norman K. Risjord, "The Virginia Federalists," *Journal of Southern History*, XXXIII (1967), 516–517.

their Posterity in more favorable Circumstances neglect them; they regarded Colleges as the best Schools of wisdom & Virtue; we consider them as nursuries of Inequality, and Enemies of Liberty; and here as elsewhere, the unnatural Genius of Equality, the arch Disturber of the moral world, is permitted to seek her visionary Level, not by elevating what Ignorance and Vice have degraded, but by degrading what knowledge and virtue have elevated.[37]

If, under a new dispensation, schools were to serve mediocrity, if "education" meant only learning to read and write, then the part of the curriculum that most obviously required changing was the old emphasis on Latin and Greek. That emphasis was heavy. Throughout the eighteenth century, virtually the only field in which applicants for college were examined was Latin and Greek. By mid-century, Yale, The College of New Jersey, and King's College had added arithmetic to their entrance tests, but Harvard did not ask for arithmetic until 1803.[38] Students continued to read the classics in college—Cicero, Horace, Sallust, and Livy at Harvard, Cicero, Horace, and Virgil at Yale—in a program that bored the best students to tears and seems to have had something less than lasting results. There is an enlightening exchange, for example, between Timothy Pickering and his son John. During his junior year at Harvard, John complained of "the slow progress we have made; . . . we don't learn half so much at a lesson as we did at school."[39] The following year, when he was assigned the English Oration instead of the more prestigious Latin Oration, he was consoled by his father: "I dare venture to say that not one fourth, even of those who are sons of Harvard [in the audience], are so prompt in that language as, on the delivery, to

---

[37] Rufus King to N. Webster, May 25, 1807, in Ford, II, 19.

[38] Theodore Hornberger, *Scientific Thought in the American Colleges 1628–1800* (Austin, Texas, 1945), pp. 16–18.

[39] John Pickering to T. Pickering, April 26, 1784, in Mary Orne Pickering, *Life of John Pickering* (Boston, 1887), p. 60. John Pickering's sentiments were shared by John Quincy Adams. See Henry Adams, "Harvard College," *Historical Essays* (London, 1891), pp. 84–85.

judge of the sentiments, and much less of the elegance or defi-
ciency of style. Like me, the greater part of the collegians, im-
prudently neglecting to read Latin daily, or at least weekly,
after they leave college . . . forget the language." [40]

The notion that the usual educational progression from the
three R's to the classics, supplemented by the sciences only when
the student had reached college, was boring to the child and of
less than optimum usefulness to the man was not original with
Pickering's generation; Locke had said as much in the seventeenth century, and Benjamin Franklin had tried to put Locke's
program into effect in a modest way in the Academy of Pennsylvania. But the removal of the classics from the curriculum was
more widely and more urgently demanded at the turn of the
nineteenth century, frequently by men of whose purposes Federalists were already doubtful. At the head of the list was of course
Thomas Jefferson himself, at whose urging William and Mary
had dropped "ancient languages" as a requirement for admission
and, indeed, from the required curriculum.[41] One of Benajmin
Rush's sons, studying Ovid, asked his father if there really was
such a river as the Nile and if Egypt really existed: the question
summed up, Rush thought, all that was wrong with "that mode
of education which makes the first knowledge of boys to consist
in *fables,* and thereby leads them to reject truth, or to esteem it
no more than gross errors and fictions of the ancient poets." [42]
Rush's essay "An Enquiry into the Utility of a Knowledge of
the Latin and Greek Languages, as a Branch of Liberal Educa-

[40] T. Pickering to J. Pickering, June 4, 1795, in M. O. Pickering,
pp. 83–84.

[41] Hornberger, pp. 16–18. See also Roy J. Honeywell, *The Educational
Work of Thomas Jefferson* (Cambridge, Mass., 1931), chapter 8. When
a *Port Folio* contributor from Richmond, who signed himself Babellophilos
[Love of Babel] quoted Plautus, he added a footnote: "I subjoin a free
translation, for the benefit of the young gentlemen of William and Mary
college, who may never have ventured beyond Terence" (*Port Folio,*
August 15, 1801).

[42] B. Rush to John Adams, February 24, 1790, APm reel 373.

tion, with Hints of a Plan of Liberal Instruction without them" was one of the earliest, and remained one of the fullest and most coherent attacks on the classics, the one whose arguments defenders of the classics would have to answer.[43]

Rush suggested that Americans had better things to do with their time, in a new country that demanded to be explored and settled, than to waste it in the useless luxury of a classical education.[44] Young people need, first of all, to know their own language and to know it well; the Greeks themselves studied Greek.[45] They need to learn about the world in which they live more than to memorize technical words: "The knowledge of things always precedes the knowledge of words. Children discover the truth of this observation every day. . . . The acquisition of words lessens the ability of the mind to acquire ideas." Classical studies had even more specific dangers: first, they were frequently immoral, full of "Indelicate amours, and shocking vices both of gods and men"; second, they were so difficult that the struggle to become competent in them might sour otherwise promising youths on education altogether; finally, and most significantly, they were undemocratic. "While Greek and Latin are the only avenues to science [i.e., knowledge], education will always be confined to a few people. It is only by rendering knowledge universal, that a republican form of government can be preserved in our country." [46] Rush and Webster had met in 1786 and discussed their ideas on educational reform. Their ideas complemented each other: in a republic, education must be as widely diffused as possible; anything which hinders that diffusion must be avoided; the classics, because both difficult and impractical, hinder the diffusion of knowledge by souring young

---

[43] First published anonymously in the *American Museum*, June, 1789, V, 525–535; reprinted in his collected *Essays*, 1798, pp. 21–56, with a new title: "Observations on the Study of the Latin and Greek Languages . . ."

[44] B. Rush, *Essays*, p. 39.

[45] *Ibid.*, pp. 26–27.

[46] *Ibid.*, pp. 22–25.

people on school and by using up time that might be more profitably employed; therefore the classics should be removed from the required curriculum.[47] "Do not men use Latin and Greek," Rush asked his old friend John Adams, "as the scuttlefish emit their ink, on purpose to conceal themselves from an intercourse with the common people?" [48]

Of all the proposed reforms, Federalists appear to have liked this one least. "Do we not fear," asked the *New England Quarterly Magazine*, "lest by removing the foundations of intellect, we should sacrifice intellect itself?" [49] Applauding John Quincy Adams's oration to the Massachusetts Charitable Fire Society, Joseph Dennie ascribed Adams's ability to write with "spirit, sense, and melody" to his familiarity with Sallust and Tacitus, and cried, "Let us hear no more of that plan of study, which should *exclude the ancients*." [50] Whereas the reformers frankly admitted that the exclusion of the classics would make the curriculum easier and therefore more widely accessible, their opponents insisted on giving the word "easier" a pejorative connotation. A watered-down education was no education at all, and the

---

[47] Shoemaker, p. 44; in "On the Education of Youth in America," written in 1788, Webster repeated many of these ideas. "The first error that I would mention, is, a too general attention to the dead languages, with a neglect of our own." Latin and Greek, he thought, were necessary only when the classics were not available in translation; but they were then widely available in English, and the progress of the arts and sciences had made "The English language . . . the repository of as much learning" as half the languages of Europe. "If children are to acquire *ideas*," Webster wrote, "it is certainly easier to obtain them in a language which they understand, than in a foreign tongue." He concluded that Latin and Greek should be studied only on an advanced basis, as preparation for the learned professions (Webster, *Essays*, pp. 3–7).

[48] B. Rush to John Adams, July 21, 1789, in *The Letters of Benjamin Rush*, ed. Lyman H. Butterfield (Princeton, 1951), I, 524. See also B. Rush, *Essays*, pp. 42–43.

[49] September, 1802, p. 124. This short-lived magazine circulated as far south as Charleston. See Charleston, S.C., *Courier*, January 10, 1803.

[50] *Port Folio*, July 31, 1802.

abandonment of the classics, as the Boston *Repertory* suggested, seemed linked to the desire for cheapened education in an intellectual as well as a financial sense:

The levity of youth, and the forbidding aspect of dead languages, to those who have not tasted their beauties, favoured the degeneracy of taste for ancient literature. It was easier to acquire a knowledge of a French writer than of a Roman or Grecian; and the licentious wit of Voltaire had more charms, for young minds than the sober morals of Cicero.[51]

Many defenses of the classics included a political theme. The note is muted in the arguments of the *Repertory's* analyst; it is more clearly present in the italics of David Daggett's complaint "that music and painting, and dancing and fencing, and *speaking French*, were the only accomplishments worth possessing; and that Latin and Greek were [assumed to be] fitted only for stupid divines or black-letter-lawyers"; and it is obvious in a *Port Folio* parody of a popular song:

> Columbia, Columbia, to discord arise,
> The world whelm in blood, and wage war with the skies;
>
> . . . . .
>
> Thy sons for science in newspapers seek,
> Neglect their own language and Latin and Greek [52]

Daggett explicitly argued that the reformers' claim that they endorsed the study of modern languages, especially French, because they were of practical use to the merchant and trader was spurious; the real purpose of encouraging the study of French was to tighten American cultural links with a land of revolution and imperialism.[53] Rush neatly turned the tables on this argument. Rome too had been an empire, and Napoleon himself was encouraging the classical studies, partly because he saw his own

[51] February 7, 1804.
[52] Daggett, p. 38; *Port Folio*, August 13, 1803.
[53] Daggett, p. 11.

empire as a descendant of Rome, but more because he probably wanted "to bring back the darkness and ignorance of the 14th and 15th centuries," when their myopic concentration on the classics had prevented monkish schoolmen from studying the problems of the real world. Napoleon encouraged classical studies, Rush suspected, as Richelieu and Louis XIV had encouraged court amusements—to divert the people "from prying into the machinations and oppressions of the government."[54] The most imaginative denunciation of the classics on political grounds, however, was furnished, with satirical intent, by Josiah Quincy. "A man is not a whit the better patriot" for a classical education, protests Slaveslap Kiddnap. Kiddnap has a friend who had long demanded the introduction of the guillotine as a particularly democratic mode of execution; he gives up the study of Greek because the letter π reminds him of the gallows. Aesop's frogs, who demanded a king from Jupiter although they already enjoyed a democracy, were obviously a bad influence on young minds; Homer was even worse. "I recollect but one town meeting, in the whole Iliad," muses Kiddnap, and even there the poet's sympathies were obviously not democratic ones. This "town meeting" occurs early in the epic when, as Kiddnap tells it, the Greeks had been in Troy for nine years "to gratify the ambition, or the lust, of eight or ten kings and aristocrats." After so many years without victory, the army "began very naturally and properly to murmur," but were stifled by the evil Ulysses, who is quoted in Pope's translation:

> Be still, thou slave, and to thy betters yield . . .
> Be silent wretch, and think not here allow'd
> THAT WORST OF TYRANTS, AN USURPING CROWD.[55]

Obviously, no good democrat should have to put up with *that*.

Much of the argument took on the flavor of the Augustan quarrel between the Ancients and the Moderns. Rush, who set

[54] B. Rush to John Adams, October 2, 1810, January 10, 1811, in *Letters of Benjamin Rush*, II, 1067, 1077.

[55] "Climenole, No. 7," March 17.

the terms of so much of the debate, seems to have suggested this theme as well. "We are told," he complained, "that the Roman and Greek authors are the only perfect models of taste and eloquence, and that it is necessary to study them, in order to acquire their taste and spirit. Strange language indeed! What! did nature exhaust herself in Greece and Rome?" The road to artistic greatness led through nature, not the classics, Rush asserted with Romantics like Coleridge and Wordsworth; he even went so far as to suggest that "Shakespeare owes his fame, as a sublime and original poet, to his having never read (as is generally believed) a Latin or Greek author. Hence he spoke from nature, or rather, nature spoke through him." [56] The *Monthly Anthology* turned to an English Augustan for rebuttal; Dr. James Beattie's "Remarks on the Utility of Classical Learning," first published in 1769, was reprinted in April, 1810 as an answer to the "weak" and "absurd" arguments of Dr. Rush. Beattie began with a sneering parody of the case against the classics:

Are we not taught by Voltaire and his editors, who, though ignorant of Greek, are well read in Madam Dacier's translations, that Tasso is a better poet than Homer . . . ? What dramatick poet of antiquity is to be compared with the immortal Shakespeare? What satirist with Pope . . . ?

Would you have your children healthy, and polite, and *sentimental?* Let their early youth be employed in genteel exercises; the theatre, the coffeehouse, and the card table, will refine their taste, instruct them in public affairs . . . and the French authors will make them men of wit and sprightly conversation.

The aim of education "should be, to teach us rather *how* to think, than *what* to think," and careful training in the classics seemed to Beattie far more likely to accomplish this goal than "an extensive smattering." Furthermore, classical studies seemed to him the most efficient guard against cultural barbarism: "How easily do ungrammatical phrases, the effect of ignorance and affectation, insinuate themselves into common discourse, and

[56] Rush, *Essays*, pp. 27–28.

thence into writing! . . . Where grammar was accurately studied, language has always been elegant and durable: witness that of ancient Greece. . . . As grammar is neglected, barbarism must prevail." [57] The *New England Quarterly Magazine* put it succinctly: "The best ages of Rome afford the purest models of virtue that are anywhere to be met with. Mankind are too apt to lose sight of all that is heroic, magnanimous and public spirited. . . . Left to ourselves, we are apt to sink into effeminacy and apathy." [58]

"Left to ourselves." The burden of the Federalist case for the classics, endlessly repeated, was that it would be foolhardy to insist on being "left to ourselves." What, after all, is education for, if it is not to enable one to take advantage of the experience of preceding generations? That replacing Latin and Greek by French might make boys better merchants they were willing to concede; but would it make them better citizens? Jealousy for the classical curriculum implied more than mere antiquarianism; as R. M. Ogilvie remarked of the English Renaissance, "Humanist education involved the attempt to recover the ancient way of life." [59]

Sometimes the claim that the classics could teach proper behavior was extremely specific, as in John Quincy Adams's querulous assertion that had he studied his classics better, James Madison would have behaved more properly in the Marbury case:

Mr. Madison has the reputation of an accomplished classical scholar. On this application to the Supreme Court, for a mandamus, he did

---

[57] *Monthly Anthology and Boston Review*, VII (1810), 228, 229, 303, 304.

[58] September, 1802, p. 125. Beattie, too, accused opponents of Latin and Greek of seeming to think "that the human mind, being now arrived at maturity, may be safely left to itself" (*Monthly Anthology and Boston Review*, VII [1810], 227).

[59] R. M. Ogilvie, *Latin and Greek: A History of the Influence of the Classics on English Life from 1600–1918* (Hamden, Conn., 1964), p. 5. See also Charleston *Courier*, September 1, 1803.

not condescend to enter an appearance. This conduct, so unnecessary for the maintenance of his official dignity, so disrespectful towards the court, ought not to pass altogether without animadversion. Had he been

> By ancient learning, to the enlighten'd love
> Of ancient glory warm'd,

he would have remembered, that in the most illustrious ages of the Roman republic, it was the proud boast of her most distinguished citizens, to manifest their veneration for the laws, and their perfect deference to the officers, invested with their authority.[60]

Adams himself recognized that this use of the classics verged on the absurd; elsewhere he poked fun at men who thought they could learn how to manage their farms by reading the *Georgics*.[61] But that, of course, was only *reductio ad absurdum*.

Properly interpreted, the lessons of the classics were more inclusive. To the complaint that the young classical scholar's head was filled only with abstract words and wordiness, Beattie had replied: "If a child find nothing but words in the old authors, it must be owing to the stupifying influence of an ignorant teacher. . . . Together with the words . . . of these two celebrated languages, they may learn, without any additional expense of time, the principles of history, morality, politicks, geography and criticism; which, when taught in a foreign dialect, will perhaps be found to leave a deeper impression upon the memory." [62] The classics, then, taught moral philosophy; what is more important, they taught what might be called "significant experience"—that is, a republican historical experience particularly appropriate for

---

[60] *Port Folio*, December 8, 1804.

[61] *Ibid.*, February 26, 1803. In this assumption Americans were squarely in the tradition of English Puritans, who had substituted the study of Horace for Ovid in the seventeenth century: "The classics were to be read not as works of literature which would teach a boy to express himself but as sources of information . . . on matters of moral and political behaviour" (Ogilvie, pp. 37–38).

[62] *Monthly Anthology and Boston Review*, VII (1810), 231–232.

the careful consideration of citizens of a new republic. When, in
1802, a depressed John Quincy Adams sought explanation for
an America which had rejected his father, he turned to Xenophon and found there "great consolation . . . that we are not
conducting worse than others have done in similar situations."
Urging his brother Thomas Boylston Adams to read Xenophon's "Treatise on the Athenian Democracy," he explained:

It shews, in the clearest light, what the spirit and the effects of Democracy were, among the most enlightened and most ingenious
people that ever existed upon earth. . . . Xenophon expressly founds
his defence of the Government upon this principle, that Democracy is, *in its nature,* the institution, best calculated to *raise the
worst men in the community to power.* Now, says he, as the Athenians *love* to have the worst men in power, Democracy must, of
course, be the Government *best suited to their purposes!*

His brother found Xenophon cold comfort: "After the disaster-
ous [*sic*] experiments made by 'the most enlightened and ingenious people, that ever existed upon earth,' are we destined to run
the same course, with a people, whose character is the very
reverse?" [63]

That the classics lent themselves to such alternative explana-
tions seemed not overly disconcerting; it was more significant
that they could be used to provide a political vocabulary, a series
of heroic examples for patriotic imitation, a sense of
proportion.[64] The Revolutionary generation had made just this
use of the classics; they, and their sons, continued to do so long
after the Revolution.[65]

[63] *Port Folio,* October 30, 1802; Thomas Boylston Adams to John
Quincy Adams, November 10, 1802, APm reel 401.

[64] Rush particularly objected to this use of the classics: "Napoleon
would have been just what he is had he never read a page of ancient
history. Rulers become tyrants and butchers from instinct much oftener
than from imitation" (B. Rush to John Adams, December 21, 1810, in
Letters of Benjamin Rush, I, 1073).

[65] See Bernard Bailyn, *Pamphlets of the American Revolution* (Cambridge, Mass., 1965), I, 22–23.

When John Adams, for example, wanted to develop a criticism of his world, he frequently turned to the ancient writers for guidance. "I should as soon think of closing all my window shutters, to enable me to see, as of banishing the Classicks, to improve Republican ideas," he rebuked his friend Rush when the latter first began to expound on his objections to the classics.[66] In 1803, now an aging ex-President, Adams furnished proof of the uses to which the classics might be put by preparing "A History of the French Revolution, by a Society of Latin Writers," in which extracts from ancient historians comprised an outline of a revolution similar to the one the French had experienced. Thus Adams quoted Tacitus on a situation he believed analogous to the opening of the Estates General:

Nor had any authority force enough to repress the seditions of a people, who believed themselves to be protecting the ceremonies of their gods, while they were defending the crimes of men. It was, therefore, ordained, that the cities should send their instructions, and their delegates.[67]

and Velleius Paterculus "on" the storming of the Bastille: "This was the first effusion of civil blood." [68] For the Vendée and the noyades, Tacitus proved disconcertingly apposite:

There was scarcely any city, without the seeds of this insurrection. But the first who broke out, were the inhabitants of Anjou and Touraine. . . . The cause of these disturbances . . . [was] their refusal to submit to the oppression of the recruiting service, and to give to our armies, the most vigorous of their youth.[69]

The freedman Anicetus . . . shews . . . how a vessel may be constructed, part of which may be opened by a mechanical invention,

[66] John Adams to B. Rush, June 19, 1789, in *Letters of Benjamin Rush*, I, 518.
[67] *Port Folio*, March 19, 1803. Identification from Athenaeum Files.
[68] *Ibid.*, April 9, 1803.
[69] *Ibid.*, April 16, 1803.

. . . and a whole cargo of prisoners sunk to the bottom, before they suspected anything.[70]

The ex-President made clear his own assessment of the French Revolution, as well as his own distrust of partisan politics in America, by his choice of Cicero for the conclusion:

The administration of a republic, like the guardian of an orphan, ought to study the interest of their constituents, not of those to whom the trust is committed. Those who consult the good of a party of the citizens, and neglect another part, introduce into society two pernicious things, sedition and discord. . . . From this source arose mighty dissensions among the Athenians; and in our republic, not only seditions but destructive civil wars; evils, which a virtuous and courageous citizen, worthy to preside in the republic, would avoid and detest. Such a man will devote himself entirely to the republic, nor will he covet power or riches. . . . He will adhere so closely to justice and equity, that, provided he can preserve these virtues, although he may give offence and create enemies by them, he will set death itself at defiance, rather than abandon his principles.[71]

The passage is worth quoting extensively for the clarity with which it reveals Adams's image of himself as The Last Roman. From the Roman experience one could learn the dangers and possibilities of republican government; from their exemplary experience we might, if we were careful, learn enough to avoid their failure. The converse readily suggests itself: if we ignore the classics, how shall we learn to save free government? [72]

History was, many Federalists feared, in the very process of repeating itself, and their frequent use of apocalyptic imagery,

[70] *Ibid.*, April 23, 1803.

[71] *Ibid.*, May 7, 1803.

[72] Cf. the Boston *Repertory*, February 7, 1804: "If even the study of Latin literature could inflame Rienzi, a person of no rank or expectation, so far as to operate his deliverance of Rome from Papal tyranny . . . surely the study of the Grecian literature, to which the other is but a shadow, hath effected, and will effect still greater things."

their overstated insistence that the nation was plunging into anarchy, were perhaps the result of a habit of restating the American experience in classical terms. The English Augustans, whom they so much admired, had assumed that the past, especially the classical past, was best employed as a source of modern parallels and cautionary examples; as we have seen, Americans habitually used the classics for a similar purpose.[73] Since the classics provided a cyclical image of historical change, the student learned that history is mainly a process of successive growth and decay of societies and civilizations. This theory denies the possibility of lasting moral progress; once the inevitable decline is begun, it is irreversible.[74] "Will you tell me," asked John Adams, "how to prevent riches from becoming the effects of temperance and industry? Will you tell me how to prevent riches from producing luxury? Will you tell me how to prevent luxury from producing effeminacy, intoxication, extravagance, vice and folly?"[75] Because history was cyclical, the historian could not help but be something of a pessimist. As the heroes of the American Revolution died, as the French Revolution became increasingly imperial rather than republican in goal, many Federalists began to feel that, despite the continuing optimistic rhetoric of the nation's press and politicians, America had reached the end of the rising curve of the cycle. They and their society were suspended on the brink of precipitous decline. The nation still might postpone disaster, but only by the wisest of policies, and certainly not by the continuation of what Federalists saw as Jeffersonian political ineptitude. Since the history and literature of the ancient world provided a touchstone of policies to be avoided, pro-

[73] H. Davis, "The Augustan Conception of History," in *Reason and the Imagination: Studies in the History of Ideas 1600–1800*, ed. Joseph Anthony Mazzeo (New York, 1962), p. 214.

[74] Stow Persons, "The Cyclical Theory of History in Eighteenth Century America," *American Quarterly*, VI (1954), p. 152.

[75] John Adams to Thomas Jefferson, December 18, 1819, quoted in Persons, p. 154.

vided political lessons as appropriate to the current historical cycle as to past ones, their practical value was immense. Any temporary convenience to be expected from eliminating the classics from the curriculum was more than balanced by the good political sense which could be assumed to be the possession of a classically-educated citizenry.

Caleb Strong, who served as Federalist governor of Massachusetts during the years of Jefferson's presidency, habitually referred to the "history of antient republics" for instruction on survival in the present one:

> In modern republicks of Europe, the scenes, which were formerly displayed in those of Greece and Rome, have been repeated. Dissention and party spirit were excited among the people, and their passions were artfully inflamed against the most able and virtuous citizens, and against those institutions and restraints, which wisdom had devised, and the experience of ages had sanctioned. These republicks, one after another have lost their freedom. . . . Let us take warning.[76]

"We are not wiser, nor more enthusiastic for liberty, nor braver, nor richer, nor stronger, than were the Greeks," protested Thomas P. Grosvenor of New York in 1808. "Has [Jefferson] . . . never heard of Philip of Macedon, and the republics of Greece? Has he never read that the latter, by yielding, one point after another, by submitting to one outrage after another, and by hugging to their bosoms the chimerical idea, that Philip would regard reason, and justice, and the rights of nations, finally became his slaves? This case presents a picture of our present situation with Bonaparte. . . . Nor is Napoleon less ambitious, less profligate, less blood-thirsty nor less powerful than was Philip. There is but one point of difference—and that is, we are separated from Napoleon by 3,000 miles of ocean, while

[76] "Speech to the Massachusetts Legislature, January 18, 1805," in *Patriotism and Piety* (Newburyport, 1808), p. 115.

Greece and Macedon were nearly contiguous. Let Bonaparte become master of the British navy, and the Atlantic is no longer a barrier." [77]

To Fisher Ames, the spectacle of contemporary Greece tyrannically ruled by Turkey called up even more distressing reflections: "Who would not prefer the republicks of ancient Greece, where liberty once subsisted in its excess, its delirium, terrible in its charms . . . to the dozing slavery of the modern Greece, where the degraded wretches have suffered scorn till they merit it, where they tread on classick ground, on the ashes of heroes and patriots, unconscious of their ancestry?" The trouble was that "the most passionate admirers" of liberty "have, generally, the least comprehension of its hazards and impediments"; the history of Greece illustrated these hazards, and the Americans were to study the classics like cautionary tales. "If it had been in the nature of man, that we should enjoy liberty, without the agitations of party, the United States had a right . . . to expect it, but [the Greek example shows] it was impossible. . . . Liberty, with all its parties and agitations, is more desirable than slavery." Ames moved easily from the classical example to the contemporary one. Those who ignored the lessons of Greece did so at their peril; it was dangerous to

expect, that an enthusiastic admiration [of liberty] . . . will reconcile the multitude to the irksomeness of its restraints. Delusive expectation! WASHINGTON was not thus deluded. . . . He had reflected, that men are often false to their country and their honour, false to duty and even to their interest, but multitudes of men are never long false or deaf to their passions. . . . Thus party forms a state within the state, and is animated by a rivalship, fear, and hatred, of its superiour. When this happens, the merits of the government will become fresh provocations and offenses, for they are the merits of an enemy. . . . The life of the federal government, he

[77] *Oration, Delivered in Christ-Church, Hudson, N.Y., on the 4th of July, 1808* (Hudson, N.Y., 1808), p. 24n.

considered, was in the breath of the people's nostrils; whenever they should happen to be so infatuated or inflamed as to abandon its defence, its end must be as speedy, and might be as tragical, as a constitution for France.[78]

Thus contemporary and ancient analogy were combined in a crude but serviceable syllogism: the history of Greece and Rome shows that when men consent to be ruled by self-seeking politicians, the result is an anarchy that invites foreign invasion; Americans are now consenting to be ruled by hypocritical and self-seeking politicians; we may, therefore, expect anarchy and foreign invasion. This syllogism took on a measure of plausibility as Napoleon's victories continued and he re-established French power in Santo Domingo.

Paradoxically, Federalists may be found espousing the argument that the way to escape the fate of the "antient republicks" was to emulate them more carefully. This idea was given its fullest expression in 1808 and 1809 by John Quincy Adams while he served as Boylston Professor of Rhetoric and Oratory at Harvard. Coming from him, there can be no doubt that the advice was given in good faith: one of John Quincy Adams's few complaints about his own education at Harvard was that the classical training had not been more rigorous, and to the end of his long political career he sought and found intellectual sustenance from classical authors and classical example.[79] His lectures on ancient oratory as Boylston Professor suggest as a subsidiary theme that democracies, like individuals, need nourishment from the classics: in the ancient example Americans may find both precedent and inspiration.

At Athens and Rome a town meeting could scarcely be held, without being destined to immortality; a question of property between individual citizens could scarcely be litigated, without occupying the

[78] "Eulogy of Washington," *Works of Fisher Ames* (Boston, 1809), pp. 123–125.

[79] H. Adams, "Harvard College, 1796–1797," *Historical Essays* (London, 1891), pp. 84–85.

attention, and engaging the studies of the remotest nations and the most distant posterity.[80]

The classical example here is the art of oratory as displayed in the works of Cicero and Quintillian, which provide, Adams insisted, all that needs to be known about the art of oratory.[81]

The excellence of the debates to be heard in the town meetings of the ancient democracies was not, Adams believed, at all accidental. In his explanation he took a sideswipe at the party caucus, a technique that was gaining popularity in Congress: "The assemblies . . . were held for the purpose of real deliberation. The fate of measures was not decided before they were proposed. Eloquence produced a powerful effect, not only upon the minds of the hearers, but upon the issue of the deliberation." [82] In other words, intelligence and lucidity had counted in a way that Adams was coming to fear they no longer did in America, in either political party. The relation of eloquence to liberty, moreover, was direct: "With the dissolution of Roman liberty, and the decline of Roman taste, the reputation and the excellency of the oratorical art fell alike into decay." The decay persisted:

In the only countries of modern Europe, where the semblance of deliberative assemblies has been preserved, corruption, here in the form of executive influence, there in the guise of party spirit, . . . has crippled the sublimest efforts of oratory, and the votes upon questions of magnitude to the interest of nations are all told, long before the questions themselves are submitted to discussion.[83]

The corruption to which Adams referred was not necessarily economic, did not imply only bribery with money or influence;

[80] J. Q. Adams, "Inaugural Oration," *Lectures on Rhetoric and Oratory, Delivered to the Classes of Senior and Junior Sophisters in Harvard University* (Cambridge, [Mass.], 1810), I, 19.

[81] *Ibid.*, pp. 28–29.

[82] *Ibid.*, I, 22. The opportunity for eloquence afforded by multiple local and national legislative assemblies is emphasized by Samuel L. Knapp, *Lectures on American Literature* (New York, 1829), pp. 209–227.

[83] *Ibid.*, I, 20, 22–23.

more significantly, and more dangerously, it was intellectual. Men who had promised their votes for partisan purposes before a debate was opened had nothing left to debate, could not be persuaded by the merits of an issue. A true republic was impossible when legislators were closed to persuasion, and unwilling to follow John Quincy Adams's own example and cross party lines.

The art of speaking must be most eagerly sought, where it is found to be most useful. It must be most useful, where it is capable of producing the greatest effects; and that can be in no other state of things, than where the power of persuasion operates upon the will, and prompts the actions of other men. The only birth place of eloquence therefore must be a free state. Under arbitrary governments . . . persuasion is of no av[a]il. Between authority and obedience there can be no deliberation. . . . Eloquence is the child of liberty.[84]

Adams, who in his old age would be known as "Old Man Eloquent," sighed for the days when "eloquence was POWER." [85] Where was political liberty if eloquence was impotence, shrugged off by politicans who were too busy log-rolling to consider the merits of a case? When God himself chose Aaron for the ministry of Israel, He did so because of Aaron's skill as a speaker. Adams quoted Exodus: "I KNOW, THAT HE CAN SPEAK WELL." [86] The modern parallels were obvious; Adams spelled them out:

Youthful Americans . . . cannot fail to remark, that their own nation is at this time precisely under the same circumstances, which were so propitious to the advancement of rhetoric and oratory among the Greeks. Like them, we are divided into a number of separate commonwealths, all founded upon the principles of the most enlarged social and civil liberty. Like them, we are united in certain great national interests, and connected by a confederation. . . . Our institutions . . . are republican. . . . Persuasion, or the influence of

[84] *Ibid.*, I, 68.
[85] *Ibid.*, I, 19.
[86] *Ibid.*, I, 30.

reason and of feeling, is the great if not the only instrument, whose operation can affect the acts of all our corporate bodies; of towns, cities, counties, states, and of the whole confederated empire. Here then eloquence is recommended by the most elevated usefulness.[87]

"My lectures," Adams confided to his brother, " . . . haunt me Night and Day." [88] Out of his toil he developed what Lewis Simpson has called "the myth of the orator in the American Republic," a myth which asserted that the tyrant never honors the orator; a myth which permitted no fear that oratory could degenerate into demagoguery.

Sons of Harvard! . . . catch from the relics of ancient oratory those unresisted powers, which mould the mind of man to the will of the speaker, and yield the guidance of a nation to the dominion of the voice.[89]

It has already been suggested that Federalist attacks on the American Philosophical Society seem more meaningful when they are viewed as part of a general effort to undermine Demo-

[87] *Ibid.*, I, 70–71. See also the comments on oratorical accomplishment in America, in Charles Jared Ingersoll, *Inchiquin, the Jesuit's Letters* (New York, 1810), pp. 56–62; and [Richard Rush] "The American Lounger, No. LXXVIX," *Port Folio*, January 28, 1804.

[88] J. Q. Adams to T. B. Adams, January 5, 1807, APm reel 405. Years later, Ralph Waldo Emerson recalled: "When he read his first lectures in 1806, not only the students heard him with delight, but the hall was crowded by the Professors and by unusual visitors. I remember . . . hearing the story of the numbers of coaches in which his friends came from Boston to hear him. On his return in the winter to the Senate in Washington, he took such ground in the debates of the following session as to lose the sympathy of many of his constituents in Boston. When, on his return from Washington, he resumed his lectures in Cambridge, his class attended, but the coaches from Boston did not come" (Worthington Chauncey Ford, ed., *Statesman and Friend. Correspondence of John Adams with Benjamin Waterhouse, 1784–1822* [Boston, 1927], p. 39n).

[89] Lewis P. Simpson, "The Era of Joseph Stevens Buckminster: Life and Letters in the Boston-Cambridge Community, 1800–1815," Unpublished Ph.D. dissertation, University of Texas, 1948, p. 406; J. Q. Adams, *Lectures*, I, 29–30.

cratic prestige within the intellectual community. Federalist so-licitude for the classical syllabus is similarly accompanied by the only thinly veiled suggestion that Democrats are seeking to shat-ter traditional forms of education as they have already shattered established political forms; the misuse of proper forms of gram-mar might well signal the coming misuse of the proper forms of intellectual discourse. Adams had said as much when he asserted the ancients had no caucus: that Americans did was symbolic of the disintegration of the American intelligence. Democrats, their enemies suspected, shared a repugnance for all form, all order; in satirizing their relaxation of rhetorical rules, Federalists were in fact predicting and denouncing a relaxation of *all* rules.

At the turn of the century, John Quincy Adams had begun to translate Juvenal's satires. He gave up the project when a com-plete translation by William Gifford was published in England and reprinted in the United States, but his two completed trans-lations were forwarded to the ever-importunate Joseph Dennie and were published in the *Port Folio*. One of these was the "Seventh Satire," in which Juvenal castigates Rome in terms analogous to John Kenneth Galbraith's strictures on a more re-cent affluent society. Rome rewards most lavishly those who per-form the most useless services: sign and symbol of the empire's decadence are the scanty rewards she metes out to her artists, poets, teachers, historians. Although there was no profit in serving

> the afflicted Muse;
> Whose darling votaries compelled for bread
> The meanest steps of drudgery must tread

the "scribbling frenzy" persists. The historian is lucky if he earns enough to pay for the paper he writes on; the poet woos the muses on an empty stomach, and the schoolteacher, whose "plastic hand must form the pupil's mind" is lucky if he earns as much as the gladiator.[90] Adams was sufficiently concerned that

[90] *Port Folio*, May 18, 1805, lines 4–6, 71, 143–146, 60.

the obvious conclusions be drawn that he provided an extended preface to his translation. The "Seventh Satire," he insisted, was as appropriate for nineteenth-century America as it had been for Augustan Rome. In America too, learning, genius, intellectuality were increasingly undervalued, poets and professors were alike underpaid, the more subtle the art the less it was honored. "If Quintillian himself were here, he would certainly escape the insult of an inadequate recompense, inasmuch as he would meet no employment at all." Rome, already in decline, had not listened to Juvenal: would "a young and rising" America listen to John Quincy Adams?

Let us reflect that this neglect of literature and contempt of learned men, in Rome, sprung up and grew, exactly at the same period, and in the same proportions as the genuine Republican spirit and manners decayed and withered. . . . That tyranny and Ignorance advanced upon them hand in hand. . . . It may be useful to many of our countrymen, to be reminded that the alliance between the love of learning and the love of genuine freedom, is indissoluble.[91]

When Adams wrote, in 1805, he was already drifting away from the Federalist party, but Federalists generally agreed with the tenor of his thought. They were convinced that Republicans who espoused radical educational reforms, including the near abolition of Greek and Latin, did not love learning; if they did not love learning, how could they claim to love "genuine freedom"? If one could undercut the Republicans'—and particularly Jefferson's own—claims to intellectuality, one would have gone far toward undercutting their claims to represent true republicanism. Thus, in Federalist parodies of Jefferson's political addresses, the satire was not merely playful. It was direct, it was vengeful, and it had clear political purpose.

In choosing to turn the rotund prose of Jefferson's First Inaugural Address into a parody of Enlightenment accounts of the state of nature, Josiah Quincy discredited both the president and

[91] *Ibid.*, Introduction to Seventh Satire.

the philosophy with which he was most frequently associated. "Man is, by nature," writes Slaveslap Kiddnap in Memorabilia Democratica, "a mighty megalonyx, produced purposely, in a philosophical view, to prowl, pillage, propagate, and putrify." When his needs came to exceed his capacity to satisfy them by himself, he entered into civil society, but kept it in turmoil by his jealousy of others' possessions. When, however, "this wild condition of civilized man" was replaced by a republican organization, "Men, restrained from injuring one another, and left otherwise free to regulate their own pursuits of industry or improvement, took not from the mouth of labour the bread it had earned, nor from the belly of industry the butter it had churned." Kiddnap's Democratic friends profess their unlimited admiration for the "sublime alliteration" parodied here, and evidenced by the assertion in *Notes on Virginia* that "a pigmy and a Patagonian, a mouse and a mammoth, derive their dimensions from the same nutritive juices." Alliteration, Quincy explained, is "words dressed in uniform, which have as great superiority, in point of effect, over the common slovenly mode of composition, as a regular army of Prussian blues would have over a beggarly mob." Since a little alliteration was so obviously useful, he hoped that books would be written "in which every word shall begin with the favourite letter." [92]

Quincy was only one of a number of Federalists who found Jefferson's rhetoric quite as distasteful as what he used it to say. A few weeks after the First Inaugural, Joseph Dennie's *Port Folio* ran a series of contemptuous critiques of the Declaration of Independence, in which it was insisted that since the subject was obviously neither inhuman events nor angelic ones, the opening phrase should be excised. Agreeing that man has a right to pursue happiness, the author doubted that he had a right to the pursuit of happiness: "Is it like a fox chase, where the whole pleasure is in *the pursuit?*" [93]

[92] "Climenole, No. 3," February 11, 1804; *Notes on Virginia*, p. 42.
[93] *Port Folio*, March 28, 1801.

The Second Inaugural Address became, in turn, a subject for parody; it was rephrased in rhymed couplets by Richard Alsop, a junior member of the Hartford Wits. The satire begins by amplifying the President's opening remark that the promises of the First Inaugural had been kept; the voice of Jefferson's conscience explains:

> What though you said, with soft persuasive tone,
> That Fed'ralists and Democrats were one;
> Yet you, and I, and Candour fully knew
> By *one* you meant nor more nor less than *two*,
> And shall a man of broad capacious mind
> Be to one meaning rigidly confined?

Alsop's couplets wander on through the Second Inaugural, with frequent references to *Notes on Virginia*, to a scathing rendering of Jefferson's final prediction of success and popularity for his administration:

> Hereafter free from care, Our skiff shall glide,
> Its compass folly, theory its guide,
> Adown the stream of state.[94]

Breaches of rhetorical rules and breaches of political tradition seemed to be opposite sides of the same coin. "It is with literature, as with government," proclaimed Theodore Dehon in a Phi Beta Kappa Address at Harvard. "Neither is a subject of perpetual experiment. The principles of both are fixed." [95] In his studies of the Anthology Society, a Federalist club which established the Boston Athenaeum and lovingly published the *Monthly Anthology and Boston Review*, Lewis P. Simpson has

[94] Alsop revived *The Echo* for this purpose, a form regularly used by the Wits in the 1790's to parody newspaper items of both political and nonpolitical nature (Richard Alsop, "Echo, No. 20, March 4, 1805," *The Echo* [New York, 1807], pp. 167, 181).

[95] *Monthly Anthology and Boston Review*, IV (1807), 472. See also Lewis P. Simpson, "Federalism and the Crisis of Literary Order," *American Literature*, XXXII (November, 1960), 264.

pointed to a widely-shared certainty that there was "an analogy between the threat of democracy to political order and the danger of democracy to the organization and control of literature." This belief had its roots "in the classical concept of a universal rational order based on 'the eternal and immutable principles of natural law' "—the same faith which lay behind the creation of a constitution for a political republic. Were that order attacked, as Federalists were certain it was being attacked by Democrats, the republic which it supported and made possible was doomed; equally certain, as Simpson suggests, was the doom of the Republic of Letters.[96] What would be lost in either case was a structured society, a structured world.

Federalists began to see a pattern: astronomers replaced by roving natural historians, aimlessly searching for curiosities—bones, salt-mountains, weird forms of animal life; the formal study of the classics replaced by an unstructured and frankly vocational curriculum; respect for learning replaced by respect for the crasser forms of success. And behind the changes, a hypocrisy which refused to admit its goals; which, while ruining American culture and drastically changing American society, had the effrontery to insist that it was doing nothing at all. "They lack but two things, I suspect, / Viz. *honesty* and *intellect*."

[96] Simpson, "Federalism," pp. 253, 264.

[5]

Concepts of Law and Justice: A Case Study

There must be much law or there will be no justice.
—JOHN RUTLEDGE, JR.

All our creditors owe us, you know, many grudges;
  'Tis because we can't pay, but we've now better times.
Now the man of the people will put down their Judges;
  For there need not be courts, where there cannot be crimes.
      —*Gazette of the United States for the Country*,
          February 19, 1802

When John Adams left the presidency in 1800, he was accompanied by a stream of abuse from his own party. Divided against itself, the Federalist party had apparently accomplished its own defeat and, after the disaster of 1800, had nothing to look forward to but its own disintegration.[1] The party was all too vulnerable to Jefferson's famous inaugural appeal: "We are all Federalists, we are all Republicans"; at least the two parties had denounced John Adams with equal venom.[2] If Jefferson was

[1] The best known of these attacks is Alexander Hamilton's *Letter . . . Concerning the Public Conduct and Character of John Adams, Esq., President of the United States, Written in the Year 1800*, in which he asserted that Adams suffered from "great and intrinsic defects in his character which unfit him for the office of Chief Magistrate" ([Boston, 1809], p. 10); Page Smith, *John Adams* (New York, 1962), II, 1058.

[2] This may explain why so many Federalists insisted on discussing the Inaugural Address in terms which implied that Jefferson had said nothing else.

going to be a Federalist, Federalists might be willing to play the Republican. Underestimating the political sagacity of the new President, a number of Federalists leaped to the conclusion that Jefferson meant the first four words of his assertion literally.[3] In this, of course, they were disappointed; within less than six months the disheveled party was ready to resume its disjointed, fragmented opposition.[4]

Ironically, the despised John Adams had left his party a gift which made it possible for its members to make their opposition meaningful; a gift which protected—if that is the word—the party against disintegration; steeled it against a precipitate establishment of an Era of Good Feelings. He left the party a standard around which to rally, a cause for which to fight, an issue on which the distinctions between the parties might be polarized in the name of principle and of the Constitution. He left it, that is, the Judiciary Act of 1801, passed by a lame-duck Congress only four days before it finally made a choice between Jefferson and Burr, signed into law by a retiring President, administered by a panel of judges whose appointments were widely thought to have been sealed in the very last moments Adams spent in the White House.

Contrary to its subsequent reputation, the Judiciary Act of 1801 had been the subject of a full and responsible debate during the preceding session of Congress, and its terms represented an attempt to correct the inadequacies of the first Judiciary Act of twelve years before. A new series of circuit courts spared ven-

---

[3] Hamilton, for example, welcomed Jefferson's words as "virtually a candid retraction of past misapprehensions, and a pledge to the community that the new President will not lend himself to dangerous innovations, but in essential points tread in the steps of his predecessors" (quoted in Wilfred E. Binkley, *American Political Parties, Their Natural History* [New York, 1943], pp. 86–87).

[4] Oliver Wolcott to G[eorge] Cabot, July 27, 1801; O. Wolcott to Fisher Ames, July 27, 1801, Oliver Wolcott, Jr., Papers, Connecticut Historical Society; William Vans Murray to John Adams, June 10, 1801, APm reel 401.

erable Supreme Court justices from the trials of riding circuit. Because they might be held more frequently than the old circuit courts, the new courts would make federal justice more readily available. As Kathryn Turner has shown, the act need not be defined primarily as a last minute expedient for providing jobs for Federalist sympathizers; it was not a foregone conclusion that once they came into power the Republicans would seek, as they did, to repeal the act.[5] But if the Judiciary Act of 1801 was in fact a reasonable one, the note of desperation that runs through the debate on its repeal remains to be explained. If we are not to be content with the superficial explanation that the furor was due to a partisan willingness to make mountains out of mole-hills, how are we to understand the ardent insistence that the continuation of the republic rested on the existence, or nonexistence, of sixteen judges, maintained at an expense to each citizen of less than a penny a year?

Some of the opposition to the new system was based on the expense of maintaining new judges and court clerks. Some of it can be traced to jealousy over party patronage—why should Republicans support lifetime sinecures for Federalist appointees?

[5] Even Gouverneur Morris admitted, however, that the act lent itself to the Republican interpretation: "I have agreed heartily and cordially to the new Judiciary Bill, which may have, and probably does, many little faults; but it answers the double purpose of bringing Justice near to men's doors and of giving additional fibre to the roots of government. . . . That the leaders of the federal party may use this opportunity to provide for friends and adherents is, I think, probable, and if they were my enemies I should not condemn them for it. Whether I should do the same thing myself is another question; I believe that I should not. . . . Can they be blamed for casting many anchors to hold their ship through the storm?" (Morris to Robert Livingston, February 20, 1801, in Anne Cary Morris, ed., *The Diary and Letters of Gouverneur Morris* [New York, 1888], II, 404–405; Kathryn Turner, "Federalist Policy and the Judiciary Act of 1801," *William and Mary Quarterly*, 3d ser., XXII [1965], 3–32). See also Abigail Adams to Jefferson, July 1, 1804, APm 403; and Erwin C. Surrency, "The Judiciary Act of 1801," *American Journal of Legal History*, II (1958), 53–65.

But the debate had other dimensions, which reveal other considerations, many of them far more serious in their implications.
To understand these, we must remember that there was a substantial amount of uncertainty in regard to the specific content of
American law in the first half century of national existence.
What is legal? What may the courts do? What are the limits of
their powers and initiative? The vagueness of the judiciary article in the Constitution served to increase the frequency and
heighten the seriousness with which these questions, natural to
any new nation and new legal system, were asked.[6]

Americans' attitude toward the law was curiously ambivalent.
On the one hand, the insistence upon written constitutions and
on the principle of a government of laws, not men, implied a
confidence in the law and in the efficacy of legal protection. But
on the other hand, it is not difficult to demonstrate a widespread
and serious distrust of "pettifogging" lawyers as men who use
the letter of the law to camouflage self-interested decisions. This
ambivalence was heightened by the lack of consensus on the
proper definition of law in America, a problem which is sometimes called "The Reception Question" and refers to the degree
to which English common law was to be absorbed into American
practice.[7]

There was no question but that statutes passed by state legisla-

---

[6] Morris, who had drafted the judiciary article in the Constitution,
admitted that the issue had been blurred in the interest of compromise
and unanimity (G. Morris to Timothy Pickering, December 22, 1814,
Gouverneur Morris Private Correspondence, Letterbook IV, Library of
Congress).

[7] A concise account of the reception problem may be found in Julius
Goebel, Jr., "The Common Law and the Constitution," *Chief Justice John
Marshall: A Reappraisal,* ed. W. Melville Jones (Ithaca, N.Y., 1955), 101–
123. See also Charles Grove Haines, *The Role of the Supreme Court in
American Government and Politics: 1789–1835* (New York, 1944), pp.
125–128, 174–175, 306–308; and Anton-Hermann Chroust, *The Rise of
the Legal Profession in America,* 2 vols. (Norman, Oklahoma, 1965), I,
11–12, 17–18, 26; II, 51, 282.

tures and by Congress after 1789 were law. Nor was there question that state courts might base their decisions on acts of their own provincial congresses prior to 1789. The basis of provincial legislation had been the common law, but, as Justice Samuel Chase explained in 1798, "Each colony judged for itself, what parts of the common law were applicable." [8] As the number of lawyers and the professionalism of legal proceedings increased during the eighteenth century, so too did reliance on common law. But this development was accompanied by a reaction: a castigation of professional lawyers as opportunists who grew rich by exploiting the suffering of their clients, and of the common law itself as overcomplicated and unsuitable for the new nation. The issue was unresolved as late as Jefferson's time; critics of the common law continued to insist that the only common law properly in force within the boundaries of the United States were the various versions which each colony had integrated into its legal system at the time of its founding. They maintained that federal courts should be content to enforce federal statutory law only, lest in claiming common law jurisdiction, they take virtually all the world for their province. Critics and defenders were not readily resolvable into Republicans and Federalists; the Republican judge Spencer Roane, for example, made use of common law precedent on occasion [9] Federalist Theophilus Parsons could be found arguing that federal courts had no jurisdiction in criminal cases, and Justice Samuel Chase, who would later be impeached by a Republican Congress, announced in 1798 "that an indictment in a Federal Court could not be supported solely at common law." [10] But just at the time when party lines were be-

[8] *U.S. v. Worrall*, 2 U.S. (Dallas) 33, 341. In colonial New York, for example, the rule had been that courts were regulated by the law of England only in cases where no provincial law was applicable (Goebel and T. Raymond Naughton, *Law Enforcement in Colonial New York: A Study in Criminal Procedure: 1664–1776* [New York, 1944] pp. xvii–xviii).

[9] *Baring v. Reeder*, 1 Hen. & Mun. (Virginia) 154, 161–164.

[10] Joseph H. Smith, *Cases and Materials on the Development of Legal Institutions* (St. Paul, Minn., 1965), pp. 491–492.

ginning to solidify a number of cases posed the issue in a more than theoretical fashion, and their outcome contributed to an increasing identification of Republicans with skepticism of the import of common law and Federalists with endorsement of its extension.

The issue was posed first in 1793, when Gideon Henfield, who had enlisted on a French privateer in defiance of George Washington's Neutrality Proclamation and of international law, was indicted even though Congress had as yet passed no statutes defining his act as a crime. Although Alexander Hamilton himself drafted the indictment, and the three Federalist judges who sat on the U.S. Circuit Court in Philadelphia announced in their charge to the jury that they were *already* unanimously agreed, on the basis of common law, that "the acts of Gideon Henfield are an offense against this country, and punishable," the jury refused to find Henfield guilty. Its position was that only a statute, not common law, could make a criminal.[11] At about the same time (1792) another seaman had accepted a commission as an officer on a French warship and subsequently had been naturalized as a French citizen. When his case came to trial in the U.S. Circuit Court in Connecticut in 1799, Chief Justice Oliver Ellsworth insisted and the jury agreed that although a government might accept any foreigner desiring naturalization, according to the common law it must consent to the expatriation of its own citizens. Even greater excitement was aroused, of course, over the Sedition Act of 1798, which Federalists defended on the ground that they were merely writing into statute a jurisdiction which federal courts already held under common law. Republican reasoning had the additional effect of reinforcing the states' rights predilections with which the party was identified at

[11] Charles Warren, *The Supreme Court in United States History* (Boston, 1922), I, 112–115; the judges were James Iredell, Richard Peters, and James Wilson. Their remarks are quoted in Mark De Wolfe Howe, *Readings in American Legal History* (Cambridge, Mass., 1949), p. 328.

least since the Kentucky and Virginia Resolutions of 1799, and of strengthening its fear that the efficient enforcement of federal law by federal courts would result in the eventual displacement of state courts and the downgrading of state law. Federalists, on the other hand, tended to be less skeptical of the possibilities of extending the jurisdiction of federal courts, even to the point of insisting that federal courts had the right to develop their own case law and to evolve the precedents that would serve as federal common law. It was not accidental, therefore, that the first major battle over a substantive issue in Jefferson's first Congress erupted over the reform of the judiciary. Behind a fight over patronage lay substantial philosophical concerns; and the debate became one on the broad question of the role of the federal judiciary in the federal republic. In the course of it the Federalists closed their ranks and developed a coherent counterattack; they began, in short, to function as an opposition party.

According to the Constitution, federal judges hold office during good behavior; the precedent was an English practice established in order to make judges independent of the Crown. Federal judges are therefore guaranteed their positions unless they can be impeached and convicted of criminal misconduct. Adams's "midnight judges" might well assume that they would outlast Jefferson in office, and the Jeffersonians feared that a one-party judiciary would have little trouble avoiding the enforcement of whatever statutes a Republican Congress might pass. As Jefferson saw it, the purpose of the Judiciary Act of 1801 was to enable the Federalist party to retire "into the judiciary as a stronghold. There the remains of federalism are to be preserved and fed from the treasury, and from that battery all the works of republicanism are to be beaten down and erased. By a fraudulent use of the Constitution, which has made judges irremovable, they have multiplied useless judges merely to strengthen their phalanx." [12] It was a situation not to be borne; although he did

[12] Jefferson to John Dickinson, December 19, 1801, in Andrew A. Lipscomb, ed., *The Writings of Thomas Jefferson* (Washington, D.C.,

not mention repeal in his inaugural address, Jefferson clearly expected a Republican Congress to revoke the law quickly.[13] John Adams received an early report of the proposed technique from his nephew William Cranch, who himself held a "midnight appointment" as associate justice of the circuit court of Washington, D.C. "They contend," Cranch wrote disapprovingly, "that a person cannot hold an office which does not exist—that congress have the power of abolishing the office—and that the meaning of the words *"during good behaviour"* is during good behaviour and *the continuance of the office*. . . . When Judges hold their office during the pleasure of a Majority of Congress, a Tyranny more despotic than that of a directory may easily follow." [14] Shortly before the lame-duck Congress adjourned, the Federalists had a more formal warning: William Branch Giles rose to demand the immediate removal of the newly appointed judges. "The revolution [of 1800]," he asserted, "is incomplete so long as that strong fortress [the judiciary] is in possession of the enemy." [15]

Thus, well before the President issued a formal demand for congressional "contemplation" of "the judiciary system of the United States and especially that portion of it recently erected," Federalists were aware of Republican plans and of at least some of their reasoning, and were beginning to prepare a defense. The day before the annual message was delivered, the Washington *Federalist* published the first of five articles signed "A Friend of the Constitution." Written by William Cranch, they

---

1905), X, 302. Jefferson himself employed similar imagery; in the same letter he remarked: "My great anxiety at present is, to avail ourselves of our ascendancy to establish good principles and good practices; to fortify republicanism behind as many barriers as possible, that the outworks may give time to rally and save the citadel, should that be again in danger."

[13] Jefferson to Archibald Stuart, April 8, 1801, in Paul Leicester Ford, ed., *The Writings of Thomas Jefferson*, IX (New York, 1897), 47.

[14] William Cranch to John Adams, May 9, 1801, APm reel 400.

[15] Quoted in Albert J. Beveridge, *The Life of John Marshall* (Boston, 1919), III, 22.

were one of the earliest statements of arguments which Federalists were to reiterate frequently during the next two years.[16]

Cranch asserted that the Republicans had not been in office
long enough to acquire the sense of responsibility that should ac-
company power; rather, they had carried their partisanship into
office with them and were motivated by "the spirit of revenge." [17]
The judiciary issue was not primarily one of patronage and ex-
pendiency, as Republicans claimed; it was more basic: "the
constitution of our country is in danger." The claim that the
abolition of new circuit courts was primarily intended to save
expense was mere camouflage for a subtle attempt to create a
federal judiciary directly dependent on Congress despite the
constitutional prohibition. "Do they really hold their offices during good behavior, or at the will of Congress?" [18] The plain
meaning of good behavior tenure, Cranch insisted, was that
"they shall hold their offices until they misbehave"; and no Republican had yet charged misbehavior. Republicans might claim
that they were interested in the courts, not the judges; that if
the judges should happen to lose their seats when unnecessary
courts were abolished, the loss was a byproduct and not a goal of
the legislation; that no personal attack on the judges was intended. The man, they would say, might not be removed from
the office, but the office could be removed from the man.[19]

[16] Identification of authorship is found in Abigail Adams to T. B.
Adams, December 27, 1801, APm 401. Federalists, in fact, found the
entire annual message distasteful. Privately, John Marshall complained that
"it reduced the strength of the Government to the old Confederation," and
Jabez Upham and Uriah Tracy worked themselves into a fever by taking
turns reading the message aloud, paragraph by paragraph, and descanting
on its inadequacies to an amused audience which included Supreme Court
Justice William Cushing and his wife (Harriet Cushing to A. Adams,
December 18, 1801, APm reel 401). For Jefferson's message, see *Annals of
Congress*, 7th Cong., 1st sess., Senate, pp. 15–16, December 8, 1801.

[17] Washington *Federalist*, December 7, 1801.

[18] *Ibid.*, December 8, 1801.

[19] Or, as *The Gazette of the United States* later put it, "When you
have sworn not to drown the man, you may sink his boat from under him"

Cranch insisted that such a precedent was too dangerous to risk setting: it meant that tenure during good behavior would never again suffice to protect an "upright judge" against his political enemies, who need not bother to collect evidence for impeachment proceedings when they might erase the office out from under him. Not even the Supreme Court would be immune: though its existence was guaranteed by the Constitution, the number of its judges was established by statute, and if the Republican interpretation of congressional powers were to be accepted, the court might be packed or purged with the fluctuation of political winds. Cranch reminded his readers that the issue had been settled by the writers of the Constitution; that even anti-Federalists had wanted to make judges *more* independent of the legislature, not less. Republican judges in Virginia had, in 1787 and 1792, sucessfully resisted legislative attempts to increase their duties on the grounds that a change in the nature of their job was in fact an infringement of their tenure. He ended by citing Montesquieu as authority for the maintenance of a clear separation between legislature and the courts, citing Jefferson to the effect that "one hundred and seventy-three despots would surely be as oppressive as one," and by asking: "Will you then my fellow citizens, for the paltry gratification of wreaking vengeance on a party so grossly calumniated and which no longer governs, destroy the constitution of your country, and deprive yourselves of the security resulting from independent judges?" [20]

The other basic statement of the Federalist position came, as was only to be expected, from Alexander Hamilton, whose response to the President's Message was a detailed refutation

---

(March 22, 1802). This statement paraphrases a remark of Gouverneur Morris, to which the Republican Senator William Cocke of Tennessee replied that if a man hires a seaman to work a boat but the boat becomes rotten, "can he come forward and say, you shall pay me for working that boat, when there is none to work" (*Annals of Congress*, 7th Cong., 2nd sess., Senate, p. 58, February, 3, 1803). All references to *The Gazette of the United States* are to the semi-weekly edition, the full title of which is *The Gazette of the United States for the Country*.

[20] Washington *Federalist*, December 8, 10, 11, 12, 1801.

printed in the New York *Evening Post* under the *nom de plume* of *Lucius Crassus*. Hamilton admitted that "it is not easy to maintain that Congress cannot abolish Courts, which having been once instituted, are found in practice to be inconvenient and unnecessary," but he believed with Cranch that the issue was a constitutional one, and that if the Constitution were to be maintained, a way would have to be found to abolish the courts without removing the judges. "The proposition, that a power to do, includes virtually, a power to undo, as applied to a legislative body, is generally but not universally true. All *vested rights* form an exception to the rule." [21] There was, however, a way out: let the judges keep their offices until they retired—and then refrain from replacing them.[22] It seemed to Hamilton that the issue was not only constitutional, but political in a sense which Republicans sought to conceal. Repeal of the Judiciary Act of 1801 represented the initiation of a general attack on the competence of the federal courts. State courts had, he asserted, proved themselves to be unreliable upholders of federal law, especially in regard to treaties. The federal circuit courts were expected to force the state courts to uphold federal law more rigorously, lest they be overturned on appeal; and, by their number and frequency of sessions, make justice more easily available to the individual claimant.[23]

[21] New York *Evening Post*, January 2 and February 23, 1802. He went on to argue that when a legislature confers permanent rights, it may not undo its grant; once it creates, for example, a new state, it cannot undo its creation. "Without doubt a legislature binds itself by all those acts which engage the public faith; which confer on individuals permanent rights . . ." (*ibid.*, February 27, 1802). Similar arguments were offered in the *Gazette of the United States*, February 5, 1802.

[22] This is what the Federalists had done in reducing the number of judges on the Supreme Court in 1801. Of course, Hamilton did not mention that by the time the judges reached retirement age, the Federalist party might well be back in power.

[23] New York *Evening Post*, December 29, 1801. Hamilton was presumably thinking of the hesitancy of state courts to restore loyalist property in accordance with the Treaty of 1783. This hesitancy had made the Jay Treaty of 1795 necessary. In 1801 the Virginia courts were still processing

As Federalists saw it, the Republicans, having gained power with something less than a clear popular mandate, now sought to make major revisions not only in federal statutes, but in the judiciary system and in the interpretation of the Constitution—changes which were so serious that they would alter the balances of power in the government, changes in the constitutional arrangements which were so substantial as to be nearly revolutionary in effect. The repeal of the Judiciary Act represented both an attempt to make the judges dependent on the will of the legislature and an attempt to abolish federal courts in order to give more jurisdiction to state courts—a tendency to favor "states rights" which led Marshall to cry that the nation was returning to the days of the Articles of Confederation.[24] And repeal was accompanied by hostility to that common law which, if embodied in federal practice, would go far toward making of the United States a single and coherent legal entity. The patronage issue may have generated the smoke, but it seems clear that the constitutional issue generated the fire.[25]

---

the case that would become famous as *Hunter* v. *Fairfax's Lessee* when Marshall finally judged it in the Supreme Court in 1810.

[24] H. Cushing to A. Adams, December 18, 1801, APm reel 401.

[25] In *The Role of the Supreme Court in American Government and Politics: 1789–1835* (New York, 1944, 1960), Charles Grove Haines castigates the Federalists for disingenuous claims to the title of the real champions of popular rights; his chapter on Judiciary Repeal may be balanced by a reading to W. W. Crosskey, *Politics and the Constitution*, 2 vols. (Chicago, 1953). Crosskey is as frankly Federalist in sympathy as Haines is Republican. Both authors emphasize the intrusion of the issue of the common law into the debate: if the federal courts were to enforce common law and to be made more extensive, the United States would have an extremely powerful national judiciary. Crosskey believes that would be precisely what the Founders had intended: "The statute was . . . repealed because the men appointed were able men, and because it seemed indispensably necessary, to Jefferson and his group, to prevent these able men from explaining, in the new national courts of first instance, what 'all Cases, in Law and Equity, under the Laws of the United States,' comprehended" (II, 764).

Repeal was quickly accomplished. The first Congress of Jefferson's administration met on December 8, 1801; a month later, on January 8, 1802, the Senate opened debate on the Judiciary Act of 1801; two months later, on March 8, the final vote was taken. In the course of the debate, each party had little trouble convincing itself that its opponent's position seriously endangered the Constitution. That the excesses of political rhetoric generally associated with electioneering spilled over into what Jefferson had hoped to make an era of good feelings may in no small measure have been due to the fact that the first major debate was on so principled and substantive an issue. Federalist newspapers gave surprisingly full coverage to what was, after all, a technical subject—publishing major speeches in full, petitions with all their signatures, lengthy and vituperative editorials, and, finally, the full text of the repealing act, generally bordered in black. Within a year of Jefferson's assumption of power, Federalists had learned much about the tactics of opposition.

The most important thing they learned, perhaps, was that the Republican party was itself vulnerable; it might, if properly handled, be split at its weakest point, which was, in 1802 as in 1804 and 1807, the enigmatic figure of Vice President Aaron Burr. Burr, after private consultation with Gouverneur Morris,[26] broke a tie vote on a proposal to send the bill to committee for further consideration, thus producing, as Roger Griswold put it, "a little delay and consequently . . . [adding] to the importance of the subject." [27] The victory, everyone knew, was only temporary; as soon as the Republican absentees should return the tie would be broken and the Vice President's casting vote no longer be usable. But as a symbol of Burr's willlingness to act independently of his own party, as a hint of possible polit-

[26] A. C. Morris, II, 417, January 15, 1802.

[27] *Annals of Congress*, 7th Cong., 1st sess., Senate, pp. 149–150, January 27, 1802; Roger Griswold to O. Wolcott, February 2, 1802, Wolcott Papers.

ical alignments to come, the gesture, and Federalists knew it was a gesture, had great value.[28] Even the cynical Abigail Adams was moved: "Burr has shown us what he will do when the fate of the Country, hangs suspended upon his veto in the National Government." [29] The tangential political results of the debate on Judiciary Act repeal, then, were the opportunity it gave Burr to display his hostility to Jefferson, and the occasion it provided for a rapproachement between Burr and the Federalists which culminated in the secessionist scheme of two years later.

Cooperation with Aaron Burr was not, Federalists soon discovered, the only possible technique of bipartisanship. In Philadelphia, thirty-six of the most prominent lawyers were induced to put their names to a petition requesting the retention of the Judiciary Act on the carefully practical grounds that freedom from extensive travel gave judges more time for reflection, and that under the old system judges had often presided in states with whose laws they were unfamiliar. The new system, they asserted, provided continuity; in the past, the judge who saw the origin of the suit had seldom pronounced the final decision. Finally, since the district courts were already overscheduled, there was little prospect that they could efficiently assume the duties of the disbanded circuit courts.[30] Most of the signers were Federalists, but then, so probably were most members of the Philadelphia bar. A number of the signers were very prominent Republicans, including Alexander J. Dallas, who would be Gallatin's successor as Secretary of the Treasury; Jefferson's

---

[28] E.g., R. Griswold to O. Wolcott, February 2, 1802: "The vote . . . was possibly given with a hope that he might not be called on ultimately to decide the principal question; or if called on his conduct might appear with the semblance of candour." Several weeks later Burr appeared at a dinner held by congressional Federalists in honor of Washington's Birthday, at which he offered the cryptic toast: "The union of all honest men." See also Henry Cabot Lodge, ed., *The Works of Alexander Hamilton* (New York, 1904), X, 428–430.

[29] A. Adams to T. B. Adams, February 7, 1802, APm reel 401.

[30] *Gazette of the United States* . . . , February 9, 1802.

good friend, Peter Stephen DuPonceau; and J. B. McKean, the
son of the Republican governor of Pennsylvania.[31] But supporters of repeal in Congress readily shrugged off the bipartisan
memorial; in the words of Senator James Jackson of Georgia, it
proved only that "there was one point upon which lawyers of all
parties agreed, that of *getting at the fees:* it was well said in this
house that the multiplication of courts multiplied litigation—
and it was natural to think that, as the Philadelphia bar expressed it, they consider it a *professional duty* to support a
source of profits." [32]

The Philadelphia memorial received bipartisan endorsement
only because it ignored the constitutional issues and stressed the
practical uses of additional federal courts. When, however, the
Philadelphia bar appealed, through Alexander Hamilton, to
their colleagues in New York, Hamilton chose not to follow
their example. He did call a bipartisan meeting of the New
York bar at Little's Hotel on February 11, but he did not hide
his lack of enthusiasm about memorials, and his remarks at the
meeting emphasized the possible unconstitutionality of the repeal bill, an issue on which the parties could not, by this time, be
expected to agree. Therefore, although leading Republicans like
Chancellor John Lansing and state Chief Justice Morgan Lewis
were critical of repeal, the Republican lawyers at Little's Hotel
stalked out of Hamilton's meeting and prepared a formal mi

[31] These signatures could not have been given lightly, for the bulk of
rank-and-file Republican opinion in Pennsylvania clearly favored repeal.
T. B. Adams, himself a lawyer in Philadelphia, was restrained from adding
his name by "the older gentlemen of the profession," who feared that an
Adams signature could only harm their cause. Nor was the signature needed
to make a respectably lengthy list. "The Bar of Philadelphia," Adams
reported, "almost to a man, signed or would have signed, if necessary"
(T. B. Adams to John Adams, February 15, 1802, APm reel 401;
Gazette of the United States, February 5, 1802; Sanford W. Higgin-
botham, *The Keystone in the Democratic Arch: Pennsylvania Politics
1800–1816* [Harrisburg, Pa., 1952], p. 42).

[32] *Gazette of the United States,* February 12, 1802.

nority report endorsing the official Republican position.[33] Other
memorials drifted into Congress—from the New Jersey bar,
from the Chambers of Commerce of New York and Philadelphia. But only the Philadelphia memorial was bipartisan, and
was discounted even there on the grounds that it was intended
to deflect Federalist attention from the multiple offices being
awarded Republican claimants for patronage. Bipartisanship
was a stillborn technique in 1802.

The notion that the repeal of the Judiciary Act in effect transferred to state courts cases that were the proper business of federal courts had first been suggested in Alexander Hamilton's
Lucius Crassus essays. Jefferson had tried to deflect this criticism; he accompanied his request for repeal with a tabulation of
the cases handled under the old system and argued that the
combination of state courts plus Supreme Court justices riding
circuit was efficient enough to obviate the necessity for new federal courts. Not even Republicans could deny that the number of
cases brought before the federal courts was increasing, but a
great number were post-Revolution lawsuits brought by British
creditors, and cases arising under the Alien and Sedition Acts—
both varieties soon likely to end. "I am inclined to think," remarked John Breckinridge, who introduced the repeal bill in
the Senate, " . . . that the time never will arrive when America
will stand in need of thirty-eight federal judges. Look, sir, at
your Constitution, and see the judicial power there consigned to
federal courts, and seriously ask yourself, can there be fairly extracted from those powers subjects of litigation sufficient for six
supreme and thirty-two inferior court judges?" [34]

[33] *Ibid.*, February 23, 1802; New York *Evening Post*, February 12, 17,
1802; Theodore Sedgwick to Rufus King, February 20, 1802, in Charles
R. King, ed., *The Life and Correspondence of Rufus King* (New York,
1897), IV, 73. In 1804 Hamilton was to urge Federalists to support
Lansing (who refused to run) or Lewis in preference to Aaron Burr for
the post of Governor of New York.

[34] *Annals of Congress*, 7th Cong., 1st sess., p. 26, Senate, January 8,
1802.

Federalists, on the other hand, pointed to the continually increasing amount of litigation as justification for an increased number of courts, questioned Jefferson's statistics, and reasoned that the attempt to abolish circuit courts was in fact an attempt to impede the efficient operation of the federal judiciary. This note was sounded in the very first Federalist speech on the subject, made by Jonathan Mason of Massachusetts on January 8, 1802: "Is it possible, that suits will go on diminishing as the gentleman seems to think? Is reason so predominant? Is the millenium so near at hand? On the contrary, is not our commerce increasing with great rapidity? Is not our wealth increasing? And will not controversies arise in proportion to the growth of our numbers and property? controversies, which will go to the federal tribunals, as soon as the judiciary system is fully established?" [35] In the House, John Rutledge, Jr., turned the contention into a matter of principle. "In a nation so great, and so growing in its greatness as ours is; among a people so commercial, so enterprising, and so attached to right as are the people of this country, there must be much law or there will be no justice." [36] The last phrase could not help but be anathema to men who believed, as a good number of Republicans did, that "the present age is in as much danger from lawyers, as the three last have been the victims of priests," but it was a graceful statement of a serious Federalist conviction.[37] Gouverneur Morris had endorsed the passage of the Judiciary Act of 1801 on the grounds that it brought "justice near to men's doors"; a writer in the Washington *Federalist* had similarly defended the act by citing the need for new courts "throughout the Union, to bring the authority of the Federal Judiciary closer to the feelings, understanding, and affections of all the citizens." [38] In the debate

[35] *Ibid.*, p. 34.

[36] *Ibid.*, House, p. 744, February 24, 1802.

[37] *Aurora*, February 12, 1802.

[38] G. Morris to Robert Livingston, February 20, 1801, in A. C. Morris, II, 405; Washington *Federalist*, February 26, 1801.

on repeal, the issue was placed in still larger perspective by Uriah Tracy:

Is the expense an object, when by that expense we extend the jurisdiction of a court over this vastly extensive, growing country, and carry law and protection to every man? This country is in a singular condition; a great tract of unsettled lands is peopling with rapidity, and numerous emigrations increase our population far beyond its natural increase; is it not of importance that courts should be located among them, early, to correct the restless spirit which is frequent in new and scattered settlements? And are not the emigrations composed of such as require the prompt assistance of the law, to preserve among them regularity? . . . to prevent crimes, is the work of a God.[39]

None of Tracy's hearers could have missed the implications of his remarks. In a brilliant chapter, Perry Miller has shown how James Fenimore Cooper's *The Pioneers* dramatized a basic conflict in the American mind, a conflict between Leatherstocking, child of nature, who trusts his instincts and acts according to them, and Judge Temple, who trusts only the law.[40] The judge can never make his peace with the wilderness—the American wilderness, by which is meant not just natural foliage but natural man. He must seek, in order to be comfortably at peace with himself, to hedge natural man about with the restraints of law much as others are at the same time restraining the wilderness, the country of dream and of nightmare, by laying railroad track and cutting canals until it is "tamed," that is, until it is wilderness no longer. If the jungle is ruined, so perhaps is the garden. Cooper was not certain which side he was on; his heart was

[39] *Annals of Congress*, 7th Cong. 1st sess., Senate, p. 54, January 12, 1802. A less orotund statement of this difficulty was made by Robert G. Harper in one of his regular letters to his constituents, February 26, 1801, in Elizabeth Donnan, ed., "Papers of James A. Bayard, 1796–1815," *Annual Report of the American Historical Association for the Year 1913* (Washington, 1915), II, 138–139.

[40] Perry Miller, *The Life of the Mind in America* (New York, 1965), Book II, Chapter 1, pp. 99–116.

with Leatherstocking, his head with the Judge. But politicians like Tracy could seldom afford ambivalence, and Tracy spoke for the Judge quite as well as Cooper would: "Is it not of importance that courts should be located . . . early, to correct the restless spirit? . . . to prevent crimes, is the work of a God."

Once again, the national consensus broke on the subject of the western wilderness. Was it an asset? Was it to be permitted to grow at its own pace, to be speculated upon by those who settled there? Or was the East to seek to make over the West (raw nature, as close to primeval chaos as it was given the American to experience) into its own image—the work, even Tracy admitted, of a God? The conflict was the old one between big government and small, states rights and nationalism, on a larger scale. The more power claimed for the federal government and the more it was proclaimed that government is capable of wielding that power, the less humble the assumption of what men can do. Was not the essence of the Republican objection to consolidated, centralized government on the Federalist model that men who could handle such enormous prerogatives would have to be gods? that the Federalist assumption that they knew what was right for the nation came perilously close to playing God?

Breckinridge was one of the few who dared attack Tracy directly, and on his own ground:

I confess I am now for the first time to learn, that to inspire terror and prevent wrongs you ought to imbody an army of judges; and that to support or discourage litigation, you ought to imbody another set of men, their general attendants, called lawyers, who, it seems, for the first time, are to become peace makers; who, with their robes and green bags, will strike such terror into the nation, that a purse of gold may hang in safety on the highway. Halcyon days these, indeed.[41]

Republicans like Breckinridge suspected that Tracy's arguments camouflaged a defense of federal common law jurisdiction. How

[41] *Annals of Congress*, 7th Cong., 1st sess., Senate, p. 97, January 14, 1802.

could more courts and lawyers prevent crime, they asked, when the courts were to be federal ones whose statutory jurisdiction was strictly limited by the Constitution? Unless, of course, it was intended that those courts claim the broader common law jurisdiction, a jurisdiction which Republicans were willing to trust only to state courts. Federalists, gingerly, claimed exactly that. "Stripped of the common law," asserted James A. Bayard in a major speech which received high praise from John Adams,[42] "there would be neither Constitution nor Government. The Constitution is unintelligible without reference to the common law. And were we to go into our courts of justice with the mere statutes of the United States, not a step could be taken, not even a contempt could be punished. Those statutes prescribe no forms of pleadings; they contain no principles of evidence; they furnish no rule of property. If the common law does not exist in most cases, there is no law but the will of the judge." [43] Bayard did not claim that the common law had been swallowed whole by the American judicial system; ". . . only such parts as were consonant to the nature and spirit of our Government. . . . What belongs to us, and what is unsuitable, is a question for the sound discretion of the judges." This was, of course, a discretion which no Republican thought a federal judge should have. Bayard, it must be added, proceeded to weaken his case, and end

[42] John Adams to Bayard, April 10, 1802, in Donnan, p. 152.

[43] *Annals of Congress*, 7th Cong., 1st sess., House, pp. 613–614, February 19, 1802. John Randolph had little difficulty reducing this argument to absurdity: "That the common law is to settle the meaning of common law phrases, few will feel disposed to deny: that when the Constitution uses the term 'court,' it does not mean 'jury,' and that by 'jury,' is not intended to express 'court,' seems plain enough. . . . But because the common law is to be resorted to for an explanation of these and similar terms, does it follow that the indefinite and undefinable body of law is the irrepealable law of the land? The sense of a most important phrase, '*direct tax*,' as used in the Constitution, has been, it is believed, settled by the acceptation of Adam Smith. . . . Does the Wealth of Nations, therefore, form a part of the Constitution of the United States?" (*ibid.*, p. 652, February 20, 1802).

all possibility of swaying the opposition, by insisting that Republicans refused common law jurisdiction to federal courts primarily as part of their general program to weaken the government wherever possible, and ended by expressing the hope that the judges would have the courage to declare a new judiciary act unconstitutional. "If, sir, I am called to take my side, standing acquitted in my conscience and before my God, of all motives but the support of the Constitution of my country," Bayard added gratuitously, "I shall not tremble at the consequences. . . . There are many now willing to spill their blood to defend that Constitution." [44]

Threats of this nature could only discredit the Federalist case. Most Federalist speakers assiduously avoided Bayard's tone, at least in their public utterances. They contented themselves with reiteration of arguments based on constitutionality, practicability, and sweet reasonableness. Let us at least give the new system a trial, begged Benjamin Huger of South Carolina. "Would it not tend to do away, in a great measure, [with] the baneful effect of party, and to promote harmony among our fellow-citizens, if in the changes of men and of parties, which must necessarily take place in the administration of public affairs, we accustomed ourselves to act with some little delicacy towards each other?" [45] In general, Federalists emphasized the inadequacies of state courts rather than the need for enlarging the jurisdiction of federal courts. If the federal judiciary were decreased in size, obviously the slack would be taken up by state courts, a prospect which Republicans often found pleasing. One senator confessed, for example,

he should feel as secure in the decision of the State judges in even federal questions, with an appeal to the Supreme Federal Court, as in

[44] *Ibid.*, p. 648. A detailed account of Bayard's role in the debate is found in Morton Borden, *The Federalism of James A. Bayard* (New York, 1955), pp. 106–125.

[45] *Annals of Congress*, 7th Cong., 1st sess., House, p. 677, February 23, 1802.

the present judges; and indeed the Constitution, in the fourth article, second section, which imposes on all State judges the oath to observe the Constitution and laws of the United States, always seemed
to him to consider the State courts in a certain degree judges of federal questions.[46]

Federalists were more distressed at the prospect. "What!" cried
Aaron Ogden of New Jersey, "are we so poor that the United
States must thus ask alms from the individual States, by declining to continue a proper provision for . . . courts?" Already
convinced that their opponents were hostile to an efficient, "energetic," government, Federalists tended to ascribe Republican
hostility to the Judiciary Act of 1801 to a desire to weaken federal agencies for the benefit of the states. Ogden warned that
the next step would be to permit state courts to decide "Constitutional questions between the General Government and State
Governments," in which event the nation would be "thrown
back. . . to that state of things which existed under the Old
Confederation." [47] In the House, Bayard and other Federalists
displayed similiar concern for the maintenance of the primacy of
federal courts, similar fears that Republicans were anxious to
permit state courts to declare federal law invalid, similar insistence that the enlarged federal judiciary system of 1801 was the
only guarantee of judicial review. If the judges were to function
as a check on Congress, then Congress, though it might check
the judges, surely might not remove them. The issue was broader
than the claim of thirty-three men to jobs and salaries. What
Congress was witnessing, in the attempt to repeal the Judiciary Act of 1801, was an attempt to make the federal government less capable, less "energetic," an attempt to make federal
justice less available—all for the benefit of local government.
The danger was a reversion to the habits of the old Confederation. "State pride," Bayard warned, "extinguishes a national sen-

[46] Robert Wright, of Maryland, *ibid.*, Senate, p. 116, January 15,
1802.
[47] *Ibid.*, pp. 173–174, February 3, 1802.

timent. Whatever is taken from this Government is given to the States." [48]

That the ready availability of federal justice operated to underwrite continued economic prosperity was a point testified to by the petitions of New York and Philadelphia merchants, and by the fluctuations of Washington real estate values. The editor of the *Gazette of the United States* complained from Washington that the sale of city lots declined during the debate, because prospective buyers feared for the stability of their property were the independence of the judiciary to be tampered with.[49] John Rutledge predicted that repeal would ruin public confidence further afield than Washington. "Who will buy your lands? Who will open your Western forests? . . . He must be a speculator indeed, and his purse must overflow, who would buy your Western lands and city lots, if there be no independent tribunals where the validity of your titles will be confirmed." [50]

The Federalist *idée fixe* that Republican programs were essentially a reflection of Virginian and southern policy inevitably

[48] *Ibid.*, p. 605, House, February 19, 1802. Robert G. Harper pointed out that the impossibility of riding circuit in the wilderness of Kentucky, Tennessee, and Maine had put an effectual stop to the system even when it was officially in force, and that state courts had in those regions informally taken over federal functions. Since "new settlements and states are perpetually forming in our frontier territories" the problem, and its unorthodox solution, might be expected to persist. The Judiciary Act of 1801 was unpopular with Republicans, he said, because of "its tendency to give stability and dignity to the general government, and to render it independent of state influence and control" (Harper to his constituents, February 26, 1801, in Donnan, II, 138–140).

[49] *Annals of Congress*, 7th Cong., 1st sess., House, p. 743 (Rutledge), February 24, 1802; *Gazette of the United States* . . . , February 23, 1802. Since the sale of city lots in Washington had never been high, it is possible the editor was indulging in wishful thinking. So too, however, was John Cotton Smith, in a letter to Tapping Reeve, March 8, 1802, E. A. Park MSS, Box 3, Yale University Library.

[50] *Annals of Congress*, 7th Cong., 1st sess., House, p. 759, February 25, 1802.

intruded itself into the economic argument. Benjamin Tallmadge thought that the debate at least had the merit of exposing "the aspiring views of the ancient Dominion." Roger Griswold, who defined repeal as a program intended to change the Constitutional balances to the detriment of the judiciary and in favor of the legislature, thought repeal had been proposed in the expectation that "the predominating influence of Virginia . . . [could be counted on to] triumph [in the House of Representatives]. . . . The Virginians have denounced the judiciary," concluded the editor of the *Gazette of the United States*, "and it must be sacrificed. The equality of the states is to be preserved by the independency of the Judiciary—and, because the Lords of the ancient dominion don't really believe the small states equal to Virginia, they have bound the Judiciary and will immolate it on the altar of ambition and resentment."[51]

This argument could hardly be expected to appeal to Virginians and other southern Federalists, and John Rutledge of South Carolina substituted one which spoke to their condition more directly. His appeal would later be associated with John Randolph of Roanoke, and eventually with John C. Calhoun; in Rutledge's speeches it appears in unlikely connection with consideration of judiciary reform. As we have seen, the argument that repeal would change constitutional balances and set unfortunate precedents had long since become standard Federalist equipment. But Rutledge gave it a new twist. If the Congress could deprive judges of seats which were constitutionally guaranteed for good behavior, it could pass other acts prohibited by the Constitution, including acts relating to slavery and the slave trade. "I call upon gentlemen from the Southern States to look well to this business," Rutledge cried. "If they persevere in frittering away the honest meaning of the Constitution by their

[51] Benjamin Tallmadge to Jeremiah Wadsworth, March 2, 1802, Jonathan Trumbull, Jr., Papers, Conn. Hist. Soc.; R. Griswold to O. Wolcott, March 5, 1802, Oliver Wolcott, Jr., Papers; *Gazette of the United States . . .* , February 23, 1802.

forced implications, this clause [re: slave trade] . . . is a mere dead letter." [52]

As the debate wore on, Federalist pronouncements became ever gloomier. "All the measures recommended by the President," sighed Oliver Wolcott, "form a consistent plan of mischief." [53] Repeal of the judiciary system, the removal of Federalist appointees, the attempt to abolish the mint, the abolition of internal taxes, were all part of a program which aimed at "breaking down all the internal Machinery of the government." [54] Federalists suspected Republicans of wanting federal justice weakened in order to free them from its restraints so that they could embark on an essentially unconstitutional political program, about whose details the Federalists were uncertain, but about whose unfortunate effects they were sure.

This interpretation inevitably encouraged the Federalist sense of righteousness. The most obvious constitutional interpretation for an opposition party is strict construction, and Federalists shifted to it without giving evidence of understanding that they

---

[52] *Annals of Congress*, 7th Cong., 1st sess., House, pp. 747 ff., February 25, 1802. Rutledge denied that his analogy was far fetched; he feared abolition might well be part of Jefferson's general program, for it was well known, he said, that Jefferson "held opinions respecting a certain species of property in my State, which . . . would endanger it." Northern Federalists criticized Jefferson for representing a slave society, and southern Federalists could as readily criticize him for his antislavery sentiments. Jefferson was in his lifetime, as he would be after his death, as much an image as a man, a political symbol as well as a practical politician. Federalists, especially those of uncompromising views, tended to treat him more as symbol than as reality.

[53] O. Wolcott to R. Griswold, February 2, 1802, Wolcott Papers.

[54] T. Sedgwick to R. King, February 20, 1802, in C. R. King, IV, 73. In *Salmagundi*, Irving denounced retrenchment as "a kind of national Starvation; an experiment how many comforts and necessities the body politic can be deprived of before it perishes. It . . . promises to share the fate of the Arabian philosopher, who proved that he could live without food, but unfortunately died just as he had brought his experiment to perfection" (March 7, 1807 [London, 1811], I, 88).

had undergone a shift. Federalist rhetoric of 1802 reveals this blindness. Sedgwick, for example, could criticize repeal on the ground that by implying easy amendment of constitutional balances and by weakening one branch of the government, it "establishes a principle of a complete consolidation of all national & state authority," without displaying the slightest awareness that Republicans could argue that the Federalists' enlargement of the court system had had precisely the same effect.[55] Gouverneur Morris became the most ardent of spokesmen for this point of view. When Republicans attacked what Breckinridge called "this pretended power of the courts to annul the laws of Congress," Morris responded both with a defense of judicial review and with the counteraccusation that his opponents sought to assign all constitutional determinations to Congress. If the courts could not rule on constitutionality, he argued, "the sovereignty of America will no longer reside in the people, but in the Congress, and the Constitution is whatever they choose to make it. . . . what safety is left for the States? . . . if a consolidated Government be established, it cannot long be republican. We have not the materials to construct even a mild monarchy. If, therefore, the States be destroyed, we must become the subjects of despotism." [56] Nor did Morris discard this contention; nearly two years after the heat of debate had dissipated he was writing privately that the result of judiciary act repeal had been

---

[55] T. Sedgwick to R. King, February 20, 1802, in C. R. King, IV, 73. Jefferson had warned, privately, in the summer of 1800: "And I do verily believe, that if the principle were to prevail, of a common law being in force in the United States (which principle possesses the General Government at once of all the powers of the state governments, and reduces us to a single consolidated government) it would become the most corrupt government on the earth" (Thomas Jefferson to Gideon Granger, August 13, 1800, in H. A. Washington, ed., *The Writings of Thomas Jefferson* [New York, 1854], IV, 331).

[56] *Annals of Congress*, 7th Cong., 1st sess., Senate, pp. 179, 181–182; February 3, 1802. See also G. Morris to R. Livingston, March 20, 1802, in A. C. Morris, II, 423–424.

to transfer "the complete sovereignty of America" to the House of Representatives. "Now, as in political affairs fact supersedes right, the Senate will not, generally speaking, have even the wish to oppose the House of Representatives. The States will, by degrees, sink more and more into insignificance." [57]

Such remarks, of course, document the truism that in the history of American political theory a concern for states rights has more frequently marked the differences between the party in power and the party out of power than it has represented permanent differences in political philosophy. But that Federalists could comfortably deliver themselves of such remarks also suggests that the two parties had begun to talk past each other in a way that vitiated the possibility of true debate. The absence of real debate in Congress may well have been the inevitable result of a two party arrangement in which one party held an overwhelming majority. But the rareness of public debate, coupled with an increasing reliance on what James Sterling Young has called the "boardinghouse caucus," [58] contributed to Federalists' disenchantment with politics. For many Federalists, the judiciary issue appears to have crystallized a growing disillusionment with Jeffersonian politics. North Carolina's four Federalist congressmen (Archibald Henderson, William Barry Grove, John Stanly and William H. Hill) ignored the instructions of their Republican state legislature to support repeal; none was reelected.[59] John Rutledge, Jr., furnished the Charleston *Courier* with a long apologia for his refusal to stand for reelection, partly because redistricting by Republicans had made his success

[57] G. Morris to Henry Livingston, November 25, 1803, in A. C. Morris, II, 442.

[58] In *The Washington Community: 1800–1828* (New York, 1966), James Sterling Young argues that party caucuses were not yet operative in the Jeffersonian period. Congressional members tended to group themselves by region and political alignment in their boardinghouses and voted with their boardinghouse colleagues fairly consistently.

[59] B. P. Robinson, *William Richardson Davie* (Chapel Hill, 1957), p. 362.

unlikely, partly because of the issues raised by the judiciary debates. The nation had declined, said Rutledge, since the days of the Constitutional Convention, which had been "filled with great and virtuous men." The current administration, in contrast, "is almost avowedly a party government. . . . The constitution itself is threatened with great alteration, tending to restrict the powers of the national government, at the expense of the smaller, and for the aggrandizement of the larger states. . . . Under the circumstances, I do not feel it incumbent on me to remain a reluctant witness of the steps by which the narrow views of a party administration may render the government imbecile at home and degraded abroad." [60] Even the indefatigable Fisher Ames, who had so cheerfully marshaled Federalists for battle in 1801, gave way to despair within two years. "I renounce the wrangling world of politics," he vowed, "and devote myself in future to pigs and poultry. I will not be a Tom Paine on the federal side." [61] In a revealing letter to Oliver Wolcott he confessed: "I am not a patriot *by trade*. I do not pretend to love my country well enough to die for it, *very soon*. At seventy or eighty, I might agree to die for it. But, *ad interim*, I would not desert my wife nor starve my children to shew my patriotism. . . . I am fated to grow, like a peach tree, in my own garden, with a vigor that wastes the root, to yield fruits that soon perish, and to give place in a few years to a cabbage stump. . . . I consider myself in this crisis of the public danger, not as one of the effectives, but as belonging to the alarm list." [62] This disenchantment was expressed in a variety of ways. The Charleston, South Carolina, *Courier* found in Addison a motto for the attitude of men like Rutledge: "When vice prevails, and impious men bear sway, / The post of honor is a private station." Others, like Roger Griswold, moved in the direction of secession, in

---

[60] Charleston, S.C., *Courier*, February 2, 1803.

[61] Fisher Ames to O. Wolcott, March 9, 1803; Oliver Wolcott, Jr., Papers.

[62] *Ibid.*, December 2, 1802.

an attempt, it may be surmised, to create a homogeneous state
where debate would be unnecessary; still others, like John
Quincy Adams, entered Republican ranks, to participate in the
debate within the Republican party as it drifted toward the Era
of Good Feelings over which James Monroe would painfully
preside.

> Who kill'd Poor Jude?
> Alas! such a band
> As disgraces the land!—
> Poor murder'd Jude! [63]

Federalists were unable to prevent repeal, which was accomplished on March 8. Their newspapers took the defeat very
much to heart: "ALL IS LOST!" mourned the *Gazette of the
United States* in a black-bordered issue.[64] The *Baltimore Anti-
Democrat* sighed "FAREWELL A LONG FAREWELL TO ALL OUR
GREATNESS," [65] and the *Port Folio* proposed a coat of arms for
the United States: "Justice bleeding couchant, her scales broken
. . . Motto, *Ruat Justitia.*" [66] Threats of secession, predictions
of civil war, accusations that there existed a "Virginia plot" to
undermine the Constitution permeated the Federalist analysis of
their defeat. "We may submit for a season," threatened the *Gazette of the United States*, "to the domination of judges whose
only law is the will of a faction on whom they are conscious of
dependence for their powers and their salaries. But this period
cannot be long. . . . Let what will ensue, the blood of our
country must be upon the heads of those who now govern." [67]
The *Anti-Democrat* jumped to the conclusion that the real purpose of repeal was to help "to bring about a general dissolution

[63] "Poor Jude, Or The Death of the Judiciary, An Amplified Parody of
the Celebrated Song of Cock Robin" (Hudson, New York), *Wasp*,
November 25, 1802.

[64] *Gazette of the United States* . . . , March 12, 1802.

[65] Reprinted in *Port Folio*, March 13, 1802.

[66] *Ibid.*

[67] *Gazette of the United States* . . . , March 12, 1802.

of the union. Virginia . . . will not be content, without holding
in hand the reins of the general government; New England will
never submit to be a colony of Virginia." The writer deplored
the prospect; he thought that "the rapid progress of America to
a state of incivilization" might be dated from the moment of
secession.[68] Nor did John Adams think radical results impossible; with repeal, he told James A. Bayard, "ambition, avarice
and revenge will snap the strongest cords of our Constitution as
a whale goes through a net." [69]

Alexander Hamilton shared Adams's view that repeal posed a
serious threat to continued constitutional stability, and added to
it the fear of an extremist reaction in the direction of secession.
"There are among us incorrect men with very incorrect views,"
he wrote guardedly to Charles Cotesworth Pinckney, "which
may lead to combinations and projects injurious to us as a party
and very detrimental to the country." Responsible leaders,
Hamilton thought, should organize the opposition to repeal,
and he called for a meeting "of leading Federalists from different States" concurrently with the next meeting of the Society of
the Cincinnati on May 1 in Washington, D.C., to devise "constitutional means to produce a revocation . . . and to restore the
Constitution." [70] But Hamilton had no practicable plan to propose, and the Cincinnati met and disbanded without taking up
the subject of the judiciary.[71]

[68] Reprinted in the *Port Folio*, March 13, 1802.

[69] John Adams to Bayard, April 10, 1802, APm reel 118.

[70] Hamilton to Charles Cotesworth Pinckney, March 15, 1802, in
Lodge, X, 429. Hamilton included a similar warning against Burrite
intrigues in a letter to Bayard, dated after April 12, 1802 (Hamilton
Papers, Library of Congress microfilm). See also Bayard to Hamilton, April
12, 1802, Hamilton Papers. Pinckney received Hamilton's letter too late
to make the trip to Washington, and Governor William Richardson Davie
of North Carolina, also invited, was preoccupied with a death in his family
(Pinckney to Hamilton, May 3, 1802, Hamilton Papers).

[71] *Gazette of the United States*, May 11, 1802. Hamilton, who offered
his draft constitution for a Christian Constitutional Society at this time, was
elected President-General; Charles Cotesworth Pinckney was elected Vice
President-General.

The apocalyptic interpretation was not, however, the only one possible. William Vans Murray explained the excesses of Federalist denunciation of repeal as part of the aftermath of the political shock of Jefferson's election. "To be in a minority is a new situation to them. Hitherto they have been a majority & have had a Chief & that Chief in Power," he explained to Rufus King. Now they needed a leader: "It may be hoped that the Feds will gain wisdom by suffering." And Gouverneur Morris provided perspective for a French friend: fulmination and overstatement were a necessary part of free debate, and not to be taken overly seriously. "Do not . . . imagine that we are on the brink of civil war, or even agitated by violent commotions. On the contrary, no republic was ever more quiet. . . . Freedom and tranquility are seldom companions." [72]

Although secession was a word with which Federalists were becoming increasingly familiar, it was probably not a real political alternative in 1802. Among those who still searched for a political answer were those most directly affected by repeal—the judges themselves. The Supreme Court justices were distressed; although their offices were not threatened, they would have to resume riding circuit. The most ardent opponents of repeal suggested that the justices force the issue by refusing to ride circuit during the next session. "How can you hold those [circuit] courts while constitutional judges remain with commissions under the constitution during good behavior," asked a letter-writer in the *Gazette of the United States*. "Could you venture to try a criminal under a doubtful authority . . . [?] You must determine between the legislature and the people." [73] John Marshall took the suggestion seriously enough to poll the court; he found them unenthusiastic about returning to the circuit, but all, except the ever-vitriolic Samuel Chase, were even more hesi-

[72] William Vans Murray to R. King, April 5, 1802, in C. R. King, IV, 95; G. Morris to the Princess de la Tour et Taxis, June 20, 1802, in A. C. Morris, II, 425.

[73] Letter signed "Z," *Gazette of the United States* . . . , April 9, 1802.

tant about refusing.[74] William Cushing, who privately believed that Adams's "System had placed the Judiciary upon the best foundation that could be easily devised," put the case for acquiescence most succinctly:

Can We, after Eleven years practical exposition of the Laws & Constitution by all federal Judges, now say, that Congress has not power to direct a Judge of the Sup Court to act with a Dt [District] Judge in an inferiour Court . . . yet making one of the Sup. bench to hold appellate Jurisdiction? I think we cannot. . . . It is not in our power to restore to them their Salaries or them to the exercise of their Offices. Declining the Circuits will have no tendency to do either. We violate not the Constitution. We only do duties assigned us by Constitutional authority. Suppose we apply or represent or remonstrate to the President; what can he say? "Gent. There is the Law. I cannot control Congress." And you & I know *We*—cannot control the Majority.[75]

If the party's political leaders and their "brethren" on the Supreme Court found it impossible to restore salaries to the circuit judges or "them to their offices," perhaps the judges could accomplish the feat themselves. While the rumor persisted that the Supreme Court might refuse to ride circuit, some circuit court judges began to think that they might be able to hold

[74] Chase took the strongest stand, but even he was ready to be voted down: "I cannot hesitate one moment betweent [*sic*] a performance of my duty, & the loss of Office. If my Bretheren [on the court] should differ from me in opinion & I should only *doubt*, what conduct I shall pursue, will readily submit my judgment to theirs . . . [*sic*]" (Chase to John Marshall, quoted in H. Cushing to A. Adams, June 25, 1802, APm reel 401).

[75] W. Cushing to John Adams, June 9, 1802, APm 401; W. Cushing to Samuel Chase, quoted in H. Cushing to A. Adams, June 25, 1802, APm 401. Refusal, of course, might well mean impeachment and, with it, the loss of office. Cushing's wife suggested that the Justices might have been more willing to act had they held separate commissions for their circuit court duties, which they might resign without endangering the more important appointment to the Supreme Court bench (H. Cushing to A. Adams, September 2, 1802, APm reel 401).

their own courts in defiance of repeal.[76] Such action however, would make them liable to impeachment, which the Senate would surely confirm, and the attempt was never made.[77] But the judges did seek to plan "uniformity of conduct in resisting repeal, justifying their opposition on the mild grounds that they wanted to establish "that they are not responsible, for the consequences, of a passive surrender of the public rights constitutionally committed to their protection." [78]

At the urging of William Tilghman of the Third Circuit, Oliver Wolcott began to prepare a brief for the ousted judges and to draft a petition which most of the "midnight judges" would eventually sign and present to Congress. Eleven copies of a petition generally similar to Wolcott's draft, each signed by a midnight judge, were presented to the Senate on January 27, 1803; they were immediately referred to a committee of three Federalists—Gouverneur Morris, Jonathan Dayton, and James Ross.[79] But even these doughty defenders of the Act of 1801 had to report that the issue had been fully settled in Congress and that debate could not be reopened. They approved, how-

[76] O. Wolcott to R. Griswold, March 23, 1802, Lane MSS, Yale University Library.

[77] *Port Folio*, May 1, 1802. Evidently John Marshall did not encourage any attempt by any Federal court to ignore repeal, but he did define the Circuit Court judges as men who still held their offices, but had to wait until the legislature should choose to *redefine* their duties and *renew* their powers. See Hamilton to Pinckney, April 25, 1802, in Warren, I, 224–225n.

[78] O. Wolcott to William Tilghman, June 25, 1802, Wolcott Papers. William Tilghman wrote to Wolcott on May 22, 1802, proposing a meeting of the Circuit judges in Philadelphia on July 17; Wolcott replied that he could not attend. Another meeting was evidently called for November, but there is no clear evidence of whether it was held or who attended it. This episode is discussed in Linda K. Kerber, "Oliver Wolcott, Midnight Judge," *Bulletin of the Connecticut Historical Society*, XXXII (January, 1967), 25–30.

[79] *Annals of Congress*, 7th Cong., 2d sess., Senate, pp. 30–32. See also *ibid.*, House, pp. 432, 434, 439.

ever, the memorialists' suggestion that their right to continuing
salaries should be tested in the courts, and therefore suggested
"that the President . . . be requested to cause an information, in
the nature of a *quo warranto,* to be filed by the Attorney General against Richard Bassett; one of the said petitioners, for the
purpose of deciding judicially on their claims." [80]

It may well be imagined that a Republican Congress (and
even those Federalist members who had not been forewarned of
the scheme) greeted the committee's report in thunderstruck silence. The proposal was so novel that basic definitions had to be
provided; Aaron Ogden of New Jersey turned to his Blackstone
to refresh failing legal memories. A quo warranto was a writ
served on one who "claims or usurps" an office, requiring him to
defend his claim in court; and an "information in the nature of
a *quo warranto,*" was a legal procedure which was originally "a
criminal method of prosecution, as to punish the usurper by fine
for the usurpation of the franchise, as to oust him, or seize it for
the Crown, but hath long been applied to the mere purposes of
trying the civil right, seizing the franchise, or ousting the
wrongful owner—the fine being nominal only." In short, the
quo warranto provided a test case.[81]

But quo warranto, as even its supporters admitted, was not
known to American statutes. It was known only to common law,
and could be justified only by arguing that according to Section
14 of the Judiciary Act of 1789, federal courts had the power to
issue standard writs not specially provided for by statute, and

[80] *Ibid.,* Senate, February 3, 1803, pp. 51–52. Richard Bassett was
probably singled out for the honor of carrying on the test case because he
alone among the judges had published an extended rebuttal of the
repealing act. Bassett was the father-in-law of Bayard, who led the opposition to repeal in the House, and to whom he was indebted for the
judgeship. See *The Protest of the Hon. Richard Bassett . . . Against the
Two Acts of Congress 8 March and 29 April 1802 . . .* (Philadelphia,
1802); Donnan, pp. 125–127.

[81] *Annals of Congress,* 7th Cong., 2d sess., Senate, pp. 61–62.

that the quo warranto was a standard writ—in England.[82] Thus
the issue of the common law was raised at the end of the affair
as it had been at the beginning. Republicans ignored Gouverneur Morris' honeyed defense of his resolution to move directly
to the substantive issues.[83] They were furious, partly because
they took it to be an infringement on the independence of the
President to order him to bring quo warranto proceedings. "We
have a good right to say whether we want the services of these
judges or not," fulminated William Cocke of Tennessee, "and if
we do not, we don't need to pay them." Even more distressing
was the Federalist attempt to proceed by the rules of common
law. "I wish to know," thundered Cocke, "where we are to stop
if we begin to authorize our courts to proceed by information.
Are there not other kinds of information known to the common
law, besides information in the nature of a *quo warranto?* If we
adopt one form of the common law may not the courts assume
more? Has the gentleman never heard of persons being seized
and put to death upon information? I wish to know where we
are to stop; and whether we are to follow this common law
until it leads us to . . . royal robes." [84]

Shortly before the vote which defeated his resolution, Gouverneur Morris tried to make light of the common law issue.

[82] *Ibid.,* p. 6a.

[83] "[The courts] will modestly conclude, that you did not mean to
abolish the offices which the Constitution had forbidden you to abolish;
and, therefore, finding that it was not your intention to abolish, they will
declare that the offices still exist. . . . those feeble judges can bring on
the inquiry [whether Congress agrees or not]. . . . Is it not better, then,
to meet them freely, fairly? to come boldly forward like men?" (*ibid.,* p.
56).

[84] *Ibid.,* pp. 58–59. By petitioning Congress, added Jackson of Georgia,
the judges had admitted the right of Congress to decide the issue.
Congress had already decided. No redundant resolutions were necessary:
"Let them take their seat upon the bench and see if the Marshal will obey
them. Let them attempt to send a man to . . . jail, and I believe that
they will find out whether they are judges or not" (*ibid.,* p. 65).

"We have heard much," he said, "of the dangerous nature of an information. Gentlemen seemed afraid of information; they are afraid, too, of the common law. They will next, I suppose, be terrified at that other hideous spectre, common sense." [85] But he could not dispose of it so easily. Its intrusion into a debate which Republicans—and most Federalists—had carefully defined as an issue primarily of expediency or, at most, of constitutional construction, had operated to broaden a debate on policy into one on principle. Republican suspicion of Federalist motives was heightened, at the very beginning of Jeffersonian ascendency, by the belief that Federalists sought to integrate into federal law principles of the English common law which had little relationship to American principles and practices. Federalist suspicion of Republican motives grew into a certainty that the attack on the judges was evidence of a more far-reaching determination to impose extremely strict limits on the operation of federal law. To Republicans, the phrase "common law" appears to have meant something *very* specific: those features of English law which the colonies had *not* adopted or which had not been rephrased into American statutes. These included reference to the established church and to writs like that of quo warranto, unknown in American custom. But Federalists tended to use the phrase "common law" as a metaphor for an extensive and reliable system of national justice which they hoped to establish in the United States. The phrase was to be taken, in its literal sense, to mean a federal law commonly enforced throughout the nation. The enlargement of the federal judiciary had been expected to help achieve this goal; in striking at the judiciary, Republicans were also attacking the Federalists' larger purpose. To require, for example, that a Supreme Court justice rule on a case twice, once on circuit and subsequently when the case was appealed before the Supreme Court, was to call into question the meaningfulness of the Court's appellate jurisdiction, and therefore to

[85] *Ibid.*, pp. 73–74. The vote was 13–15 because of the close balance of parties in the Senate.

weaken the Court as an institution. Who stood to gain if the federal courts' jurisdiction was diminished? Most obviously, the state courts. Many Republicans, both in 1802 and subsequently, preferred state courts and believed that judicial review worked both ways: if the federal courts could declare acts of state legislatures unconstitutional, state courts could block the enforcement of federal decisions within state bounds. Federalists found themselves vigorously defending the propriety of Supreme Court review of Congressional decisions; two years before *Marbury* v. *Madison* it was clear that the issue would soon have to be faced.

The debate on the Judiciary Act repeal served as a particularly revealing episode in the continuing interparty confrontation. The debate was not only a political contretemps over the loaves and fishes of patronage; it epitomized a number of substantial differences in attitude which help explain why the rift between the parties was perceived by contemporaries as wide. A better guide to the central issue than the epithet "midnight judges" was the assertion of John Rutledge, Jr.: "There must be much law or there will be no justice"—law to set limits to the excesses of democratic individualism, law to guard against the demagogery that traditional Republicans fully expected to arise as American society grew less sensitive to traditional social restraints. Within the Supreme Court these concerns were absorbed in the issue of the extent of judicial review, as John Marshall sought "to establish . . . the authoritative place of a liberal Constitution kept authentic by the courts." [86] But the expansion of the role of the federal courts and of national law was a matter of concern to other branches of government, and the exact nature of the balance to be established between federal and state law a problem that remained unsettled.

During the debate, Federalists found themselves able to act as a coordinated opposition party (although they found little joy in it); they developed the uses of strict construction to the needs

[86] Robert Kenneth Faulkner, *The Jurisprudence of John Marshall* (Princeton, New Jersey, 1968), p. 221.

of an opposition party, and they added to their collection examples of Republican hypocrisy. Those phases of the debate which
concentrated on the "reception" of the common law went far toward solidifying the Federalist conviction that their opponents'
purpose in espousing repeal was both anti-intellectual (in the
sense that Republicans were thought to prefer that cases be decided more on the emotional response of the judge than on the
letter of the law), and conspiratorial (in the sense that repeal
seemed to be the first step in a projected demolition of federal
courts in order to prevent the further development of a federal
law). Once again, if there was one word Federalists would have
chosen to define their opponents, that word would have been
"hypocrite." The Charleston, South Carolina, *Courier* printed a
parable:

Sir John Cutler had a fine pair of SILK STOCKINGS which his maid
darned so often with worsted, that they at length became a vile pair
of WORSTED STOCKINGS. . . . Sir John's maid did not set about darn-
ing with more carelessness and levity than the anti-federalists exercise
in the business of amendment. . . . If we will not change the Constitution till it says that courts may be abolished and Judges removed
at the pleasure of Congress and the President, they will undertake to
say that it means so now. . . . —It is the singular policy of the present administration to call its measures precisely what they are not;
and its singular assurance to suppose the public incapable of detecting
the deception. . . . When Mr. Jefferson drew the attention of Congress to the judiciary, he did not say to us, "I am going to lay a
heavy hand on the Constitution; I am about sacrificing one of its
most important provisions to my pride, and my resentment. —No—
he has only talked about "economy" and "saving," and left the real
design to be explored through many pages of patriotic profession, and
all the soft notes in the lullaby song about oppressed humanity, and
the blessings of self-government. . . . Thus the Constitution becomes one thing, and the actual government another.[87]

[87] Charleston *Courier*, November 21, 1804.

[6]

Images of the Social Order

There is . . . a strong connexion
between literature, morality,
politics and religion.
—*New-England Palladium*
January 12, 1802

"Little whirlwinds of dry leaves and dirt portend a hurricane," warned Fisher Ames.[1] The Federalist saw these little whirlwinds everywhere in America: in the ineffectuality of Jeffersonian foreign policy, in the willingness to embark on projects as unpredictable as the acquisition of Louisiana, in Jeffersonian expressions of confidence in the political amateur. As the Federalist read his current events, one after another of the sources of cultural stability was being undermined by Jeffersonian enthusiasms: by the shift in the grounds and goals of scientific inquiry, by the rejection of the classical curriculum, and by what was believed to be a hostility to the institutions of social order, manifested by the revision of the judiciary system and the subsequent impeachment of judges.

The Jeffersonian approach to politics struck the articulate Federalists as dangerously naive. The optimism, the ready professions of faith in popular democracy, seemed to mask a failure to comprehend the ambivalence of the American social order. To

[1] Fisher Ames to Thomas Dwight, August 24, 1795, *Works of Fisher Ames*, ed. Seth Ames (Boston, 1854), I, 172.

these Federalists, American society, for all its surface stability and prosperity, was torn by internal contradiction. A population which had proved its capacity for revolutionary violence would not necessarily remain tranquil in the future. Moreover, even the early stages of industrialization and urban growth were providing the ingredients of a proletariat; there already existed a volatile class of permanently poor who, it was feared, might well be available for mob action. Finally, the expectation that the republic might deteriorate into demagogery and anarchy was given intellectual support by the widely accepted contemporary definitions of what popular democracy was and the conditions necessary to its stability. "I assure you," Jonathan Jackson told John Lowell, Jr., "that I feel quite satisfied in having had to pass through one Revolution. One is full enough for mortal man." [2] It was a common Federalist fear that the Jeffersonians were insufficiently conscious of the precariousness of revolutionary accomplishments, and that this laxity might well prove disastrous.

Their conviction of imminent disaster made Federalists and Augustans intellectual bedfellows. They shared the sense that an ordered world was disintegrating; that a cherished civilization was imperiled. The Federalist handbook was less *Hudibras* than it was *The Dunciad*. Pope's image of the advance of Dulness from country to country, leaving disorder in its wake, refers, of course, to the literary world and literary disorder, whereas Federalist references were primarily to political disorder; but the pessimism was equally deep, and the forecast of cultural chaos similar.[3]

This expectation of chaos so characteristic of Federalist satire also appeared in the work of contemporary English inheritors of the Augustan tradition. It is not accidental that Joseph Dennie

[2] February 17, 1805, in James Jackson Putnam, *A Memoir of Dr. James Jackson* (Boston, 1906), p. 59.

[3] Lewis P. Simpson, *The Federalist Literary Mind* (Baton Rouge, 1962), pp. 37–38.

admired the anti-Jacobin satirist William Gifford, or that John
Quincy Adams reviewed Gifford's translation of Juvenal. Both
literary circles paid homage to Augustan models, but the later
satire was less personal, more political; less reasonable, more
strident; and its tone was often defensive.[4] Battered by both political and intellectual revolution, those who longed for the continuance of the Old Republic often found it difficult to retain
their critical perspective. But that weakness should not blind us
to the fact that they did have comprehensible ground for their
distrust.

Substituting Democracy for Dulness, John Sylvester John
Gardiner fashioned an ode in celebration of Napoleon's defeats
at Spanish hands in which Democracy is apostrophized as the
"Hag-Seed of Hell," whose origins could be traced to the time

> When erst the arch fiend from blest obedience fell,
>   And the whole rebel rout to ruin ran,
> Thee he engendered in the caves of hell,
>   The inexorable foe of envied man.

Appearing in Athens, Democracy forced the Goddess of Freedom to find on "Albion's cliffs . . . a blest asylum"; subsequently the transit of democracy, like the transit of civilization,
was to be westward. Leaving "the Roman eagle writhing," Democracy made for France; the ode ends with a cheer for the Ibe-
rian victories of 1807 and the return of Democracy to her in-
fernal home. Should she ever be released to continue her
westward journey, the next step was obvious.[5]

Gardiner's mock ode includes several themes that frequently
appear in Federalist rhetoric. Democracy for example, is associated with violence and chaos, an association which was habitual
among Federalists, as indeed it had been among socially conser-

[4] Martin Roth, "Satire, Humor and Burlesque in the Early Works of
Washington Irving" (unpublished Ph.D. dissertation, University of Chicago, 1966), pp. 165–167.

[5] *Monthly Anthology and Boston Review*, V (1808), 495–497.

vative critics since Aristophanes. Martin Roth has perceptively remarked that Chaos and Orgy, metaphysical and sexual disintegration, "are and always have been the comic archetypes of the Conservative mind"; certainly Federalist satirists, from Gardiner and Richard Alsop to Josiah Quincy and Washington Irving, made extensive use of chaotic imagery. In *Salmagundi* the disorder permeates the entire social and political scene: from Congress, "a blustering, windy assembly, where every thing is carried by noise, tumult and debate"; to the militia, which finds it impossible to obey the simplest order (" 'Right, about, face!' cried the officer: the men obeyed, but bungled—they faced *back to back*"); to elections, which convulse the community like a civil war.[6] The image of Pandemonium, lifted bodily from John Milton's *Paradise Lost,* appeared in another set of verses by Gardiner. He used it so effectively to link the Republican political style with the Satanic slander of free discussion that Federalist satirists came virtually to regard it as their own. "At *Pandemonium,*" wrote Gardiner, "meets the scoundrel throng, / Hell in their heart, and faction on their tongue." [7] An anonymous satirist equated Abijah Adams, a Republican newspaperman convicted of libeling the Massachusetts General Court, with Milton's Satan:

> HIGH, in a room of legal state, which far
> Outvied the strength of *Dedham,* or of *York,*
> Or e'en the *Concord,* which with heavy hand
> Clanks on her slaves her barb'rous chains, and bars,
> 'BIJAH exalted sat, by merit rais'd
> To that bad eminence . . . [8]

Even the standards by which heroes were to be judged could be taken from Milton: Washington was honored, George F. Sensa-

---

[6] Washington Irving *et al., Salmagundi* (London, 1811), I, 136 (April 4, 1807); I, 90 (March 7, 1807); I, 33 (April 4, 1807); II, 2 (June 2, 1807).

[7] J. S. J. Gardiner, *Remarks on the Jacobiniad* (Boston, 1798), p. 9.

[8] *The Demos in Council; Or 'Bijah in Pandemonium, Being a Sweep of the Lyre. In Close Imitation of Milton* (Boston, 1799), p. 3.

baugh found Federalists arguing, as a figure of "awful goodness" because he had ruled the "wild uproar" and brought order where there had been confusion. "Through Miltonic symbols the Father of his Country had already begun [by the early nineteenth century] to assume the image of greatness that history has so firmly secured." [9]

The expectation of violence and disintegration permeated Federalist political conversation in the opening years of the nineteenth century. "The power of the people, if uncontrolled, is . . . mobbish," remarked Fisher Ames in 1802. "It is a gov't by force without discipline." [10] When Thomas Boylston Adams undertook to follow his brother John Quincy's advice and reread Xenophon, he expected no surprises: "The Athenians doubtless afford an excellent example of the *violence* to which a Democratic government necessarily leads a people." [11] Josiah Quincy's Slaveslap Kiddnap proclaimed his vision of "the tempestuous sea of liberty":

now tossing its proud waves to the skies, and hurling defiance toward the throne of the almighty; now sinking into its native abyss, and opening to view its unhallowed caverns, the dark abodes of filth and falsehood, and rapine and wretchedness. . . . From the top of Monticello, by the side of the great Jefferson, I have watched its wild uproar, while we philosophised together on its sublime horrors. There, safe from the surge . . . I have quaffed the high crowned cup to this exhilirating toast—TO YON TEMPESTUOUS SEA OF LIBERTY . . . MAY IT NEVER BE CALM.[12]

H. L. Mencken once distinguished two varieties of democrats —those who see liberty primarily as the right of self-government,

[9] George F. Sensabaugh, *Milton in Early America* (Princeton, N.J., 1964), pp. 243–254. Sensabaugh traces the use of Miltonic imagery with considerable subtlety.

[10] F. Ames to Oliver Wolcott, Jr., December 2, 1802, Oliver Wolcott Papers, Connecticut Historical Society.

[11] Thomas Boylston Adams to John Quincy Adams, November 10, 1802, APm reel 401.

[12] "Climenole, No. 7," March 17, 1804.

and those who see it primarily as the right to rebel against governors. American political theory usually denies the necessity to choose between the two options, but in the early years of the republic it was widely assumed that a choice had to be made. The former concept, of "positive" liberty, or the freedom to follow a "higher" pattern of behavior, has its analogues in Puritan thought, and is comparable to the elitist definition of the social order which many Americans, perhaps the majority, held in the half-century following 1770.[13] The widespread assumption among Federalists that their opponents espoused the alternate concept of "negative" liberty, or individual immunity from restraint, was derived in part from some of the better-known Jeffersonian aphorisms, but it was also based on the Federalists' own experience. Primarily, it reflects their sense of the precariousness of the American social order. Every age is one of anxiety; Jacksonians might look back on the the Old Republic as a period of placidity and social stability, but their vision was fictitious and illusory.[14] All around them, the Federalists of the Old Republic saw familiar social habits decaying. The most obvious sign of changing social balances was the decline of deferential behavior. After the social dislocations of the 1770's and 1780's fewer people had a pedigree of gentility and fewer still were willing to recognize such pedigrees where they existed. Surely there had always been in America egalitarians who refused to defer to their social superiors: the Quakers, for example, or the unchurched men and women who had accompanied John Winthrop to Boston and had made it so difficult for him and his associates to establish the tightly structured community

[13] H. L. Mencken, introduction to James Fenimore Cooper, *The American Democrat* (New York, 1956), p. x. The distinction between positive and negative liberty is Isaiah Berlin's; see Mark DeWolfe Howe, "Problems of Religious Liberty," in *Nomos IV: Liberty: Yearbook of the American Society for Political and Legal Philosophy*, ed. Carl J. Friedrich (New York, 1966), pp. 262–273.

[14] See Marvin Meyers, *The Jacksonian Persuasion* (Stanford, Cal., 1957).

of which they had dreamed. The egalitarian current of the Revolutionary era turned exceptions to the rule into harbingers of a trend; by the first decade of the nineteenth century, gentlefolk all over the nation, except perhaps in the South, were complaining that they were treated with far less respect and awe than they were accustomed to. Men who saw sullen or, at best, bland countenances where formerly they had received broad smiles and a bow, took the sullenness as a personal affront. Their insistence that America possessed the social ingredients for a "mobocracy" may have been something of a rhetorical overstatement, but it was not mere fulmination: people who would not defer to anyone seemed unpredictable and capable of "mobbishness." [15]

What the Federalist meant by "mob" appears most clearly in a long satire called "Morpheus," which Timothy Dwight, the president of Yale, published in the *New-England Palladium* at the end of 1801. In a dream, the author visits the city of Perfectability, where William Godwin has become a sort of philosopher-king and is seeking to put his ideas into practice. When Dwight arrives, Godwin is addressing a crowd:

"Order! How can I do you any service . . . unless you keep order, and consent to hear me?"

Order? (Murmured a grave man at my elbow) a command of order is a restraint. It is beneath the dignity of man to submit to restraint.

"I beseech you, then, my friends and fellow-citizens, to hear me."

[15] The notion that American society was always free of class-consciousness is one of the more persistent of American myths. In *Gentlemen Freeholders* (Chapel Hill, 1952), Charles S. Sydnor explains the extent to which even the processes of voting in eighteenth-century Virginia were grounded in the expectation that the common folk would follow the lead of their social betters. Similar patterns existed further north; see Richard J. Purcell, *Connecticut in Transition: 1775–1818* (Middletown, Conn., 1963), pp. 135–137. The decline of deference in the early national period is extensively explored in David Hackett Fischer, *The Revolution of American Conservatism: The Federalist Party in the Era of Jeffersonian Democracy* (New York, 1965).

We will think of it (replied the grave man.)

We will not think of it (exclaimed a boy.)

Hear him, (roared out a great number of voices.)

"I say, my friends and fellow citizens (proceeded the philosopher) I say, the present is an auspicious day."

You said that before, (replied a lad at my left hand.)

Hear him, (cried a multitude.)

You have said it twice already (rejoined the boy.)

"I say, (said the philosopher, in some confusion) this is an auspicious day. . . . With your kind cooperation I will here begin a new system of human things; in which every sentiment and action shall unite to advance the perfection, and secure the rights of man. Human perfectibility.

Fudge, Fudge-man, (growled a brawny fellow).

Godwin goes on to advocate the abolition of private property, and to denounce marriage as "a narrow and unwarrantable monopoly":

Who will take care of the children? (cried an old man.)

"Who?" (exclaimed the philosopher,) "The public, doubtless . . ."

The public shall never take care of my children (screamed a delicate woman behind me). I know too well how the public takes care of children. We had a poor-house filled with children, just in our neighborhood.

In the end the philosopher declares one John Gaston's house common property. The mob attacks and destroys it, and then moves on to tar and feather the philosopher himself.

What infinite diversion you furnish us, (cried the mob.) In no way could you possibly so promote the public good.[16]

[16] *New-England Palladium*, November 27, December 8, 1801. There were other installments on November 24, December 11 and 15, 1801; March 9, 1802 (identification of author by Robert Edson Lee, "Timothy Dwight and the Boston *Palladium*," *New England Quarterly*, XXXV [1962], 229–239).

The portrait of the mob Dwight furnishes is a three-dimensional picture of crowd behavior. These people are good folk; good-humored, and in some moods, eminently commonsensical. But they can also be turbulent and destructive; they can turn on and destroy even the men who, like Godwin, had most confidence in their judgment. The mob, as the Federalist envisioned it, was not composed of a particular social group, nor was it a permanent organization; rather the word described a type of behavior of which the entire public, under appropriate conditions, seemed capable. The mob is the people in their worst mood—boisterous, giddy, impassioned, unreasonable, destructive.

The republic itself had been born in turbulence; that their nation had been created by rebellion and secession was never far from the Federalist mind. Eighteenth-century America had been a society in which violence was endemic; as Howard Mumford Jones has recently reminded us, mob action was common during the revolutionary era. "American mobs were amenable to cunning leadership, sometimes disguised, sometimes demogogic; they pillaged, robbed, destroyed property, defied law, interfered with the normal course of justice, legislation, and administration, occasionally inflicted physical injuries." [17] After the Revo-

---

[17] Howard Mumford Jones, *O Strange New World* (New York, 1964), p. 209; Bernard Bailyn, ed., *Pamphlets of the American Revolution* (Cambridge, 1965), I, 581–584; R. S. Longeley, "Mob Activities in Revolutionary Massachusetts," *New England Quarterly*, VI (1933), 98–130. "Beginning in 1769," writes Alan Heimert, "when a 'formidable' mob of some 2,000 to 3,000 persons formed in Boston (thus, according to Hutchinson, setting the stage for the confrontation of wills that issued in the Massacre), Boston Liberalism was seldom without a multitude to be disturbed by . . ." (*Religion and the American Mind: From the Great Awakening to the Revolution* [Cambridge, Mass., 1966], pp. 418n, 518). "There will be always a *Shays*, a *Bradford*, or *Fries*, for every provoked occasion, to pour their hosts in hostile array from the mountains," predicted Samuel Blodget in 1806 (*Economica* [Washington, D.C., 1806], p. 16). See also Pauline Maier, "Popular Uprisings and Civil Authority in Eighteenth-Century America," *William and Mary Quarterly*, 3d ser., XXVII (1970), 3–35.

lution, similar violence was experienced in Boston, New Haven, Philadelphia, Charleston. It may well be that Shays' Rebellion was, in contemporary context, an anomaly; as one of the few episodes in which mob violence was forcibly resisted by a state legislature, Shays' Rebellion is merely better remembered than the numerous other occasions on which legislatures were more easily intimidated. Americans were not necessarily more temperate than their French contemporaries; since they met less resistance from constituted authority, they may simply have felt less need for extreme action.[18]

The national government, only a dozen years old when Jefferson took office, was daily insulted, at home and abroad, by men who acted as though the republic were merely a temporary expedient. The Articles of Confederation, after all, had been in force for a dozen years before they had been abandoned; there was no guarantee in 1800 that the document which replaced the Articles would have a longer life. The federal government was insulted by the British, who had refused to honor all the terms of the Peace of 1783 until required to by the Jay Treaty; by the French, whose regular seizure of American shipping resulted in a "Quasi-War," and even by the Dey of Algiers, whose Barbary pirates exacted regular tribute. It was insulted at home by men who similarly refused to regard the new government as permanently established. Critics of national policies habitually spoke as though the Union did not deserve to survive; a threat of secession was a standard response of the frustrated politician.[19]

[18] Gordon S. Wood, "A Note on Mobs in the American Revolution," *William and Mary Quarterly*, 3d ser., XXIII (1966), 641.

[19] The concept of the Union as a wartime experiment "coolly carried over into peace as an expedient response to a crisis of the moment" is described in Paul C. Nagel, *One Nation Indivisible: The Union in American Thought, 1776–1861* (New York, 1964), pp. 13–31. The idea that Union was of absolute value developed only gradually; this gradualness may account for the ease with which men could entertain disunion sentiment prior to the antebellum decade. "Those who so talked of dismemberment reflected the experimental mood: usually they planned

When William Blount thought he was being permitted to wield too little power in North Carolina, he attempted to arrange for the secession of the Western Territory; when Virginia objected to the Alien and Sedition Acts, she made sure her protests would be listened to by including a veiled threat of secession. Secession was the response of a group of New England Federalists to the prediction of Jefferson's re-election in 1804, of Aaron Burr to his isolated position after the Hamilton duel. And all through the early national period, the nation was insulted by men who seemed to cherish democracy primarily as a guarantee of their right of rebellion. The best known of these insults had been the violent demonstrations headed by the "whiskey rebels" and by John Fries, but there were many other occasions of riot in the early years of the republic.[20] These riotous demonstrations generally accomplished little, but they are not unimpor-

---

simply to wipe the slate clean, beginning afresh with more insight" (Nagel, pp. 14, 23).

[20] Sometimes noisy crowds congregated at jails, demanding harsher sentences for prisoners of whom they disapproved (e.g., William Duer in New York City in 1792) or the freedom of those with whom they sympathized (e.g., William Keteltas in New York in 1796 and Jason Fairbanks in Dedham, Massachusetts in 1801). Often the motives were political, election days were usually full of boisterousness and drunkenness, which sometimes flared into destruction. When Arthur St. Clair, governor of the Northwest Territory, opposed the drive for Ohio statehood, his official residence was invaded by a crowd of armed and probably intoxicated citizens who disrupted a dinner of the members of the Territorial Assembly. (Arthur St. Clair to James Ross, January 15, 1802, in William Henry Smith, ed., *The St. Clair Papers* [Cincinnati, 1882] II, 555). To show its hostility to the Jay Treaty, a Boston mob burned a Bermudian privateer (Samuel Eliot Morison, *The Maritime History of Massachusetts* [Boston, 1941], p. 174); to show its hostility to Federalist politicians, a New Hampshire mob assaulted a local merchant (James Sheafe in 1795). See David Fischer, *The Revolution of American Conservatism* (New York, 1965), p. 231. Fischer lists a series of politically inspired mobbish demonstrations in 1810 and 1812 (pp. 157–158); among the towns affected were Boston, New Haven, Litchfield, Plymouth, Newburyport, New York, Philadelphia, and Baltimore.

tant; Federalists worried about them because they provided evidence that Americans had not lost the capacity for violence which they had demonstrated during the Revolution. "If there is no country possessed of more liberty than our own," the *Palladium* remarked, "there is probably none where there are more formidable indications of the error, prejudice and turbulence that will render it insecure." [21] The nation had malcontents enough for Gouverneur Morris to conclude: "There is a moral tendency, and in some cases even a physical disposition, among the people of this country to overturn the Government. . . . The habits of monarchic government are not yet worn away among our native citizens, and therefore the opposition to lawful authority is frequently considered as a generous effort of patriotic virtue." [22] The Whiskey Boys, Fries, the men who successively raised and tore down liberty poles in New England as late as 1798, made it impossible for Federalists to relax in Arcadia.[23] They could not assume that the New World would escape the disastrous cycle of European history; they could not assume that the pastoral landscape of the Old Republic, settled by contented yeomen, would not be replaced by the congested landscape of the Old World, occupied by malcontented *canaille*.[24]

---

[21] *New-England Palladium*, January 16, 1801.

[22] Gouverneur Morris to Uriah Tracy, January 5, 1804, in Anne C. Morris, ed., *The Diary and Letters of Gouverneur Morris* (New York, 1888), II, 450–451.

[23] F. Ames to Timothy Pickering, November 22, 1798, in Seth Ames, I, 242–243.

[24] Kenneth Lockridge's demographic studies of colonial New England confirm that the Federalist diagnosis had more than a grain of truth in it. The pressure of population on land resulted, in many eastern towns, in an average landholding no better than what the English yeoman had originally fled to the New World to escape. With this development came class polarization and a tendency toward social stratification; in short, there was some reason for the prevalent fear of a "Europeanization" of American society ("Land, Population, and the Evolution of New England Society: 1630–1790," *Past and Present*, No. 39 [April 1968], pp. 71, 80). See also Jonathan Jackson to John Lowell, Jr., February 17, 1805, in Putnam Papers, Massachusetts Historical Society.

There was reason to fear that the capacity of the American people for mobbishness was increasing. One analysis of the American scene which Federalists found almost disarmingly appropriate had been provided, ironically enough, by Thomas Jefferson as early as 1787. The passage appears in *Notes on Virginia,* and follows Jefferson's famous remark that "Those who labour in the earth are the chosen people of God, if ever he had a chosen people." Jefferson goes on to explain the contrast he had in mind and the reasons for his preference for the husbandman:

Dependence begets subservience and venality, suffocates the germ of virtue, and prepares fit tools for the designs of ambition. . . . The mobs of great cities add just so much to the support of pure government, as sores do to the strength of the human body. It is the manners and spirit of a people which preserve a republic in vigour. A degeneracy in these is a canker which soon eats to the heart of its laws and constitution.[25]

Jefferson could easily have found Federalists to agree with his statement, point by point. They would have changed the application from prediction to statement of fact, and they would not have limited their fear to "the mobs of great cities"; rather, mobbishness was a quality of which the Federalist feared all were capable. But they would have agreed that the urban poor were particularly restless, and they would have added that there seemed to be increasing numbers of poor people in America. Boston had slums by 1810; New York's seventh ward was swampy, stagnant and an unhealthy slum as early as the 1790's.[26] Poor people were, by eighteenth-century definition,

[25] Thomas Jefferson, *Notes on the State of Virginia,* ed., Thomas Perkins Abernethy (New York, 1964), pp. 157–158.

[26] R. B. Nye, *The Cultural Life of the New Nation* (New York, 1960), pp. 126, 131; Staughton Lynd and Alfred Young, "The Mechanics and New York City Politics, 1774–1801," *Labor History* V (1964), 219; Alfred Young, "The Mechanics and the Jeffersonians: New York, 1789–1801," *Labor History* V (1964), 260–261.

dependent on those who had jobs to offer and salaries to pay; the "manners and spirit" of the economically dependent, it was feared, could not possibly be as stalwart as those of the independent and self-sufficient yeoman. "You would never look at men and boys in workshops," said the Maryland Federalist Philip Barton Key, "for that virtue and spirit in defense [of the nation against an aggressor] that you would justly expect from the yeomanry of the country." [27]

Now it is true enough that early America was an agricultural country; nine out of ten of her citizens still worked the land. But as Leo Marx has perceptively pointed out, we may not therefore jump to the conclusion that Jefferson's definitions are adequate for our own understanding of the American farmer. The noble husbandman is a mythical image, not a description of sociological reality: "He is the good shepherd of the old pastoral dressed in American homespun." Both shepherd and yeoman are models of beings who live in a word from which economic pressures are absent. The self-sufficient yeoman on the family-sized farm seeks not prosperity and wealth, but stability, "a virtual stasis that is a counterpart of the desired psychic balance or peace." Only in a world like his, free of economic tension, can the omission of a class structure seem believable. [28] The image is mythical because it ignores economic fact; it draws life from the assumption that Americans could live independent of the international marketplace. Suppose one should deny the possibility; what then becomes of the image? "Let our workshops remain in Europe," Jefferson had counseled. "It is better to carry provisions and materials to workmen there, than bring them to the provisions and materials, and with them their manners and principles. The loss by the transportation of commodities across the Atlantic will be made up in happiness and perma-

---

[27] *Annals of Congress*, 11th Cong., 2d sess., House, p. 1906, April 18, 1810.

[28] Leo Marx, *The Machine in the Garden: Technology and the Pastoral Ideal in America* (New York, 1964), p. 127.

nence of government." [29] But America's workshops were not to remain in Europe. The men who counseled agricultural self-sufficiency, Fisher Ames sneered, were themselves "clad in English broadcloth and Irish linen, . . . import their conveniences from England, and their politics from France. It is solemnly pronounced as the only wise policy for a country, where the children multiply faster than the sheep." [30] Although the major boom in American industrialization is generally dated 1830–1865, it was rapidly becoming apparent in the early years of the nineteenth century—and to men like Tench Coxe and Alexander Hamilton and Oliver Wolcott much earlier—that the nation's destiny lay with the machine. It was inescapably obvious that with the machine would come further changes in the quality of American social life, changes in "manners and spirit."

Consciousness of the nation's industrial destiny may be said to have begun with Alexander Hamilton's great "Report on Manufactures" of 1791, the same year in which Samuel Slater began the operation of his spinning mill in Pawtucket. But American manufactures did not start with Slater; Hamilton's correspondence as he requested information for the Report reveals that manufacturing operations were already extensive. [31] The social structure of the United States, however, seemed ill-suited to the development of an industrial society; available land, prosperous commerce, the heavy demand for handcrafted items meant that few men would be content to remain day laborers. How to industrialize without workers? To this question Hamilton offered three comments: first, the increased efficiency of machinery would enable it eventually to *replace* human hands, thus cutting

[29] Jefferson, p. 158.

[30] F. Ames, "Falkland, No. 2," in S. Ames, II, 132.

[31] This correspondence has been reprinted in Arthur H. Cole, *Industrial and Commercial Correspondence of Alexander Hamilton* (Chicago, 1928). So great a quantity of nails, iron utensils, shoes, and hats were produced in America as early as 1789 that the British consul had begun to fear American competition. See John C. Miller, *Alexander Hamilton: Portrait in Paradox* (New York, 1959), p. 283.

the need for labor to a great extent; second, new hands could be encouraged to emigrate to America; and finally, more extensive use could be made of an as yet barely tapped source of labor. In England, Hamilton explained, "all the different processes for spinning cotton, are performed by . . . machines, which are put in motion by water, and attended chiefly by women and children." [32]

Hamilton was not the progenitor of child labor in America; he was endorsing a trend, not initiating one. To get the information on which the Report was based, he had instructed Treasury agents throughout the country to report to him on the state of manufactures in their area; they, in turn, polled local businessmen and sent their letters on to the Secretary of the Treasury. The information thus collected showed that child labor was already extensive in certain segments of the economy: in yarn manufacture, in cotton and woolcarding, and in the making of nails.[33] By 1803, Oliver Wolcott was finding it difficult to re-

[32] Cole, p. 258. See also "Report on Manufactures," in Harold C. Syrett and Jacob E. Cooke, eds., *Papers of Alexander Hamilton* (New York, 1966), X, 253.

[33] Syrett, IX, 374, 446; X, 316. See also Cole, p. 77; Joseph Stancliffe Davis, *Essays in the Earlier History of American Corporations* (Cambridge, Mass., 1917), II, 259–261. The use of child labor was regularly defended and even advocated on the grounds that it not only spared pauper children from becoming public burdens, but taught them to be responsible and productive. When the Connecticut Federalist David Humphreys built a model factory town in 1806 and staffed it with women who were paid less than a dollar a week and unpaid apprentices and orphan boys, he (and the Connecticut legislature which granted Humphreysville a ten-year tax exemption) thought of himself as a benefactor rather than an exploiter of children and women. In *A Poem on Industry* (Philadelphia, 1794) Humphreys had written:

> "Teach little hands to ply mechanic toil,
> Cause fading age o'er easy tasks to smile . . .
> So shall the young, the feeble find employ,
> And hearts, late nigh to perish, leap for joy!"

(Joseph Dorfman, *The Economic Mind in American Civilization* [New York, 1946] I, 327–328; Leon Howard, *The Connecticut Wits* [Chi-

cruit boys to work in his cousin's nail factory, not because children were not working, but the contrary: "Children who have health and are not utterly depraved in their morals," he explained, "are worth money and can easily find employment." [34] Samuel Slater's factory opened with nine workers—seven boys and two girls, none older than twelve years; the youngest was seven.[35] When, in 1801, Josiah Quincy visited one of Slater's mills, he found that the machinery was tended by over a hundred children from four to ten years old, under a single supervisor, who were paid from 12 to 25 cents a day. "Our attendant was very eloquent," Quincy remarked in his diary, "on the usefulness of the manufacture, and the employment it supplied for so many poor children. But an eloquence was exerted on the other side of the question more commanding than his, which called us to pity these little creatures, plying in a contracted room, among flyers and coggs, at an age when nature requires for them air, space, and sports. There was a dull dejection in the countenances of all of them." [36] The children who worked in the mills did not have air, space, and sports as an option; if they were not in the textile factories they joined the "abundance of poor children" which Noah Webster reported to be wandering about the streets, "clothed in dirty rags, illy educated in every respect." [37] By 1809, the nation's cotton mills employed four

cago, 1943], pp. 242, 250–251; Richard J. Purcell, *Connecticut in Transition: 1775–1818* [Middletown, Conn., 1963], pp. 80–81, 108–111).

[34] O. Wolcott, Jr., to Frederick Wolcott, December 20, 1803. Huntington-Wolcott MSS., Mass. Hist. Soc.

[35] Edward C. Kirkland, *A History of American Economic Life*, 3d. ed. (New York, 1951), p. 314.

[36] "Account of Journey of Josiah Quincy," *Proceedings of the Massachusetts Historical Society*, 2d ser., IV (May, 1888), 124.

[37] Noah Webster, "Patriot, No. III," May 2, 1791, in Harry R. Warfel, ed., *Letters of Noah Webster* (New York, 1953), p. 95. The founders of the Society for Establishing a Free School in the City of New York declared in 1805 that they were motivated by a desire to educate the children who were "wandering about the streets, exposed to the influence of corrupt example" (Timothy L. Smith, "Protestant Schooling and American Nationality" *Journal of American History*, LIII [1967], 681–682).

thousand workers, of whom thirty-five hundred were women and children under age sixteen. Labor statistics, and especially statistics of child labor for the years before 1820, are very scattered, vague, and impressionistic. But they do indicate that child labor, especially in the textile regions, continued and increased. Typically whole families worked in the mills; the men were paid something less than a living wage, and families made ends meet by adding the labor of wives and children, much as Hamilton had predicted.[38]

The prevalence of woman and child labor in early American industry is generally assessed in the context in which Hamilton had placed it. It is taken as an indication of scarcity of labor, as evidence of an expanding economy which offered most men something better to do than to work as factory operatives. Treated in this manner, child labor is seen almost as an index of American prosperity. All this may be true. But we should not ignore the other social conditions of which child labor may be an index; we should not ignore what it tells us about the men who *were* common laborers, and whose dollar a day salary, which made them the best paid common laborers in the West, did not provide for a family sufficiently so that it did not have to send its children into the mills.[39] An American working class was

[38] Albert Gallatin, "Report on the Subject of Manufactures," *American State Papers: Finance* II (Washington, D.C., 1832), 427. See also Harvey Wish, *Society and Thought in Early America* (New York, 1950), I, 266–267; William A. Sullivan, *The Industrial Worker in Pennsylvania* (Harrisburg, Pa., 1955), pp. 18, 19n, 40; Edith Abbott, "The History of the Industrial Employment of Women in the United States: An Introductory Study," *Journal of Political Economy* XIV (1906), 461–501; Kirkland, p. 316.

[39] Skilled artisans could make more than a dollar a day: the organized shoemakers of Philadelphia earned nine dollars for a six-day week between 1806 and 1815, and in 1808 a skilled carpenter in Massachusetts earned as much as $10.50. But shoemakers in Massachusetts were paid only 67 to 85 cents a day during the same period, and the daily wages of unskilled urban workers fluctuated from a low of 25 cents a day in 1805 to a high of $1.67 in 1809. The average wage of unskilled urban workers, without

being formed in the early national period, and while class lines were far more flexible, and living conditions were far better than those prevalent in Europe, they were severe enough.[40] The number of people in the early republic who might be labeled members of a proletariat was relatively small, but the conditions of their lives were grim, for all the open-endedness and social mobility of American life. Men do not live by comparisons, but by the conditions of their own lives.

"The time is not distant when this Country will abound with mechanics & manufacturers who will receive their bread from

board, was estimated to be 75 cents in 1805. Massachusetts farmers were paying their hired hands nine to fifteen dollars a month plus board. Wages were lowest for unskilled factory labor because, as Victor S. Clark explains, the women and children who worked in the factories and lived on nearby farms constituted a virtually captive labor supply. "No other occupation for these workers then existed except household pursuits, and many such occupations were disappearing before factory competition. The rise of the factory system, therefore, transferred labor from the home to the mill, rather than created a new labor demand" (Clark, *History of Manufactures in the United States* [New York, 1929], I, 391–395); Curtis P. Nettels, *The Emergence of a National Economy: 1775–1815* (New York, 1962), p. 392; Samuel Blodget, *Economica: A Statistical Manual for the United States of America* (Washington, 1806), p. 142; U.S. Department of Labor, Bureau of Labor Statistics, Bulletin #499, *History of Wages in the United States from Colonial Times to 1928* (Washington, D.C., 1929), pp. 84, 120, 127, *passim*.

[40] In *The Social Structure of Revolutionary America* (Princeton, N.J., 1965), p. 271, Jackson Turner Main estimates the American poor in the revolutionary era as 30 per cent of the total population, 20 per cent of the whites, with a permanent proletariat of perhaps 5 per cent of the white population. Lynd and Young (pp. 215–224) describe New York City mechanics as "more proletarian in character" in 1800, as the number of common laborers on the docks, wage workers in factories, and petty tradesmen increased in connection with an influx of poor immigrants. In Kent, Connecticut, there had emerged by 1796 "a significant number of men destined to remain poor. . . . There were twenty-two permanent proletarians [11 per cent of the adult male population]" (Charles S. Grant, *Democracy in the Connecticut Frontier Town of Kent* [New York, 1961], pp. 83–103).

their employers," Gouverneur Morris had predicted in the Constitutional Convention. Two decades later Morris was sounding like Montesquieu: "The strongest aristocratic Feature in our political organization is that which Democrats are more attached to, the Right of universal Suffrage." [41] Montesquieu had suggested that universal suffrage worked to strengthen the power of the rich because the employer or landowner could command the votes of those who were economically dependent on him; Thomas Jefferson himself had warned that "Dependence begets subservience and venality." Would America be transformed when her working population became a salaried one? Would there be an American proletariat? And if there were, would it behave any differently from the European? The pastoral idea was predicated on the continued *absence* of certain things: factories, urban concentrations of population, the presence of the extremely poor. If these things were not absent, pastoral America could not exist; and wherever the northern Federalist leader looked, it seemed more and more apparent that these conditions would not be absent much longer.[42]

The Federalist anticipated violence, in short, because his countrymen had demonstrated their capacity for it during the Revolution, and because he saw developing a class of poor and unskilled laborers who might easily be encouraged to indulge what the Federalist knew to be a general human capacity for turmoil. Over and over, Federalist spokesmen identified their greatest fear: the experimental republic would be destroyed, as the French republic had been, by the "turbulence" and "mobbish-

[41] G. Morris to Robert R. Livingston, October 10, 1802, in G. Morris, Private Letterbook II, Library of Congress.

[42] It is characteristic of Federalist ambivalence on the subject of industrialization that while the social side effects of industry were deprecated, the industrial process itself was not, and, of course, many Federalists invested heavily in the new factories. For the political implications of alternative evaluations of manufactures, see Richard J. Purcell, *Connecticut in Transition: 1775–1818* (Middletown, Conn., 1963), pp. 85–88.

ness" of which the public was capable. To curb this tendency to "mobbishness," then, was to save the republic, and an act of patriotism. "Every friend of liberty," explained one editorial writer, "would be shocked if the people were deprived of all political power. . . . But . . . if the people will not erect any barriers against their own intemperance and giddiness, or will not respect and sustain them after they are erected, their power will be soon snatched out of their hands, and their own heads broken with it—as in *France.*" [43]

"An hundred years hence," Benjamin Rush predicted in 1789, "absolute monarchy will probably be rendered necessary in our country by the corruption of our people. But why should we precipitate an event for which we are not yet prepared? Shall I at five-and-twenty years of age, because I expect to be an old man, draw my teeth, put on artificial gray hairs, and bend my back over a short cane? No . . . I will husband my strength and vigor, and try to keep off old age as long as I can by temperance, proper clothing, simple manners, and the practice of domestic virtues." [44] That democracy had tendencies dangerous to the stability of the state no one denied. Federalists took particularly great pains to spell out these tendencies, drawing not only on the demonstrable growth of an unpropertied class of American citizens, but also on a large body of political theory dating back to the ancients. Aristotelian political theory warned that the standard fate of democracy was to decline into demagoguery; the Founders had displayed a great deal of courage in challenging this prediction. Federalists did not propose to let the grandeur of the challenge or the size of the risk be forgotten; even democracy modified into representative government might succumb to the cycle. "What, think you, but the turbulence and in-

---

[43] *New-England Palladium,* January 30, 1801.

[44] Benjamin Rush to John Adams, July 21, 1789, in Lyman H. Butterfield, ed., *The Letters of Benjamin Rush* (Princeton, N.J., 1951), I, 522–523.

constancy, the folly and presumption of the Roman and Athenian commonwealths, so fatally illustrated in their history, brought those states into decay, and the very name of republic into disrepute?" asked William Crafts of a South Carolina audience. "And what is there in our atmosphere or situation, what but the wrecks of those illustrious republics, which still lift their shattered fragments above the waters of oblivion to warn us of our dangers, what is there in a peculiar manner to preserve the political integrity of our states? Nothing, nothing but the virtue of our citizens can afford us a bulwark or a barrier." [45]

A republican democracy was assumed to be a contradiction in terms; Democratic-Republican as a party label a non sequitur.[46] It was Federalism and Republicanism, they insisted, which went together; both defined a version of popular government characterized by the built-in, self-limiting features which popular government required if it was to endure. In categorizing Americans as "all Federalists, all Republicans" Jefferson was seen either to be making an unexpected and complete capitulation or, what was more likely, deliberately befogging the issues. The former alternative did not seem inconceivable to Federalists, who still regarded the two-party arrangement as novel. The first party to be in power had the firmly established habit of identifying itself with the government, its personnel with the national administration, and its members with the heroes of the American Revolution.[47] Opposition to party was easily equated with a near-treasonable opposition to the government, and the development of an opposition party was often viewed as the cause, rather than the reflection, of "political rancour &

[45] William Crafts, "Oration Delivered in St. Michael's Church, Before the Inhabitants of Charleston, on the Fourth of July 1812 . . ." in *Selections in Prose and Poetry* (Charleston, 1828), p. 36.

[46] *Weekly Inspector*, September 20, 1806.

[47] See Seymour Martin Lipset, *The First New Nation* (New York, 1963), pp. 36–40; and Richard Hofstadter, *The Idea of a Party System: The Rise of Legitimate Opposition in the United States, 1780–1840*, (Berkeley, Calif., 1969), pp. 74–169.

malevolence." [48] The difficulty historians have in tabulating congressional votes of the period, the frequent regrouping of political cliques, remind us that for a long time it was unclear that the nation had a two-party destiny. Until Jefferson's election, many continued to indulge the hope that a permanent party division could be avoided. To Judge William Paterson, the fact that Jefferson and Adams found themselves in the same Philadelphia boarding house in 1797 was a hopeful sign. "It carries conciliation and healing with it, and may have a happy effect on parties. Indeed, my dear sir," he told Supreme Court Justice James Iredell, "it is high time that we should have done with parties. . . . If we were one and true to ourselves, we should be in peace at home, and respected abroad." [49] To men convinced, like Edward Rutledge, that "Unanimity, is . . . absolutely essential, to the happiness, & I had almost said, Independence of America," Jefferson's inaugural words were ones they had long hoped to hear.[50]

"We believe, with Mirabeau, that 'words are things,'" declared Thomas Green Fessenden. "If false, they give a wrong direction to the public mind, and of consequence to the physical powers of the community." [51] If words were things, definitions counted. Jefferson's words sent Federalist publicists off on a veritable orgy of definition. Congressman William Henry Hill of

[48] Thomas Pinckney to John Rutledge, Jr., September 23, 1800, John Rutledge Jr., Papers, Southern Historical Collection, University of North Carolina Library, Chapel Hill, N.C.

[49] William Paterson to James Iredell, March 7, 1797, in Griffith J. McRee, *Life and Correspondence of James Iredell* (New York, 1858), II, 495.

[50] Edward Rutledge to John Rutledge, Jr., June 9, 1797, John Rutledge, Jr., Papers, Duke University Library. Jefferson was equally anxious to erase the line between the parties, but of course by absorbing the moderate Federalists. See Jefferson to James Monroe, March 7, 1801, *The Writings of Thomas Jefferson*, ed. H. A. Washington (Philadelphia, 1854), IV, 366–368.

[51] "Prospectus," *Weekly Inspector*, August 30, 1806.

North Carolina explained to his constituents that the President was correct only in his acknowledgement that Federalists were Republicans. "The federalist prefers the federal constitution, to all other forms of government; he values it for its republicanism. . . . It is to be lamented that there are republicans among us who are not federalists." [52] The editor of the Washington *Federalist* counseled that the opposition should be called Jacobin. To call them republican was "a gross misrepresentation. . . . If they are republicans, . . . federalism must be something different from republicanism, which you ought to be rather ashamed than proud of." [53] Two years after the inaugural, the editor of the Charleston *Courier* was still playing with Jefferson's phrases: "Federalism is republicanism—republicanism calculated alike to support the rank and dignity of the country as an independent nation, and the just rights, liberty and privileges of the people . . . the pretended republicanism of the party who are [in power] . . . is in reality naked jacobism." [54]

Round and round the editorials went (Federalism is Republicanism, is Republicanism Democracy?) until the arguments lost clarity and the tone became shrill. Federalists saw clearly that reasonable debate could not begin until the opposition ceased to equate Federalism with monarchy. They failed to realize that they would have to offer an equivalent concession; at the very least they would have to cease equating Republicans with Jacobins (as serious an error of definition as the one of which they so loudly complained). Meanwhile words divorced from definition flew about like missiles, and did nearly as much damage. "Words without meaning, or with wrong meaning have especially of late years done great harm," mourned Rufus King. "Liberty, Love of Country, Federalism, Republicanism, Democracy, Jacobin, Glory, Philosophy and Honor are words in the mouth of

[52] Charleston, S.C., *Courier*, March 16, 1803.
[53] Washington *Federalist*, January 8, 1801.
[54] Charleston *Courier*, April 18, 1803.

everyone and used without precision by any one; the abuse of words is as pernicious as the abuse of things." [55] In this politically poisoned atmosphere, no one seemed to listen to anyone else. The American government, Washington Irving declared in exasperation, had become a "pure unadulterated *logocracy,* or government of words."

The whole nation does everything *viva voce,* or by word of mouth; and in their manner is one of the most military nations in existence. Every man who has what is here called the gift of gab, that is, a plentiful stock of verbosity, becomes a soldier outright; and is forever in a militant state. The country is entirely defended . . . by force of tongues. . . . This vast empire, therefore, may be compared to . . . a mighty windmill, and the orators, and the chatterers, and the slang-whangers [newspaper editors], are the breezes that put it into motion; unluckily, however, they are apt to blow different ways, and their blasts counteracting each other—the mill is perplexed, the wheels stand still, the grist is unground, and the miller and his family starved.[56]

But beneath the slang-whanging lay real concern. The Federalist insistence that unrestricted liberty is not true freedom, that Democracy is not the same as Republicanism, has been unfashionable in American historiography for so long as to have become unrespectable. But it had respectable origins. The distinction between a democracy in which "the people meet and exercise the govenment in person" and a republic in which "they assemble and administer it by their representatives and agents" was one upon which Alexander Hamilton had insisted; the argument that "the progress of a democracy [is] to strip the

[55] Essay on "Words," *The Life and Correspondence of Rufus King,* ed. Charles R. King (New York, 1900), V, 96. "Names & appearances," remarked F. Ames, "are in party warfare arms & ammunition." F. Ames to J. Rutledge, January 26, 1801, John Rutledge, Jr., Papers.
[56] Irving *et al., Salmagundi,* April 4, 1807, I, pp. 132, 138.

people of all power" because it tends to degenerate into despotism had respectable classical origins in Aristotle, and Napoleon was at that moment demonstrating its validity.[57] Many years later, reflecting on the political situation of 1806, John Quincy Adams commented: "It may be laid down as a law of political gravitation governing the universe of man, that democracy must and will have a master, and that master must be a soldier." [58] The map of Europe in 1942 sufficiently resembles the map of Europe after Tilsit to make Federalist hysteria comprehensible to a modern generation.

The terms "democracy" and "republic" have long been subject to confusion. Montesquieu had offered a clear definition, but, despite the widespread familiarity with *The Spirit of the Laws,* it was seldom used in the United States. Republican government, he said, was any form in which authority rested with the people. An aristocratic republic was ruled by a select group of the people; a democratic republic was one in which all ruled directly. According to this definition, the United States was an aristocratic republic; if the Jeffersonian's charge that his opponents were aristocrats had any validity, it was in this sense. In general, however, and with disastrous results for the clarity of political dialogue, the terms were used interchangeably to indicate any government which derived its power from the people; both were applied to the United States, but with different overtones. The democratic republic seemed to be one which sought, by increasing the number of voters and of participants in political decisions, to approximate as closely as possible the direct democracy of the ancients; this system was considered prone to turbulence and chaos. Republicanism, Robert W. Shoemaker has explained, "stood apart from democracy and was rarely if ever

---

[57] *The Weekly Inspector,* September 20, 1806; February 21, 1807 (reprint from Boston *Repertory,* n.d.). See also Alexander Hamilton," Speech on the Constitution," excerpted in Richard B. Morris, *Alexander Hamilton and the Founding of the Nation* (New York, 1957), pp. 136 ff.

[58] J. Q. Adams, *Parties in the United States* (New York, 1941), p. 51.

associated with violence and disorder." [59] Rejecting the universal political participation which was identified with democracy, Federalists stressed accountability and selectivity, a choice of emphasis consonant with their concern for the maintenance of the intellectual credentials of the republic.

Despite the rancors of the debate over definitions, Americans of both parties were aware that theirs was the only republic of the time, and that it was an extremely perilous experiment. In his examination of the causes of the War of 1812, Roger H. Brown has pointed to the American's fear that there may have been "some fatal weakness inherent in the republican form of government that accounted for its rare and fleeting occurrence." [60] Both parties were intensely concerned for the continuation and security of their holy experiment, but their jealous protectiveness of that experiment was displayed in varying fashion. The early years of the republic were years of great accomplishment and also of tremendous frustration. It seems to have been habitual among Republicans to place the blame for that frustration on foreign nations and the conduct of foreign affairs, a way of thinking which, Brown suggests, eventually led them to justify the War of 1812. But one may also speculate that one of the sources of Federalist resistance to that war was a well-established habit of thought which tended to place blame for political failure, even in foreign affairs, on the nation's own internal weaknesses.

Repeatedly the Federalists insisted that Americans interpret the French Revolution as a cautionary tale. Democracy was never static; constant vigilance was required to keep popular government stable. And many Federalists had come to fear that

[59] Robert W. Shoemaker, " 'Democracy' and 'Republic' as Understood in Late Eighteenth-Century America," *American Speech* XLI (1966), 83–95; Charles de Secondat, Baron de Montesquieu, *The Spirit of the Laws,* trans. Thomas Nugent (Chicago, 1952), Book II, sec. 1, p. 4.

[60] Roger H. Brown, *The Republic in Peril: 1812* (New York, 1964), pp. 2–3.

Americans lacked that vigilance. "We are in fact a much altered[?] people," complained Edward Rutledge to his nephew John Rutledge, Jr., in 1798, "& are no more like what we were some Twenty years ago, than . . . the Italians are like the Romans." [61] In 1805 John Rutledge, Jr., sent a similar complaint to Uriah Tracy; his standard of comparison was ten years. Complaints like these were generally linked to glowing memories of the past and to the image of George Washington. "In former times, & in the days of Washington," said Uriah Tracy flatly, "the leading men were virtuous." [62] "For what did you go thro' the fatigues, the sufferings, the perils of a seven years' war?" Timothy Pickering asked old Rufus Putnam in 1803. "You thought you were fighting for liberty & independence. Alas! mistaken soldier! You find, after the lapse of only twenty years, that *liberty* is the right of adopting implicitly the political opinions of our present chief ruler. . . . Firm in virtue, and inviolably attached to the correct policy of Washington, you could not descend to the degrading level of *modern patriotism. . . .*" [63] "I have been disappointed certainly in the moral character of this Government which I assisted to form," complained William Richardson Davie.[64] Federalists typically spoke of the national failure as a moral one; editorial diatribes habitually slighted other subjects in order to dwell on the lack of moral fiber which the opposition had allegedly displayed. This habit tended to give Federalist political writing in the nineteenth century a vague and repetitive tone, but the editors were not

[61] Edward Rutledge to J. Rutledge, January 23, 1798, John Rutledge, Jr., Papers, Duke University Library.

[62] Uriah Tracy to J. Rutledge, January 12, 1805, John Rutledge, Jr., Papers, South. Hist. Coll. "You say that the people *now* are unlike what they were ten years ago . . ."

[63] T. Pickering to Rufus Putnam, December 6, 1803, Timothy Pickering Papers, Mass. Hist. Soc.

[64] To John Haywood, May 14, 1816, quoted in Blackwell P. Robinson, *William R. Davie* (Chapel Hill, 1957), p. 392.

merely dodging the issues: to the Federalist mind, morality was the issue. Federalism had been founded, explained Fisher Ames, "on the supposed existence of sufficient political virtue, and on the permanency and authority of the public morals." [65]

Americans of both parties were fond of the notion that the virtue of the citizen and the stability of the republic were linked. "Virtue . . . is the foundation of Republics," explained a contributor to the *Gazette of the United States* who signed himself "Serranus." "In these, all Power emanating from the people, when they become corrupt, it is in vain to look for purity or disinterestedness, in the administration of their affairs. A polluted fountain must necessarily pour forth a foul and turbid stream. Hence, Morals [,] of great importance in every scheme of government, are of indispensable necessity in a free Commonwealth." [66] Sustenance for this point of view might be found by reading Montesquieu, who taught that whereas what makes the laws effective in a despotism was fear, a republic must depend on the virtue of its citizens. "There is no great share of probity necessary to support a monarchical or despotic government; the force of the laws in one, and the Prince's arm in the other, are sufficient to direct and maintain the whole. But in a popular state one spring more is necessary, namely, virtue." [67]

[65] F. Ames, "On the Dangers of American Liberty" (1805), in Seth Ames, II, 379.

[66] *Gazette of the United States* . . . , January 5, 1802. See also "Reply of Massachusetts Senate to Governor Strong's Speech of June 3, 1800," in Caleb Strong, *Patriotism and Piety* (Newburyport, Mass., 1808), p. 15.

[67] *The Spirit of the Laws*, trans. Thomas Nugent, p. 9. This translation was quoted in Thomas Green Fessenden's *The Weekly Inspector*, September 20, 1806, and subjected to Fessenden's versification:

> "Moreover Montesquieu
> Points out with a fescue,
> That truth in all cases
> Is Liberty's basis."

The debaters in the Constitutional Convention had cited Montesquieu more often than Locke, and he continued to be quoted —and misquoted—in the popular press.[68] During the Convention, his arguments in favor of the separation and balance of powers had proved most useful; after the form of government was settled, emphasis shifted to his insight that only a virtuous and moral citizenry could make a republic viable.

If one is willing to assume that men are naturally virtuous, then the foundations of a healthy republic were already present in American society and could be counted on to persist. But few Federalists were able to share this cheerful Jeffersonian assumption. Their attitude stemmed partly from the old Puritan awareness of man's natural depravity, but even more it stemmed from an understanding of the extreme fragility of their experiment in democracy and an awareness of the substantial demands for self-restraint and individual responsibility that republican government places on its citizens. Theirs was a style of consciousness that had been characteristic of the members of the Constitutional Convention, who had been frank in their acknowledgement— even insistence—that the sort of government they had devised depended for its continued existence on a public superior in its political sophistication to any other public, anywhere on the globe. There were to be checks and balances to restrain the corrupting influence of power, but in the last analysis it was citizens, not devices, who would have to guard the republic. The Founders were equally frank in their acknowledgement that the average American might not be able to sustain the burdens placed on him. Because the American public was better educated,

[68] H. M. Jones, p. 431, note 39. Two other concepts associated with Montesquieu were familiar in America. Gouverneur Morris shared Montesquieu's fear that universal suffrage resulted in giving "undue Influence to those of great Wealth." Montesquieu's suggestion that governments should be appropriate to climatic conditions was subjected to Fessenden's satire in "A Character" in the *Port Folio*, October 3, 1801 (identification by R. Randall, "Authors of the Port Folio . . ." *American Literature*, XI [1940], 396).

more endowed with landed property than any other, the risk seemed worth taking. Americans had shown in their state governments that they were capable of self-rule, but they were also capable of riot. He had taken democracy, Gouverneur Morris said, "not only . . . as a Man does his Wife for better or worse, but what few Men do with their Wives, . . . knowing all its bad Qualities."[69]

Rousseau was thought to have encouraged the worst qualities to which democracy was prone. Fessenden described him as "a gaunt Genevan priest," who

> madly theoriz'd,
> That men were best *unciviliz'd*
> Like those philosophers, who prate,
> Of Innocence in savage state.
> E'en took it in his crazy noddle,
> A *savage* was *perfection's* model.

Although Fessenden offered only a crude reading of *Emile,* he was able, in one of the many lengthy footnotes that turn *Democracy Unveiled* from satire into polemic, to identify precisely the crucial problem of *Le Contrat Social.* "We . . . are informed that the general will cannot err, (*vox populi, vox dei,*) and that it tends invariably to the public advantage. Yet we are told almost in the same breath that the people . . . are *often deceived.* That is that the expressions of the will of a *fallible* body

[69] G. Morris to John Dickinson, May 23, 1803. Modern liberals continue to be concerned by the demonstrated willingness of local majorities to brush aside constitutional and traditional guarantees of civil rights and civil liberties in favor of curbs on the expression of views they find distasteful. "The attempt to reconcile values which are essentially aristocratic with a social structure which is democratic is as old as Aristotle," comments Andrew Hacker. "The democrat's problem is to reconcile what are essentially aristocratic values with an open society." This was also the task assumed by both Federalists and Republicans in the early national period; the difference between them lay largely in the particular issues and fears each group made its special concern (Hacker, "Freedom and Power: Common Man and Uncommon Men," in C. J. Friedrich, pp. 313, 333).

are always *infallible*." [70] The Federalist lament was not simply that their government was founded on the popular will, but that this will was not invariably correct; they agreed with Rousseau that "men always desire their own good, but do not always discern it."

Had they read Rousseau more carefully and sympathetically (one suspects they did not because of his association with the French Revolution), Federalists would have found other features of his thought with which they were in substantial agreement. Rousseau's concept of the General Will was not quite the same thing as transient numerical majority desires on specific issues; the *volunté générale*, by definition, in all cases operated for the general good. Cecelia M. Kenyon has perceptively identified Hamilton as the "Rousseau of the Right" for his view that "the will of the community toward its corporate good, [was] something quite distinct from the will of all." For men of this persuasion, "the public good was morally and politically prior to private, individual ends, with which it was occasionally if not frequently in conflict." [71] In Rousseau's vision, it was the task of the Legislator to bridge the gap between the transient majority will and the true and permanent will of the entire

----

[70] [Thomas Green Fessenden,] *Democracy Unveiled or Tyranny Stripped of the Garb of Patriotism, by Christopher Caustic, L.L.D.* 3d ed. (New York, 1806), I, 17, 26–28, 41n. John Adams had reservations about the same concept when he found it in the article on "Economie politique" which Rousseau wrote for the *Encyclopedie:* "If the majority is 51 and the minority 49, is it certainly the voice of God? If tomorrow one should change to 50 vs 50, where is the voice of God? If two and the minority should become the majority, is the voice of God changed?" (Haraszti, p. 93). G. Morris similarly objected to "the dangerous doctrine that the public will, expressed by a numerical majority, is in all cases to be obeyed. . . . That numerical majority not only may, but frequently does, *will* what is unwise and unjust. Those, therefore, who avow the determination strictly to comply with it, acknowledge themselves the willing instruments of folly and vice" (G. Morris to U. Tracy, January 5, 1804, in A. C. Morris, II, 451–452).

[71] Cecelia M. Kenyon, "Alexander Hamilton: Rousseau of the Right," *Political Science Quarterly*, LXXII (June, 1958), pp. 166, 161.

community, in obedience to which true freedom is to be found. In the best of all possible worlds, the individual will and the general will would always coincide: "The most free of all governments," remarked a *Port Folio* essayist in unwitting paraphrase of Rousseau, "would be that of a despotic authority in the hands of an Angel sent from Heaven to controul us, provided it were also administered [and, he might have added, populated] by Angels." [72] The fallibility of the general will seemed to account for a variety of unpalatable popular movements, from the Reign of Terror in France to the successes of Jeffersonian Democracy in America. "It would be, indeed," Fessenden remarked, "a most infamous aspersion on the People of the United States, to insinuate, that *if they had known* that many men who now fill the highest offices in government, were destitute of common honesty, they would have honoured them with their suffrages." [73] But at the same time, Fessenden and his colleagues were quick to insist that if America were not to submit to monarchy or an unprincipled dictatorship, the general will, or some approximate expression of it, would have to be accepted. "The pillars which secure the fabric of society in America are placed on a less solid foundation than in older countries," Fessenden explained. "In America *public opinion* must, in a great measure, supply the place of long established precedents, and form the chain which binds together society." [74] In Europe unpopular governments might be propped up by standing armies, clerical hierarchies, or patronage. "Other governments may stand, though not very steadily, if public opinion be only neuter," said Fisher Ames, "but our system has so little intrinsic energy, that this soul of the republic's soul must not only approve but cooperate." [75] How might the nation guard against the fallibility of the general will?

In this dilemma Federalists appealed to Montesquieu, and

[72] *Port Folio*, November 27, 1802.
[73] Fessenden, I, iv.
[74] *Ibid.*, I, xxiii.
[75] F. Ames, "Laocoon, No. I" in S. Ames, II, 115.

found in his thesis that public virtue is the safeguard of republics support for a repeated insistence (which they were probably unaware echoed Rousseau) that only the dictates of a virtuous general will were binding. In the United States politicians were bound by the dictates of the popular will; it was obviously necessary to ensure that the popular will be virtuous. As John Adams's nephew William Smith Shaw explained, "To establish a government, founded on *public opinion,* and then allow this opinion to be misled and corrupted by the lowest miscreants of society, who have talents to invent falsehood, is not my system." [76]

Only a virtuous citizenry would sustain a republic and, in a sinful world, a virtuous citizenry was made, not born. Could the Jeffersonians, who seemed so ready to ignore the issue altogether, be trusted to educate the people to virtue and enlightenment? Federalists had their doubts; for their part, the press and the pulpit seemed the most promising means of reinforcing what tendency to virtue and morality already existed. It was through the press, Thomas Green Fessenden thought, that the French had been persuaded to endorse the Revolution and the English persuaded to eschew it. "LITERATURE, well or ill-conducted . . . is the great engine, by which . . . all civilized States must ultimately be supported or overthrown," he asserted. [77] Federalists treated the triumph of Thomas Jefferson, David H. Fischer has remarked, as "an object lesson in the power of the printed word," and bent their energies to establishing newspapers and increasing their circulation in an attempt to ensure that as many printed words as possible were of Federalist origin. [78] In this

---

[76] William Smith Shaw to Arthur Maynard Walter, January, 1801, in Joseph B. Felt, *Memorials of William Smith Shaw* (Boston, 1852), p. 131. A similar thought appears in Washington's Farewell Address: "In proportion as the structure of a government gives force to public opinion, it is essential that public opinion should be enlightened."

[77] Fessenden, I, xxi–xxii.

[78] Fischer, p. 134.

they perhaps overestimated the Word, a tendency not unusual among men who believed that "words are things," [79] who measured the success of a republic by the excellence of its literature and oratory, and who defined their opponents as anti-intellectuals. But the effort also suggested the variant of democracy that was Federalism. Federalists insisted that they would have retained their office had the American people not been deceived. The fault lay not with republican government, but with the capacity of the opposition for deceptive techniques, and with the understandable human propensity to listen to those who spoke of happiness rather than of stern duty or of rectitude.

"I am willing you should call this the Age of Frivolity as you do; and would not object if you had named it the Age of Folly, Vice, Frenzy, Fury, Brutality, Daemons, Buonaparte, Tom Paine, or the Age of the burning Brand from the bottomless Pit: or any thing but the Age of Reason," John Adams told a friend.[80] In an age of unreason, something more than newspapers was required to sustain the virtue that alone could sustain the republic; something more than a liberal education was required to counteract the disorderly passions that threatened to disrupt the state. William Crafts typically warned that a nation "subject to its passions" could not possibly be virtuous; "Passion, so far as it prevails, destroys reason," counseled Tapping Reeve, "and when it gains an entire ascendancy over men, it renders them bedlamites." [81]

---

[79] Cf. Jonathan Swift, *Travels into Several Remote Nations of the World. By Captain Lemuel Gulliver* (London, 1726), II, 75–76.

[80] John Adams to Benjamin Waterhouse, October 29, 1805, in Worthington Chauncey Ford, ed., *Statesman and Friend: Correspondence of John Adams with Benjamin Waterhouse, 1784–1822* (Boston, 1927), p. 31.

[81] William Crafts, "An Oration on the Influence of moral causes on national character . . . August 28, 1817," p. 6; Tapping Reeve, *The Sixth of August* (Hartford, Conn., 1806), p. 5. Faced with a similar dilemma, German Romantics like Schiller proposed to strengthen moral instincts by aesthetic education. This prescription was not appealing to Americans, who retained a suspicion of artistic endeavor and a tendency to associate

In this context, Faith had a political as well as a supernatural function; the God of the Federalists often appears to behave like a fourth branch of Government. "Where is the security for property, for reputation, for life, if the sense of religious obligation desert the oaths which are the instruments of investigation in courts of justice?" George Washington had asked in the Farewell Address. "Give religion to the winds," wrote Abigail Adams, "and what tye is found strong enough to bind man to his duty, to restrain his inordinate passions? Honour is phantom. moral principal [*sic*] feeble and unstable—nothing but a firm belief and well grounded assurance that man is an accountable being, and that he is to render that account to a Being who will not be mocked, and cannot be deceived, will prove a sufficient Barrier, or stem the torrent of unruly passions and appetites." [82]

Religious obligation would reinforce moral obligation; moral obligation would make popular government orderly and stable. This paradoxical insistence that religious faith was a necessary ingredient in a social order which forbade the establishment of religion was both widespread and persistent. The concept is essentially a Puritan one; it reappears in the Massachusetts Bill of Rights of 1780: "the happiness of a people and the good order and preservation of civil government essentially depend upon piety, religion and morality." It was reasserted by Washington in the Farewell Address ("Of all the dispositions and habits which lead to political prosperity, religion and morality are in-

---

the arts with luxury, effeminacy, and corruption. See Neil Harris, *The Artist in American Society: The Formative Years 1790–1860* (New York, 1966), pp. 28–41.

[82] Abigail Adams to T. B. Adams, July 6, 1802, APm Reel 401. The prevalent idea that legal order, especially the order embodied in the common law, and religious tradition were interdependent helps explain the force of Federalist resistance to the repeal of the Judiciary Act of 1801. See Mark DeWolfe Howe, *The Garden and the Wilderness: Religion and Government in American Constitutional History* (Chicago, 1965), pp. 27–31.

dispensable supports. . . . Virtue or morality is a necessary spring of popular government"); by Arthur St. Clair in his addresses to the legislature of the Northwest Territory ("good laws [are those] tending to the promotion of religion, patriotism, and virtue, without which the happiness of no people can be durable"); [83] and repeatedly by Caleb Strong in his annual addresses to the Massachusetts General Court, which are collected, appropriately enough, under the title of *Patriotism and Piety*.[84] Alexis de Tocqueville found it still an integral part of American culture a generation later. "The Americans," he wrote, "combine the notions of Christianity and of liberty so intimately in their minds that it is impossible to make them conceive the one without the other." He was impressed by clergymen who accepted hardship and expense "lest religion should be allowed to die away in . . . remote settlements, and the rising states should be less fitted to enjoy free institutions than the people from whom they came. . . . Thus religious zeal is perpetually warmed in the United States by the fires of patriotism. These men do not act exclusively from a consideration of a future life; eternity is only one motive of their devotion to the cause. If you converse with these missionaries of Christian civilization, you will be surprised to hear them speak so often of the goods of this world, and to meet a politician where you expected to find a priest. . . . How is it possible, [they ask] that society should ca-

---

[83] Address to the Territorial Legislature, November 5, 1800, in Smith, II, 501.

[84] Newburyport, Mass., 1808. The First Amendment bound only the Federal Government; the states might, and often did, use public funds to support worship and the teaching of distinctly religious concepts in the public schools. Not until 1867 did the passage of the Fourteenth Amendment make the Bill of Rights directly binding on the states. For the concept of religious liberty as freedom *to* worship (as opposed to freedom *whether* to worship) in the early national period, see Mark DeWolfe Howe, "Problems of Religious Liberty," in C. J. Friedrich, pp. 262–273. Jefferson's support of the latter definition seems to have placed him among a minority of his countrymen.

cape destruction if the moral tie is not strengthened in proportion as the political tie is relaxed? And what can be done with a people who are their own masters if they are not submissive to the Deity?" [85]

The moral tie must be strengthened as the political tie is relaxed. This was Montesquieu all over again. The only available, if imperfect, measure of morality seemed to be the extent of religious commitment. "The great pillars of all government and of social life," Patrick Henry characteristically remarked in the course of explaining his opposition to Jefferson, were "virtue, morality, and religion." [86] At a Washington's Birthday Dinner, Timothy Pickering proposed a toast to *"Religion* and *Morality,* essential supports [of] a *free government."* [87] That other forms of morality existed Federalists were generally willing to admit, but none of these was measurable, and all seemed too vague to be trusted. "Let us with caution indulge the supposition that morality can be maintained without religion," Washington had warned. "Whatever may be conceded to the influence of refined education on minds of peculiar structure, reason and experience both forbid us to expect that national morality can prevail in exclusion of religious principle." [88] Because Federalists placed so

[85] *Democracy in America* (New York, 1945), I, 306–307. The intimate connection between Christianity and liberty was expounded by the clergy during the era of the American Revolution. Perry Miller argues that the revolutionary emotion was as much a religious emotion as a political one, if not more so. The revolutionary jeremiad was not merely political preaching, Miller thinks; rather it was "imparting a sense of crisis by revivifying Old Testament condemnation of a degenerate people." See "From the Covenant to the Revival," in James Ward Smith and A. Leland Jamison, *The Shaping of American Religion* I (Princeton, 1961), 340. For the equation of the American Revolution with the archetypal struggle in Heaven between Good and Evil, see Sensabaugh, pp. 241–242.

[86] Patrick Henry to Archibald Blair, January 8, 1799, quoted in Fischer, p. 375.

[87] Boston *Repertory,* March 9, 1804.

[88] Farewell Address. The *Palladium* called "the principle of Washington's FAREWELL ADDRESS . . . the great Exhibit of the Federal System"

much reliance on traditional religious behavior as the measure of the morality which all agreed must buttress a republic, they were severely distressed at Jeffersonian endorsement of vaguer forms of religious identification. "The federalists are dissatisfied," Timothy Pickering explained, "because they see the public morals debased, by the corrupt and corrupt[ing] system of our rulers. Men are tempted to become apostates, not to federalism merely, but to virtue, and to religion, and to good government." [89]

The Jeffersonians were dangerous, Simeon Baldwin explained, because their influence was used to break down the "barrier of habitual morality . . . both as it respects our civil & our religious institutions . . . if the restraints of Law, of education, of habit & [of what the opposition was pleased to call] superstitions and prejudice [i.e., religion] shall be entirely removed, I am confident we shall have more *positive* vice, than is even now exhibited at the South. The human propensities when released from those restraints will like the pendulum vibrate & when urged by precept & allowed by Example they will vibrate to an extreme." [90] They were vibrating, even then, in the camp meetings of the Great Revival. Cane Ridge, Kentucky, in the

---

(January 1, 1802). On another occasion, it denounced the notion that morality or virtue could exist independently of religion, because in that case, "every man becomes his own judge of moral good, and his own standard of moral rectitude. . . . All the hostile, and selfish passions will be nourished, and fed; all that is decent will be numbered; and the human mind will be left to assert its native dignity" (January 6, 1801). See also Purcell, pp. 25–29.

[89] T. Pickering to George Cabot, January 29, 1804, Timothy Pickering Papers. For the generally acknowledged link between Jeffersonianism and religious latitudinarianism see G. Adolf Koch, *Republican Religion: The American Revolution and the Cult of Reason* (New York, 1933), pp. xv, 3–27, 285–298; Charles Roy Keller, *The Second Great Awakening in Connecticut* (New Haven, 1942), pp. 13–35. See also Alan Heimert, *Religion and the American Mind* (Cambridge, Mass.), pp. 535–538.

[90] Simeon Baldwin to Elizabeth Baldwin, February 7, 1804, in Baldwin Family Papers, Yale University Library.

summer of 1801 set the pattern for subsequent revivals, at which salvation was demonstrated by ranting, twitching, fainting and other behavior closely resembling the cataleptic fit.[91] The revivalists were not only saving themselves, they explained, they were redeeming the entire nation.[92] But some people could not be comfortable in a nation so redeemed. The revival encouraged the free play of passions quite as much as militant deism did; like so many other disturbing trends in American life, it came out of a western wilderness which had voted for Jefferson and which the purchase of Louisiana had done much to enlarge. Religious liberty should mean that men were free to choose the institutional form of their faith, Federalists thought, but they feared if it were also construed to encourage the growth of deism on the one hand or of noninstitutional evangelicalism on the other, then not only the churches, but the entire national establishment would be threatened.

In the years after the Revolution, the American walked a strange tightrope between optimism and pessimism. The Revolution had been both a radical break with the past and a conservative affirmation of it; that ambivalence persisted through the early years of the national experience. The Federalist characteristically searched the American social order to find the stability that would justify the Revolution; for the same purpose the Democrat searched it to find flexibility. The Jeffersonian, at

---

[91] John Bach McMaster, *History of the People of the United States* (New York, 1883), II, 580–582; Catharine C. Cleveland, *The Great Revival in the West* (Chicago, 1916), pp. 62–159; John Melish, *Travels in the United States of America* (Philadelphia, 1812), I, 36–37. For the distress with which the Methodist clergy were viewed in New England, see Purcell, pp. 55–58.

[92] See Perry Miller, *The Life of the Mind in America* (New York, 1965), pp. 3–20; and Heimert, p. 534. Heimert suggests that the congruence of "The Revolution of 1800" with the revival movement is not accidental: "The political-religious explosion of 1800 represented the culmination of a full generation of intellectual turbulence."

least in theory, endorsed flexibility, unpredictability, open-endedness; he led the Federalist to wonder how a society so characterized could endure. The Virginia democrat lived in one of the least flexible of American social arrangements; when the Federalist found him endorsing unpredictability he logically concluded that the Virginian was a hypocrite. Men long for what they do not have; the Federalist's glorification of social stability —his castigation of the decline of deferential behavior, his objection to the annexation of the "howling wilderness" of Louisiana, his jealous maintenance of an extensive federal judiciary, his concern for the advancement of intellectuality, virtue, and traditional religious observance—may well have come out of his appreciation of the forces that were operating to increase the anxieties of American life.

"I appeal to the wise and dispassionate of this House," declared Archibald Henderson in the North Carolina House of Commons, "and ask them if the general character of this President's administration has not been to corrupt and demoralize the public mind. By corruption, I do not mean that he has bribed the people with money; by demoralization, I do not mean that he has made them thieves or robbers: I mean to say that he has suffered to evaporate that manly pride and spirit of independence which conducted us through the revolutionary war. . . . The people have become impatient of governmental restraint, and have lost all reverence for established usages and the settled order of things." [93] As Henderson confessed, the harsh things which Federalists said of their opponents were often not to be taken literally. But it would be unwise not to take them seriously. Federalist accusations of corruption and subversion referred not so much to specific felonies as to the impact of Jeffersonian attitudes upon the cultural life of the nation.

Certain cultural developments were taken to be indices of a

[93] Archibald Henderson, Speech in the North Carolina House of Commons, December 11, 1807; in Raleigh, N.C., *Minerva*, December 24, 1807.

nation's progress that were quite as significant as economic statistics and census data, and it was in these developments that the Republicans were held to be most seriously deficient. "There is . . . a strong connexion between literature, morality, politics and religion," maintained the *Palladium*. "It is usually true, that he, whose mind is filled with visionary theories, on any of these subjects, either is at present, or will soon become equally visionary concerning the rest."[94] "Visionary" theories of literature led Republicans to endorse educational reforms that smacked of the theories of William Godwin and threatened to undercut the classical studies which were thought to be essential to the maintenance of a vigorous intellectual life and of the proper attitudes toward popular government. "Visionary" theories of politics encouraged Republicans to weaken the restraints which were relied on to inhibit popular government from declining into riotous assemblies: in this sense, the weakening of the federal judiciary and the encouragement of the growth of deism were opposite sides of the same coin. The Laputa analogy was never far from the Federalist mind. "Philosophism is a poor thing in the [presidential] chair," complained Fisher Ames. "Those who spin cobwebs are poor spinners of common thread."[95] The Republicans were expected either to destroy themselves or to transform the nation. Their inexperience in government encouraged some

[94] *New-England Palladium*, January 12, 1802. The idea was a common one among Federalists and frequently repeated; virtually the same words appear in *The Ordeal*, January 7, 1809: "The strong connexion which subsists, in all good governments, between politicks, religion, and literature, renders it . . . important to detect the fallacy of such literary hypotheses as may have a tendency to subvert our understandings or undermine our principles of action."

[95] F. Ames to J. Rutledge, July 20, 1801, John Rutledge, Jr., Papers. On another occasion, Ames remarked: "A statesman of this [Republican] sect will poise himself in his chair, like an alchymist in his laboratory, pale with study, his fingers sooty with experiments, eager to make fuel of everything that is precious, and sanguinely expecting that he shall extract everything precious from the cinders and dross that must be thrown away." ("Falkland, No. II" [February, 1801], in *Works*, II, 135).

Federalists to hope it would be the former; if it were to be the latter, the Federalists could only resist and pray that their resolute stand would serve to delay the attainment of Republican goals. A set of verses in the Charleston *Courier* succinctly expresses a characteristic Federalist attitude in the difficult years of the Jeffersonian ascendancy:

THE OAK AND THE WILLOW

I am an Oak, tho' fall'n, indeed
Thou still a *vile* and skulking weed!
Rais'd by no merit of thy own,
But by the *blast* that laid me prone,
Say! if thou canst, what plant or tree,
Except a sycophant like thee,
Devoted to *intrigue* and *strife*,
Would e'er prefer a *dastard's* life,
Preserv'd by guile and crafty saws,
To falling in A GLORIOUS CAUSE.[96]

[96] Reprinted in the *Port Folio*, April 3, 1802.

A Note on Sources

The Federalists of the Jeffersonian era have not endeared themselves to historians. Their grumbling makes it easy to characterize them as merely complainers and obstructionists; among the most persuasive of such characterizations is that of Vernon Louis Parrington, who discussed Fisher Ames, Robert Treat Paine, Harrison Gray Otis, and Josiah Quincy under the scornful heading of "The Tie-Wig School," and described them as citizens of a "testy little world" (*Main Currents in American Thought* [New York, 1927], II, 275–295). A more recent holder of similar views is Elisha P. Douglass ("Fisher Ames, Spokesman for New England Federalism," *Proceedings of the American Philosophical Society*, CIII [1959], 693–715). Other influential historians who shared Parrington's views were Charles Beard, Frederick Jackson Turner, and, before them, John Bach McMaster and Edward Channing. Their assessments have percolated into modern monograph and textbook literature, especially that which focuses primarily on Thomas Jefferson and his accomplishments.

In the classic works of Richard Hildreth and Henry Adams, however, the Federalists are paid the compliment of being taken seriously, and their fulminations are treated as expressions of sincerely held belief. The usefulness of Emerson's rule that "every scripture should be read in the light of the spirit which brought it forth" has recently, and most effectively, been demonstrated by David Hackett Fischer in *The Revolution of American Conservatism: The Federalist Party in the Era of Jeffersonian Democracy* (New York, 1965). He indicated that Federalist resentment of Republicans had ingredients other than the obvious one of sour grapes, and was founded in part on opposing definitions of the social order appropriate to the new republic. In three related essays, Paul Goodman has shown that party differences also rested on personal attitudes, ethnic identification, and particular economic interests. See Paul Goodman, "The First American Party System," in *The American Party Systems: Stages of Political Development*, ed. William Nisbet Chambers and Walter Dean Burnham (New York, 1967), pp. 56–89; "Social Status of Party Leadership: The House of Representatives, 1794–1804," *William and Mary Quarterly*, 3d ser., XXV (1968) 465–474; and "Social Sources of Political Behavior in the Early Republic," unpublished paper delivered at the 81st Annual Meeting of the American Historical Association, New York, December 28, 1966. Other historians in this group are John C. Miller (*Alexander Hamilton: Portrait in Paradox* [New York, 1959]); William Nisbet Chambers (*Political Parties in a New Nation: The American Experience 1776–1809* [New York, 1963]); Roger H. Brown (*The Republic in Peril: 1812* [New York, 1964], especially pp. 1–15, 199 note 12); Norman K. Risjord ("The Virginia Federalists," *Journal of Southern History* XXXIII [1967], 486–517); John R. Howe, Jr., ("Republican Thought and the Political Violence of the 1790's," *American Quarterly* XIX [1967], 147–165); Marshall Smelser (*The Democratic Republic: 1801–1815* [New York, 1968]); Richard Hofstadter (*The Idea of a Party System: The Rise of Legitimate Opposition in the United States, 1780–1840* [Berkeley, Calif., 1969]); and James M. Banner, Jr., whose book, *To the Hartford Convention: The Federalists and the Origins of Party Politics in Massachusetts, 1789–1815* (New York, 1970), gives a particularly perceptive interpretation of Federalist politics and ideology.

Two students of the cultural patterns of the early republic from whom much can be learned are Lewis P. Simpson and Perry Miller. See Lewis P. Simpson, "The Era of Joseph Stevens Buckminister: Life and Letters in the Boston-Cambridge Community, 1800–1815," unpublished Ph.D. dissertation, University of Texas, 1948; *The Federalist Literary Mind: Selections from the Monthly Anthology and Boston Review, 1803–1811* (Baton Rouge, La., 1962); "Federalism and the Crisis of Literary Order," *American Literature* XXXII (1960), 253–266. The most helpful of Perry Miller's works are *The Life of the Mind in America: From the Revolution to the Civil War* (New York, 1965); *The Legal Mind in America: From Independence to the Civil War* (New York, 1962); "From the Covenant to the Revival," in *The Shaping of American Religion*, ed. James Ward Smith and A. Leland Jamison, I (Princeton, N.J., 1961), 322–368.

The most revealing sources for the study of science in the early republic are the most basic ones: *Transactions of the American Philosophical Society, held at Philadelphia, for Promoting Useful Knowledge*, vols. IV, V (Philadelphia, 1799, 1802); *Memoirs of the American Academy of Arts and Sciences*, vol. II, part II (Charlestown, Mass., 1804), and the records of the two societies at the American Philosophical Society in Philadelphia and the Boston Athenaeum. The Records of the Society for the Study of Natural Philosophy at the Boston Athenaeum should be supplemented by the diary comments of John Quincy Adams in the Adams Papers microfilms reel 30. See also *Memoirs of the Connecticut Academy of Arts and Sciences*, I (New Haven, 1810); Samuel Miller, *A Brief Retrospect of the Eighteenth Century*, 2 vols. (New York, 1803); I. Bernard Cohen, *Science and American Society in the First Century of the Republic* (Columbus, Ohio, 1961); and Daniel Joseph Boorstin, *The Lost World of Thomas Jefferson* (New York, 1948).

The sources on which my analysis of Federalist thought is based are identified in the footnotes, but it may be useful to indicate some which have been of particular value. The task of the historian of the early national period is being made immeasurably easier by the Readex Microprint edition of the pamphlet titles in Ralph R. Shaw and Richard H. Shoemaker, *American Bibliography: A Preliminary Checklist for 1801–1819*, 19 vols. (New York, 1958–1963), and those in Charles Evans, *American Bibliography*, 13 vols. (Chicago, 1903–1955). The microprint editions, produced by the American Antiquarian Society, are: Clifford K. Shipton, ed. *Early American Imprints: 1639–1800* (Worcester, Mass., 1956–1964), and *Early American Imprints, 2nd Series, 1801–1819* (Worcester, Mass., 1964—). They should be used with the awareness that no checklist of such ephemeral material can be definitive.

Another major source is, of course, contemporary newspapers. Many, though worth scanning, are so full of mercantile announcements and reprints from other newpapers that their usefulness is limited. In some, however, the majority of the articles are original, and tremendously revealing of Federalist concerns and interests. Those which I have used most extensively and found most informative are: *The Mercury and New-England Palladium*; Boston *Repertory*, Boston *Columbian Centinel*, *New-York Evening Post*, Hudson, New York, *Balance*, *Gazette of the United States*, Hartford *Connecticut Courant*, Washington D.C., *Federalist*, Releigh, N.C., *Minerva*, and Charleston, S.C., *Courier*.

American periodical literature was in an embryonic state in 1800. The *Port Folio* and *Monthly Anthology and Boston Review* were, however, substantial journals which will repay careful reading. In both, contributions were usually published anonymously, but most of the authors of the *Monthly Anthology* have been identified by M. A. DeWolfe Howe, ed., *Journal of the Proceedings of the Society Which Conducts the Monthly Anthology and Boston Review, October 3, 1805 to July 2, 1811* (Boston, 1910). Identification of authorship in the *Port Folio* is far less complete, but a certain amount may be pieced together from the following sources: Albert H. Smyth, *The Philadelphia*

Magazines and their Contributors: 1741–1850 (Philadelphia, 1892); Ellis Paxson Oberholtzer, *The Literary History of Philadelphia* (Philadelphia, 1906); Harold Milton Ellis, *Joseph Dennie and his Circle: A Study in American Literature from 1792 to 1812* (Austin, Texas, 1913); Randolph C. Randall, "Authors of the *Port Folio* Revealed by the Hall Files," *American Literature* XI (1940), 379–416; Linda K. Kerber and Walter John Morris, "Politics and Literature: The Adams Family and the *Port Folio*," *William and Mary Quarterly*, 3d ser., XXIII (1966), 450–476; G. Thomas Tanselle, *Royall Tyler* (Cambridge, Mass., 1967). Other journals that are useful include *The Ordeal: A Critical Journal of Politics and Literature, The New England Quarterly Magazine, The Weekly Inspector, The American Review and Literary Journal, The Wasp, The Weekly Corrector, The Baltimore Weekly Magazine* and *Polyanthos.*

A large number of manuscript collections have been examined. The most exciting and fruitful are often the largest: the Adams Family Papers, available to researchers in a microfilm edition provided by the Massachusetts Historical Society, which owns and is gradually printing the originals; the Oliver Wolcott Papers at the Connecticut Historical Society, Hartford, Conn., the Papers of John Rutledge, Jr, in the Southern Historical Collection, University of North Carolina Library, Chapel Hill, N.C. But some smaller collections must be mentioned here, and the unfailing helpfulness of their curators acknowledged: John Adams Letters, Historical Society of Pennsylvania, Philadelphia; Records of the American Association of Arts and Sciences, Boston Athenaeum; Baldwin Family Papers, Yale University Library, New Haven, Conn.; David Campbell Papers, Duke University Library, Durham, N.C.; Joseph Dennie Papers, Houghton Library, Harvard University, Cambridge, Mass.; Henry William DeSaussure Papers, Duke University Library; William Gaston Papers, Southern Historical Collection, University of North Carolina Library; Gratz

Collection, Historical Society of Pennsylvania; Roger Griswold Papers, Yale University Library; Ernest Haywood Papers, Southern Historical Collection, University of North Carolina Library; Archibald Henderson: Papers Relating to the Henderson Family, Southern Historical Collection, University of North Carolina Library; Huntington-Wolcott MSS, Massachusetts Historical Society, Boston, Mass.; Ephraim Kirby Papers, Duke University Library; Rufus King Papers, New-York Historical Society, New York, N.Y.; Lane Family Papers, Yale University Library; James Russell Lowell Papers, Houghton Library, Harvard University; McKean Family Papers, Historical Society of Pennsylvania; Gouverneur Morris Papers, Library of Congress, Washington, D.C.; Meredith Family Papers, Historical Society of Pennsylvania; Harrison Gray Otis Papers, Massachusetts Historical Society; E. A. Park Papers, Yale University Library; Timothy Pickering Papers, Massachusetts Historical Society; Putnam Family Papers, Massachusetts Historical Society; Josiah Quincy Papers, Washburn Collection, Massachusetts Historical Society; Josiah Quincy Papers, Library of Congress; Josiah Quincy Papers, Houghton Library, Harvard University; John Rutledge, Jr., Papers, Duke University Library; Sedgwick Family Papers, Massachusetts Historical Society; William Smith Shaw Papers, Boston Athenaeum; John Cotton Smith Papers, Connecticut Historical Society; Records of the Society for the Study of Natural Philosophy, Boston Athenaeum; Benjamin Tallmadge Papers, Litchfield Historical Society, Litchfield, Conn.; William Tilghman Papers, Duke University Library; Jonathan Trumbull, Jr., Papers, Connecticut Historical Society; John Vaughan Papers, American Philosophical Society, Philadelphia, Pa.; Oliver Wolcott, Jr., Papers, Connecticut State Library, Hartford, Conn.; Oliver Wolcott, Jr., Papers, New York Public Library, New York, N.Y.

Index

Federalists in Dissent

IMAGERY AND IDEOLOGY
IN JEFFERSONIAN AMERICA

Designed by R. E. Rosenbaum.
Composed by Vail-Ballou Press, Inc.
in 11½ point linotype Caslon Old Face, 2 points leaded,
with display lines in monotype Caslon Old Style.
Printed from type by Vail-Ballou Press, Inc.,
on Warren's No. 66 Antique Text, 60 pound basis,
with the Cornell University Press watermark.
Bound by Vail-Ballou Press, Inc.
in Columbia Bayside Linen
and stamped in imitation gold foil.